DATE DUE

NOV 1 88	
~~APR 24 72~~	
~~MAY 1 '72~~	
APR 15 '74	
APR 1 2 1982	
~~MAY 1 0 1982~~	
~~NOV 1 1 1985~~	
~~DEC 1 5 1986~~	
~~DEC 0 9 1991~~	
MAR 3 0 1998	

THE PSALMS ARE CHRISTIAN PRAYER

To
A. J.
with sincere gratitude
for the generous guidance and encouragement
of the past
25 years

THE PSALMS ARE
CHRISTIAN PRAYER

T. WORDEN

SHEED & WARD—NEW YORK

Nihil obstat : Bernardus Can. Patten S.T.D., L.S.S., *Censor Lib.*
Imprimatur : Liverpolii, die 7a Sept, 1961. Thomas Adamson,
Vic. Gen.

The Psalms included in this work are taken from the
Revised Standard Version of the Bible, Copy-
righted 1946 and 1952, and are quoted by kind
permission of Messrs. Thomas Nelson & Sons Ltd.

Manufactured in the United States of America

Contents

Introduction

The title of this book *The Psalms are Christian Prayer* states a truth for which there is no lack of evidence throughout the history of the Church. From the earliest days when Peter and John went up to the Temple at the ninth hour of prayer (Acts 3, 1), until the present time when many thousands of priests and religious recite the Divine Office daily, the Psalter has been the inspired source of the Church's worship. During the early centuries it was the Church's one prayer-book, used not only by monks and clerics but also by the simple and unlettered, who memorised the psalms in order that they might take part in the liturgy. The place of the Psalter in the prayer of the Church is well portrayed by St John Chrysostom: 'When the faithful have a vigil at the church, David is at the beginning, in the middle and at the end. If at dawn they wish to sing hymns, it is again David who begins, continues and concludes. In funeral processions and at funeral services, it is David who is first and last.' (Hom VI *De Poen.*) An inspection of the Church's official prayer-books, the missal and the breviary, will confirm that David has never lost this pre-eminence.

But an inspection of the popular prayer-books would tell a different story. Probably there are few which do not contain the *De Profundis* and the *Miserere*; but the vast majority do not contain any other of the one hundred and fifty psalms. The truth is that the psalms are no longer in practice Christian prayer. This would not of itself be particularly significant, for there is necessarily a place in the Christian life for more personal devotions, as the Church has recently reaffirmed. Yet the balance has been so considerably upset, that many of those who are obliged to recite the Divine Office find it difficult to do so in the spirit of prayer, and many of the faithful completely unfamiliar with the psalms, are reluctant to respond to the exhortations of the present liturgical movement, because they find both its spirit and its formularies completely alien. It would be a step forward towards the solution of such difficulties if we could assent with real conviction to the truth that the psalms are Christian prayer.

In order to acquire this conviction a certain change of outlook is required, and a re-orientation. In particular we need to re-orientate our ideas of the Old Testament, and change our outlook towards Israel. The aim of this book is to help towards the formation of this outlook or mentality, without which the Psalter cannot be used as the Christian prayer-book.

The title therefore explains the end in view. But it is a misleading indication of the contents of this book. Very little is here written about the psalms themselves. The many problems which face the student of the Psalter, problems of text, authorship, date, and the constantly-recurring problems of interpretation, are all left to the detailed commentaries and the accurate modern translations. Whilst these are indispensable, they often fail to create that mentality without which even a thorough understanding of the text gives no conviction that the psalms are Christian prayer. It is necessary to consider the nature of Israelite prayer in general, and to realise the faith which inspired it. In order to do this, we must inevitably draw our material from the Old Testament and in particular the Pentateuch, since the psalms are the epitome of what is contained at length in the Old Testament revelation.

There is a second general question which is indeed less important, but on the other hand more directly connected with the psalms. This concerns the basic patterns of Israelite prayer.

The stereotyped character of the psalms makes it possible without undue simplification, to consider two basic forms which in greater or less degree are to be found in all the psalms. Almost every one of them is either a song of praise or a lamentation or a combination of both. A consideration of these two forms may throw some light on the whole Psalter, and since both forms are to some extent alien to our mentality, it may help towards that re-orientation which seems demanded if the psalms are to be our prayer.

Yet general considerations cannot wholly solve our problems. The actual subject matter of the psalms raises its own difficulties, and it is therefore necessary to consider the main themes of the Psalter. Unfortunately it has proved possible to deal with only two of these, the redemption of Israel, and the conquest of Israel's enemies. The recital of the so-called historical psalms often seems to us the very antithesis of prayer, whilst the violence and vindictiveness of the psalms which plead for the destruction of Israel's enemies usually arouse strong feelings of repugnance. A consideration of these two groups of psalms therefore, may remove certain obstacles to our use of the Psalter, and encourage us to think that other psalms may in similar fashion be used as prayer, without the need of any artificial interpretation.

The psalms are to be understood according to the meaning they had when they were first written and used as the prayer of Israel. There is no need to do violence to our modern mentality with its strongly historical outlook and its insistence on the literal sense of what is written, according to the time and circumstances of writing. The allegorising interpretation of the Fathers was a reflection of their own particular age and not, as is sometimes thought, the inescapable condition for the Christian understanding of the psalms. There is no need for us to sacrifice the principles of historical and literary criticism which are so integral a part of our mentality. What we need though, is a comprehensive appreciation of the whole of Divine revelation, and a strong realisation of the continuity of Israel in the Church. Seen in this light the psalms will be the expression of our faith in God's consummation of His promises through Our Lord Jesus Christ. What is said in the psalms will inevitably lead our thoughts to what remains unsaid, and yet is implied and indeed demanded by our faith in God's fidelity to His Chosen People. In this way we will rejoin by the path best suited to our modern historical outlook, the Fathers' understanding of the psalms, which constantly spoke to them of Christ, the Redeemer and the fulfilment of God's promises for which the Israelites had so long hoped and prayed in the psalms.

Chapter I

The Basic Pattern of Israelite Prayer

The Complexity of the Term 'Prayer'

Our English word 'Prayer' is very inadequate to express the complex notion we wish it to convey. Its immediate meaning is 'request, demand or petition': to pray is to ask for something. And unfortunately there are those who in fact do nothing other than ask God for things when they pray. But many realise that they ought not to spend all their time of prayer in asking God for benefits; they realise that they must also think of His power and His goodness; that they must also express their admiration and love and gratitude towards Him; that they must also express their sorrow for having offended Him, and their determination to live in the way He wishes. All these other aspects are part of their prayer but how inadequately they are described by this word.

The Israelites, wisely it would seem, did not have any one word which was applied to all the various aspects of what we term prayer, or at least they were not willing to make any extensive use of a general term.[1] Instead they used such an indefinite expression as 'to speak words', leaving the particular aspect of prayer to become apparent from the words of the prayer itself. Or they used such expressions as 'to cry out', 'to call or invoke', 'to moan or groan', in order to underline the sincerity and urgency of their prayer. But their prayer was by

[1] cf Herrmann, in *Theologisches Wörterbuch zum Neuen Testament* II, pp. 782-787.

1

no means confined to petition or to urgent appeals for some benefit. Very important aspects of their prayer were expressed by such terms as 'to praise', 'to acknowledge'—or 'confess' as translations sometimes misleadingly put it. Other synonyms were 'to recall or commemorate', 'to make known', 'to recount or narrate', 'to magnify', 'to extol' and 'to bless'. All such terms, and even an expression such as 'to meditate' implied praying aloud, or vocal prayer, to use our expression. This quality is emphasised in other expressions, such as 'to rejoice or jump for joy', 'to sing', 'to play musical instruments'—the word Psalm is derived from this last idea, for the Greek verb *Psallō* means first to pluck the strings of a harp, and therefore etymologically a Psalm is a song sung to the accompaniment of the harp.

This great variety of words should be some indication that if we are to make the Psalms our prayer, we must realise in practice what perhaps we already acknowledge in theory, namely that to pray includes other things besides petition. Many of the Psalms do not strike us as prayers simply because our idea of prayer is far too limited. To take just one simple example, we are accustomed to the distinction between hymns and prayers, and such a distinction has its obvious justification; but in practice it may well obscure the fact that the former are prayer just as much as the latter.

The Basis of Israelite Prayer

Many people consider that prayer is a waste of time. They might grant that it is a harmless pastime for the ignorant who seem very often to derive comfort from it, but they would judge it to be an excercise in self-deception which is unworthy of an intelligent man. Even though they admit the existence of God as the least unsatisfactory answer to the problems of their existence, He is not in their eyes someone with whom they can communicate in a personal way, nor someone who is interested in their individual needs. To suggest that He can by prayer be led to change the circumstances of a man's life, giving health for

2

instance to the sick man, or happiness to the depressed, seems to stultify their notion of God as the omniscient and immutable creator.

There are some indeed who are led by their own powers of reasoning to a truer concept of God, and this evokes from them the sincere acknowledgement and the fervent praise which is prayer. But this phenomenon is so rare and this prayer so limited, that it is difficult to see how the vast majority of the human race can in practice have either the will or the capacity to pray if their prayer is not based on divine revelation. An intelligent contemplation of the universe may evoke the cry:

> O God, how manifold are Thy works!
> In wisdom hast Thou made them all;
> the earth is full of Thy creatures. (cf Ps 104, 24)

It may call forth the humble acknowledgement:

> When I look at Thy heavens, the work of Thy fingers,
> the moon and the stars which Thou hast established;
> what is man that Thou art mindful of him,
> and the son of man that thou dost care for him?
> Yet Thou hast made him little less than God,
> and dost crown him with glory and honour.
> Thou hast given him dominion over the works of Thy
>   hands;
> Thou hast put all things under his feet,
> all sheep and oxen,
> and also the beasts of the field,
> the birds of the air, and the fish of the sea,
> whatever passes along the paths of the sea.
> O God, how majestic is Thy name in all the earth!
>   (cf Ps 8, 3-9)

But it cannot evoke either Psalm 104 or Psalm 8, for the former exclaims: 'O *Yahweh,* how manifold are Thy works!' (v. 24), and the latter 'O *Yahweh* our Lord, how majestic is Thy name in all the earth!' (vv. 1. 9). In his reasoning man has not encountered Yahweh, *our* Lord. God remains for him the creator of the universe whose name he does not know. And it is so difficult to pray until we enjoy that intimacy with God in which He reveals to us His own name.

God revealed His name to Israel, and the whole basis of Israelite prayer is God's revelation of Himself, unfolded in Israel's history, expounded by the prophets and preserved in the sacred books. For this reason the psalms lose their meaning if they are separated from the rest of the Old Testament. Fragments of them still retain their beauty of language and serve to express religious sentiments, but for the most part the psalms will be incomprehensible. The Psalter in its entirety is the prayer book only of those who believe in the divine revelation contained in the Old Testament as well as in the New. Forgetful of their limitations there are many Christians who consider that they have no need of those glimpses which God gave of Himself before He came to us in the flesh, and this is largely the reason why the Psalter so often fails as the Christian prayer book. It demands not only a knowledge of the Old Testament, but a fervent belief that in the Old Testament our Christian faith is nourished and increased.

To appreciate the psalms therefore it is vital to understand the nature of the revelation God made of Himself to Israel. Now a study of the Old Testament makes it clear that the fundamental revelation is not that God is the almighty creator, but that God is He Who chose Israel for His own private property, leading them out of Egypt into a land He reserved for them, and there making them His mouth-piece as it were, in order to reveal Himself to the rest of the world. It is instructive to compare the Israelites' creed with the opening statement of our own, namely 'I believe in God the Father Almighty, creator of heaven and earth'. When the Israelite offered the first-fruits of his harvest he had to make the following solemn declaration,

4

which amounts to the recital of his creed[2]: 'A wandering Aramean was my father; and he went down into Egypt and sojourned there, few in number; and there he became a nation, great, mighty, and populous. And the Egyptians treated us harshly, and afflicted us, and laid upon us hard bondage. Then we cried to the Lord the God of our fathers, and the Lord heard our voice, and saw our affliction, our toil, and our oppression; and the Lord brought us out of Egypt with a mighty hand and an outstretched arm, with great terror, with signs and wonders; and He brought us into this place and gave us this land, a land flowing with milk and honey' (Deut 26, 5-9). In other words the Israelites' creed begins 'I believe in Yahweh our God, Who brought us out of the land of Egypt, to be His own special people.' God had explained His action of rescuing this small and insignificant group of people from the powerful nation of Egypt: 'You have seen what I did to the Egyptians, and how I bore you on eagles' wings and brought you to myself. Now therefore, if you will obey my voice and keep my covenant, you shall be my own possession among all peoples; for all the earth is mine, and you shall be to me a kingdom of priests and a holy nation' (Ex 19, 4-6). The Israelites were constantly reminded: 'You are a people holy to the Lord your God: the Lord your God has chosen you to be a people for his own possession, out of all the peoples that are on the face of the earth. It was not because you were more in number than any other people that the Lord set His love upon you and chose you, for you were the fewest of all peoples; but it is because the Lord loves you, and is keeping the oath which He swore to your fathers, that the Lord has brought you out with a mighty hand and redeemed you from the house of bondage' (Deut 7, 6-8; cf Deut 14, 2; 26, 18; Ps 135, 4).

That Israel believed in God as the creator of heaven and earth there can be no doubt since she recognised Him as the supreme and only God. But this aspect was not of primary

[2]cf G. Ernest Wright, *God Who Acts,* London 1952, pp. 71-72.

importance for Israel, and the extensive literary expression of this belief does not appear in the earliest sources.[3] The early prophets of the eighth and seventh centuries always describe Yahweh in terms of the liberation from Egypt, and this is the foundation of Israel's claim for protection and the source of her hope of salvation. They are not concerned with Yahweh's creative power nor with His position in relation to the universe. Their horizon is limited to their own small land.

But historical circumstances made any continuance of this isolation impossible. Their geographical position alone was sufficient to make them aware of a greater world outside. The force of the Assyro-Babylonian empire made itself felt with ever greater insistence, and by the latter half of the eighth century it was threatening Israel's very existence. This was bound to have a twofold effect: it not only brought them into contact with Mesopotamian beliefs concerning the origin of the universe, but more especially it made them consider the relation of Yahweh to this greater world around them. He was their protector, and therefore greater than the gods of their enemies, and His superiority over them and over the world began to take on an importance not previously felt. The greatness of Babylonian gods depended upon their powers over Nature, and upon the part they played in the origin of the universe. In this atmosphere Israel became conscious of the fact that Yahweh's greatness derived not merely from His salvation of Israel, but also from His creation of the universe. Thus it is that in the Book of Jeremias we find for the first time any real insistence on Yahweh's position as creator of the world. But even here, Jeremias does not consider the question for its own sake: his teaching is concerned with the fate of Israel at the hands of the Assyro-Babylonian empire, and the most important title of Yahweh remains that of saviour of Israel. According to Jeremias the Israelites were being punished because their fathers

[3]cf J. Lambert, 'La Création dans la Bible', *Nouvelle revue théologique* 1953, pp. 252-282.

failed to ask: 'Where is the Lord who brought us up from the land of Egypt, who led us in the wilderness, in a land of deserts and pits, in a land of drought and deep darkness, in a land that none passes through, where no man dwells? And I brought you into a plentiful land to enjoy its fruits' (Jer 2, 6-7). But, Jeremias reminds them, Yahweh is also He who can claim to be the creator of the world: 'I placed the sand as the bound for the sea. . . .', and they ought to say: 'Let us fear the Lord our God who gives the rain in its season, the autumn rain and the spring rain, and keeps for us the weeks appointed for the harvest' (Jer 5, 22-4). He is the one Who fills heaven and earth (23, 24), and makes the claim 'It is I who by my great power and my outstretched arm have made the earth, with the men and animals that are on the earth, and I give it to whom-ever it seems right to me' (Jer 27, 5-6; cf 31, 35).

The belief in God the creator of heaven and earth, there-fore, was far from absent in the Old Testament, and indeed it finds expression in Pss 8; 18, 1-8; 28; 88; 148 and especially in the great creation hymn, Ps 104. But it was never the first and the most basic expression of Israel's faith. God's choice of Israel always remains the root of Israel's faith, and it is this fact which gives its shape to the whole of Israel's prayer. It is true that by the time the Old Testament writings were collected and edited in their present form, the logical method of begin-ning with the creation was followed, and therefore the reader is presented first of all with the image of God the creator. But it would be misleading to draw any theological conclusion from this arrangement. The first question in the Israelite catechism was not 'Who made you?', but 'Who is your God?'. And the answer was not 'Yahweh, creator of heaven and earth' but 'Yahweh Who brought us out of the land of Egypt.'

Thus we are immediately presented with a concept of God which only revelation can give us. The philosopher must reject such a notion as an anthropomorphism: the first cause and prime mover, having created and ordered the universe cannot at one stage in time differentiate between certain groups of the same species. They may evolve according to the laws of nature, and by their own efforts; but God does not intervene in the manner of a changeable man. But the God of revelation exercises a free choice. He has His preferences and He favours whomsoever He wishes to favour. Whatever the difficulties raised for the philosopher, God is He who chose Israel out of all the peoples of the earth. The fundamental revelation concerning God therefore, is that He can and does choose. He is a person with as it were special interests. He is someone who is active in pursuit of His wishes. He is someone who works to bring about the fulfilment of His intentions. And since that choice was manifested initially in His freeing the Israelites from Egypt, He is first and foremost the Rescuer or the Saviour; and He is Israel's protector from that day onwards.

The object of God's special choice is Israel: a group of people descended from Abraham and Jacob to whom the name Israel had been given (Gen 32, 29; 35, 10). The primary object of God's choice is this group or nation, and not the individual man, even though he is an Israelite. The object of God's choice is not the individual, who along with other chosen individuals can then be grouped into one nation. The primary object is the group, and therefore the individual is a chosen individual only because and only insofar as he belongs to this group. Because the fundamental truth of faith is that God chose Israel, it follows that fundamentally the relationship expressed by prayer is not between a man and God, a creature and his creator, but between the group or community of Israel and Yahweh, God the deliverer from Egypt. The individual cannot pray unless he first of all establish that he belongs to Israel. On this depends his belief that God loves him, that God wishes to protect him, that God intends to exalt him. His relationship to God and his future for good or evil is intimately bound up with that of the group. It is for this reason that the past history of Israel and the future hope of Israel are of so great importance for each individual Israelite. It is also for this reason that success or failure, the hopes or fears, and the prosperity or misfortunes of other individual Israelites are of so great importance. They are all members of the one body Israel. To be cut off from that body is to be destroyed; to remain part of that body makes everlasting life certain. Insofar as that body is threatened in any of its members the whole body is endangered; insofar as that body prospers in any of its members, that whole body grows stronger. The primacy of the community over the individual is never in doubt.

Israel the Corporate Person

This has such far-reaching consequences that it calls for proof, and there has been much discussion centring on the notion of Israel as a 'corporate person'.[4] Does the evidence in fact support the claim that the word 'Israel' frequently refers to a group of people considered not as a number of individuals but as so closely bound together that they in reality are a close unity, so close that they can be regarded as in some way one person? The notion may strike us as very strange, since the first object for our consideration is always the individual. We consider that the individual is of greater importance than the group. But a study of the Old Testament shows us that the distinction between individual and group was not so important, nor too obvious.

[4]Admittedly the term 'corporate personality' is open to objection, but it has become widely accepted, and no wholly satisfactory alternative exists. The term was first used by T. W. Manson (cf *Bulletin of the John Rylands Library*, t. xxxii, 1949-50, p. 188), but it is more readily associated with H. W. Robinson and the well-known article he wrote: 'The Hebrew conception of Corporate Personality' in *Zeitshrift für die alttestamentliche Wissenschaft*, 66 (1936) pp. 49-61. An alternative expression 'Inclusive personality' is used by E. Best in *One Body in Christ*, London 1955. One of the latest studies of the whole question of 'corporate personality' is by J. de Fraine S.J., *Adam et son Lignage*, Bruges 1959.

The close unity of a group of people, whether a family, clan, tribe or nation is to a varying degree common to all mankind. But nowhere else it is so strongly insisted upon as in the Old Testament. We have early examples of this in the patriarchal stories, where such men as Abraham and Jacob are regarded not only as individuals, but also and more especially as the eponymous representatives of their descendants, and to whom therefore the experiences of their descendants over a long period can be attributed as their very own. There is no valid reason for supposing that these men did not exist as individuals, with each his personal history.[5] But our knowledge of this is scanty and uncertain, precisely because these men are presented in our sources not as individual persons, but as corporate persons. They *are* their descendants, and the whole group is personified in them.

A perfect example to illustrate this lies to hand in the story of Esau and Jacob (Gen 25, 19-34; 27, 1-45). Even before their birth Rebecca is told: 'Two nations are in your womb, and two peoples, born of you, shall be divided; the one shall be stronger than the other, the elder shall serve the younger' (Gen 25, 23). Jacob and Esau are two nations, namely Israel and Edom. That Jacob is Israel is not mentioned in the story for it is so well known a fact (cf Gen 32, 29; 35, 10), but a reminder of Esau's identification with Edom is given us in a parenthesis (v. 30).

In order to appreciate this story, we must first see what information history gives us concerning the Edomites. They were a nomadic people of semitic stock and practising circumcision (cf Jer 9, 25), with a reputation for wisdom (cf Jer 49, 7). They inhabited the region which lies south of the Dead Sea, and extends from the Sinai peninsula to the desert east of the high plateau. Certain groups of this people became sedentary, settling on the mountainous plateau south of the Wadi Hasa, a river

[5]cf R. de Vaux, 'Les Patriarches hébreux et les découvertes modernes', *Revue biblique* 1946, p. 321ff.

which runs westward into the Dead Sea at its southern end. Here a kindgom was set up with its capital at Bosra, about twenty miles south of the W. Hasa. Other groups of Edomites occupied the region south of the Negeb and west of the Araba, which is probably the localisation of the mountainous region of Se'ir, a district with which the Edomites are frequently associated.[6] The whole of this territory is extremely barren, and is for the most part covered with deposits of reddish stone.[7]

The historical contacts between Israel and these groups of Edomites, partly nomad, partly sedentary, but all included under the one name Edom, began at the time of the Exodus. Moses sent messengers to the king of Edom: 'the brother of Israel', seeking permission to pass through his territory. This was refused: 'And Edom came out against him (Israel) with many men and with a strong force' (Num 20, 20 cf 20, 14-21). More than two hundred years later David defeated the Edomites and imposed his yoke upon them (2 Sam 8, 13), but they were still hostile in the reign of Solomon (1 Kgs 11, 14-22). They were compelled to help Joram in a campaign against Moab (2 Kgs 3, 9), but later they rebelled (2 Kgs 8, 20-22), and Amasias made war on them (2 Kgs 14, 7). As a last indication of the relations that existed throughout history between Israel and Edom we must recall that one of the blessings promised by the prophets to Israel on its restoration, was the conquest and final destruction of Edom (cf Jer 9, 25; 25, 21; 49, 7-22; Ezek 25, 13-15; 32, 29; 35, 1-15; 36, 5; Joel 4, 19; Amos 1, 11-12; 9, 12; Abd 1, 5-18; Mal 1, 2-5).

Clearly therefore the Edomites, though a semitic people, were the enemies of Israel throughout history. Living in an arid region where the red-coloured rock and the scanty rainfall forced them to hunt for their food, they were always eager to migrate northwards where the more fertile soil and the greater rainfall enabled men to settle down, well provided with food by

[6]F. M. Abel, *Géographie de la Palestine,* Paris 1933, I, pp. 282-3.
[7]*ibid.*, pp. 102-3.

their crops and their cattle, and to reach a land which to them seemed flowing with milk and honey (cf Deut 8, 7; 10, 11).

Such are the facts which the Israelites learned gradually in the course of history. But this knowledge, acquired only gradually, over a long period of time, is put to use in telling what appears on the surface as the story of two individuals, the twin sons of Rebecca.[8] These facts decide the details of the story at every turn, and if we remember also that the Israelites could never resist inventing popular etymologies for words, and rarely missed the chance of a pun, we are in a position to appreciate the brilliantly composed story of Esau and Jacob.

Esau is born red, because the word Edom reminds the hearers of the Hebrew *'adom* which means red, and anyway the Edomites lived in the red country, Esau is born covered with hair, because Edomites occupied the mountainous district of Se'ir, a word so close in sound to *se'ar*, the Hebrew for hairy. He is the elder of the twins, for as we saw, Edom was already established in its territory when Israel was still on its way to the promised land.[9] Jacob (*ya'aqob*) is born grasping the heel of Esau, for his name echoes the Hebrew word *'aqeb* meaning 'heel'. Esau became a hunter, for the Edomites were hunters. Jacob was a quiet man, for the Israelites were a sedentary people. Though Edom was the elder, Israel was chosen by God and blessed with the divine favour. It was a case of the elder losing his birthright, and so Edom, not only situated in the red country, but having a name that sounds like 'red', is portrayed

[8]It is not easy to date Gen 25, 19-24; 27, 1-45. Both stories belong to J (with the exception of additions from P cf vv. 19-20. 26b), commonly thought to belong in its essentials to the period of Solomon, cf A. Clamer, *La Genèse*, Paris 1953, pp. 38-9; R. de Vaux, *Genèse* (*Bible de Jérusalem*), Paris 1951, p. 18. If this dating is accurate, which is open to question, then some of the historical contacts mentioned are later and therefore did not affect the composition of the story. But this makes no great difference, since they followed the same pattern as earlier experiences of Edom.

[9]cf G. Ernest Wright, *Biblical Archaeology*, London 1957, p. 73.

12

as selling his birthright for a plate of 'red-stuff'.[10] In spite of the boasted wisdom of the Edomites it is clear that Israel is vastly superior, for was not Jacob so much cleverer than Esau, and so much more appreciative of God's blessing, than Esau the glutton?

The superiority of Israel is further shown by the clever ruse of Jacob and his mother. Having obtained two kids from the flock, just as any Israelite would, and whilst Esau was still out hunting for food, as the Edomites had to do, Jacob made himself hairy, and by a clever trick obtained the first and best blessing from his father Isaac. By this blessing he was given a land where the soil germinated crops, and the rains and dew watered them, just as it was in Canaan, and he was made master of all the surrounding peoples, as Israel was, or would certainly be one day. For Esau there only remained the blessing of living a wild nomadic live in an arid land; a life of submission to Jacob: but only for a time. History could not be denied, and the Edomites eventually shook off the yoke imposed upon them by David.

Such is the story of Esau and Jacob, having the superficial appearance of a family anecdote involving two individuals, but in reality portraying the fortunes of two peoples. Neither the Israelite story-teller nor his hearers saw anything incongruous in this procedure, much less did they consider themselves to be propagating falsehood or deception.[11] To have asked them whether the events described were 'historical' would have been a stupid and indeed an unintelligible question. The story was wholly true, precisely because Jacob *is* Israel, and Esau *is* Edom. Their individuality is of no importance, and whatever incidents took place in their individual lives are quite insigni-

---

[10]Such translations as 'red *pottage*' (*Revised Standard Version*) are *ad sensum*, whereas the Hebrew text has simply: 'Please feed me some of the red, this red.'

[11]cf John L. McKenzie, S.J., *The Two-Edged Sword*, Milwaukee 1956, ch. IV.

ficant. In these two individuals are embodied the two nations, and the vicissitudes of these nations' history *are* the lives of Esau and Jacob. These two peoples are two persons to whom are given in this instance the personal names Esau and Jacob.

Israel is a Corporate Person

The name Israel, which of itself first appears as the proper name of one individual, formerly called Jacob, is used to denote that group of people whom we more naturally refer to as the Israelites, a form of the name which has no corresponding term in Hebrew: to call attention to the plurality, Hebrew must use the expression 'Sons of Israel'. This in itself shows to some degree that the aspect of unity is stressed. But the unifying of many in the one person Israel is particularly evident from the epithets used to describe this unity. Thus Israel is God's son—not 'sons'. Moses is commanded to say to Pharaoh : 'Thus says the Lord, Israel is my first-born son, and I say to you: Let my son go that *he* may serve me. If you refuse to let *him* go, behold, I will slay your first-born son' (Ex 4, 22-3). Israel, God's son, had no reason to fear the might of Pharaoh : 'If thou dost say in thy heart: These nations are greater than I; how can I dispossess them?, thou shalt not be afraid of them, but thou shalt remember what the Lord thy God did to Pharaoh and to all Egypt, the great trials which thy eyes saw, the signs, the wonders, the mighty hand, and the outstretched arm, by which the Lord thy God brought thee out; so will the Lord thy God do to all the peoples of whom thou art afraid' (Deut 7, 17-19). Israel is as one man, challenging many nations, he is God's first-born son, so he ought to fear nothing. God's choice of him gives him every confidence: 'He found him in a desert land, and in the howling waste of the wilderness; He encircled him, He cared for him, He kept him as the apple of His eye. Like an eagle that stirs up its nest, that flutters over its young, spreading out its wings, catching them, bearing them on its pinions, the

14

Lord alone did lead him, and there was no foreign god with him' (Deut 32, 10-12).

The way in which these texts speak of Israel as one person is striking; but it might be thought that it is merely a figure of speech without further significance. Yet the very inconsistencies lead us to suspect so simple an explanation. Within the same passages there is often a strange oscillation between the singular and the plural which we have no reason to think the writers found impossible to avoid, if they simply intended to use a figure of speech. The truth is rather that they were struggling to give expression to a deeper truth, too great to be kept within the bounds of logical speech: Israel was in some mysterious way one person in whom many individuals were to be found. We have a clear example of this oscillation in a passage telling of the negotiations with Edom, to which we have already referred. In an attempt to overcome the resistance of the king of Edom to their passing through his territory, the people of Israel say: '*We* will go up by the highway; and if we drink of thy water, I and *my* cattle, then I will pay for it; let *me* only pass through on foot, nothing more. But he said: *Thou* shalt not pass through me. And Edom came out against *him* with many men, and with a strong force. Thus Edom refused to give Israel passage through his territory; so Israel turned away from him' (Num 20, 19-21). Thus the small group of families emigrating from Egypt, a group which in historical fact was far from constituting the nation Israel, is here spoken of, partly as a plurality and partly as one person.

The opening words of the Israelite creed give us another example of this oscillation between singular and plural: 'A wandering Aramean was my father; and *he* went down into Egypt and sojourned there, *few in number,* and there *he* became a nation' (Deut 26, 5). God rescued his son from Egypt, but he became wayward, and Moses disclaimed responsibility for this dissatisfied people: 'Did I conceive *all this people?* Did I bring *him* forth, that thou shouldst say to me, Carry *him* in thy bosom, as a nurse carries the sucking child, to the land which thou didst swear to give *their* fathers? Where am I to get meat to give to all this people? For *they* weep before me and say, Give *us* meat, that *we* may eat' (Num 11, 12-13). God's son is ungrateful: 'When Israel was a child I loved *him*, and out of Egypt I called my son. The more I called *them*, the more *they* went from me' (Os 11, 1-2). Israel was frequently the prodigal son, but God was always ready to welcome him home when he cared to turn back from his wickedness: 'The Lord *thy* God will restore thy fortunes, and have compassion upon thee, and he will gather thee again from all the peoples where the Lord thy God has scattered *thee*' (Deut 30, 3). The final clause of this quotation is particularly revealing: sinful Israel is as one person scattered among many peoples.

The Individual Israelite Inherits all that is Israel's

Israel is one person, whose life has lasted for many hundreds of years, and through many vicissitudes, and which is destined to continue for ever. But Israel is on the other hand a plurality of individuals whose separate lives are limited to one short period in a longer historical experience. Insofar as an Israelite is an individual he can experience, either for good or for evil, only those things which come his way during the short span of life allotted him. But insofar as he is part of the corporate person who is Israel, he can lay claim to all the experience, for good or for evil, which has been Israel's in the past, is Israel's in the present, and will be Israel's in the future.

This notion is particularly prominent in the book of Deuteronomy. We must remember that this book was composed with the help of earlier traditions and earlier written sources, in the seventh century B.C.[12] The traditions of ancient Israel were presented in the form we find in Deuteronomy, for the benefit

[12]cf A. Clamer, *op. cit.*, pp. 44-7; H. Cazelles, *Le Deuteronome* (*Bible de Jérusalem*), Paris 1958, pp. 13-16; G. Ernest Wright, *God Who Acts*, London 1952, p. 75.

of the Israelites of that period. And yet no incongruity is felt in adopting the literary framework of speeches by Moses, addressed to the Israelites on their way from Egypt, a journey which had in historical fact taken place some five hundred years before. Such a literary device emphasises the role of Moses as first and paramount lawgiver; but it also emphasises that the experiences of Israel five hundred years ago are in truth the experiences of the Israelites living in the promised land in the seventh century. Only occasionally is any attention paid to the time factor involved, by a reference to this present day,[13] and more especially to the exile which in the seventh century had already overtaken the northern kingdom, and was threatening Juda.[14] The Israelites have indeed grown numerous as the stars of heaven (Deut 1, 10), but this gradual growth does not alter the perspective of Israel, however few or however many, making its way through the wilderness.

The seventh century Israelites are told therefore that they

[13]Deut 4, 20. 38; 5, 3; 6, 24; 8, 18; 10, 8; 11, 4. Notice particularly how in Deut 4, 38 Moses tells his people that they have been led into the land God has given them as their inheritance, for so it is 'even today'. Yet on the other hand Moses is supposed to be addressing them whilst they were still on the east side of the Jordan (Deut 1, 1), and he was to die before they entered the promised land (cf Deut 31, 21; 34). In Deut 8, 18 Yahweh is said to be observing today, the covenant He made with 'our fathers', though in 5, 3 He is said to have made the covenant, not with 'our fathers' but with 'us, ourselves, who are here, all alive today'. The constant repetition of the word 'today' in the discourses of Moses, e.g., 'Keep His laws and His commandments, which I prescribe for thee *today*' (Deut 4, 40; cf 6, 6; 7, 11; 8, 1. 11; 10, 13; 11, 8. 13. 27. 28. 32; 13, 19; 15, 5; 19, 9; 30, 3. 8) is clearly a literary device for emphasising that all laws originate from Moses, though many of them, in the form in which they are to be found in Deuteronomy, are the result of a long experience of life in Canaan, e.g., the law of the one sanctuary (Deut 12, 2-28), a law which had not been in force previously cf Jud 6, 28; 13, 16; 1 Kgs 14, 23; 2 Kgs 16, 4; 17, 10. The prescriptions concerning the monarchy (Deut 17, 14-17) are worded in the light of sad experience (cf 1 Kgs 10,28-9; 11).

[14]Deut 4, 25-31; 28, 36-7. 47-68; 30, 1-10. These passages show the unmistakable influence of the prophets.

17

refused to penetrate into the valley of Eshkol, and complained that Yahweh planned to destroy them (1, 27). They were at Horeb when Yahweh spoke to them from the midst of fire (4, 10-12). It was before their very eyes that Yahweh performed the prodigies in Egypt (4, 34), and they are warned not to forget the God who led *them* out of Egypt (6, 12). When their children ask why they observe the laws and customs they must reply: *'We* were slaves of Pharaoh in Egypt, and Yahweh brought us out of Egypt by His mighty power' (6, 21). But Yahweh chose from among all the nations of the earth the descendants of the patriarchs, the Israelites *of today* (10, 15 cf Ex 13, 8). That these events historically speaking took place hundreds of years before makes no difference, for insofar as the Israelites of the seventh century are to be found within the corporate person Israel, then all these events are as vitally significant to them as those which happen during the short span allotted to them individually.

They not only share in what historically speaking took place long before their birth. Israel's experiences in the future are in a real sense theirs, and have a vital part to play in their final destiny. Israel will for instance be dragged into exile, and there suffer great hardships; but she will benefit by it, for she will realise that God is her only salvation. She will be reconciled with Him, and He will save her. All this will happen to Israel, and therefore all this will happen to everyone who is truly an Israelite. Only those, and unhappily they are many, who cut themselves off from Israel have no claim to the future experiences of Israel. 'Yahweh will scatter you among the nations, and only a small number of you will remain among the nations where Yahweh takes you. There you will serve gods made by the hands of man, gods of wood and stone, unable to see or hear, to eat or feel. From there *thou* wilt seek Yahweh thy God again; and thou wilt find him if thou dost seek him with all thy heart and soul. In thy distress all these words will come to thee, but at the end of the time thou wilt return to Yahweh thy

God and hear His voice; for Yahweh thy God is a merciful God, who will not abandon thee nor destroy thee' (4, 27-31; cf 30, 3-5). The fact that at this time the exile of the northern kingdom had already lasted a hundred years, and that the exile of Juda had not yet begun, did not make these words meaningless.

The gradual fulfilment of Israel's destiny over a long period of time is expressly indicated when the Israelite is told: 'It is little by little that Yahweh thy God will destroy these nations before thee; thou wilt not be able to exterminate them immediately, for fear the wild beasts increase to thy harm' (7, 22). But however long this takes it will be for the benefit of all Israel, for the covenant is made with Israel whose life is not limited to that of any individual's: 'It is not with you only that I today make this covenant, and that I pronounce this imprecation, but as much with the one who stands here with us in the presence of Yahweh our God, as with him who is not here today' (29, 13).

Israel is affected by the actions of the individual

Whilst the individual is affected for good or evil by the total experience of Israel, Israel on the other hand is affected for good or evil by the experience of the individual. The influence of such men as Moses and David on the future of Israel as a whole is readily understood, and there were many others, kings and prophets who played a decisive part. But of far more importance to us here is the establishing of the principle that every individual does in some measure affect the destiny of the corporate person Israel.

God had promised to bless all who blessed Abraham, and to curse all who cursed him. In other words many were to share in the blessing of Abraham, and not only his descendants, but 'All the nations of the earth will in thee be blessed' (Gen 12, 3; 18, 18; 26, 4; 28, 14). It is true that this last saying is often understood as indicating simply that Abraham will be a byword

19

among the nations for his good fortune, and therefore another translation is often adopted : 'By thee all nations of the earth will bless themselves', that is, they will wish Abraham's blessing on themselves or their friends (cf Gen 48, 20; Zach 8, 13). But von Rad is surely right when he maintains[15] that the climax of God's blessing on Abraham must mean something more than this. In fact the call of Abraham heralds the approach of God's salvation for the whole world. Abraham is God's instrument, and through him and because of him God will save Israel and all the nations (cf Is 2, 2-4). The time will come when Yahweh will say: 'Blessed be my people Egypt, Assyria the work of my hands, and Israel my inheritance' (Is 19, 25).

That the individual may benefit the group is clearly shown in the story of Sodom and Gomorrha, for although God had decided to destroy the cities with all their inhabitants, He was nevertheless willing to change His plans if fifty, or forty-five, or forty, or thirty, or twenty or even ten good men were found there.

But the influence of the individual upon the group is more frequently seen in those cases where the group suffers on account of the individual's wickedness. Perhaps the best known example is the punishment meted out to the families of Dathan and Abiram. These two sons of Eliab revolted against the authority of Moses, and the latter called upon God to punish them, in a spectacular way which would be proof that God upheld the authority of Moses. Consequently: 'The ground split asunder, beneath their feet. The earth opened its mouth and swallowed them, *along with their families* as well as all Korah's men and all their possessions. Thus they and all that belonged to them went down alive to Sheol; the earth closed over them, and they perished from the midst of the assembly' (Num 17, 31-33). The revolt of Dáthan and Abiram therefore led to the destruction of their wives, their sons and their little ones (Num 17, 27). This incident reminds us of the divine state-

[15]Gerhard von Rad, *Das erste Buch Mose,* Göttingen 1956, p. 133.

ment: 'I the Lord your God am a jealous God, visiting the iniquity of the fathers upon the children to the third and fourth generation of those who hate me' (Ex 20, 5; 34, 6; Deut 5, 9). Hence the descendants of Reuben lost their birthright because of Reuben's sin (1 Chron 5, 1-2).[16]

Israel inherited much suffering from its kings. Thus because of David's sin in carrying out a census of the people, seventy thousand Israelites died of the plague (2 Sam 24, 15). David knew well enough that his actions affected the whole of Israel, for when Abner was murdered he hastily cried: 'I *and my kingdom* are innocent of the blood of Abner, son of Ner, before Yahweh for ever. Let it fall upon the head of Joab *and on all his family*' (2 Sam 3, 28-9). Because of the wickedness of king Manasses God said: 'See, I am bringing on Jerusalem and Juda evil such that both ears will tingle of whoever hears about it' (2 Kgs 21, 12; Jer 15, 4).

From these examples it is clear that the actions of certain individuals had a profound effect upon the group, either for good or for evil. Israel, the corporate person, was enriched or impoverished by the goodness or wickedness of her members. Without doubt the evidence is only concerned with outstanding individuals such as Abraham, Moses, David and the kings. But a theological principle is thereby established, which applies in due measure to every individual. The life and deeds of every individual affect to some extent the corporate person Israel: hence the warning: 'Beware lest there be among you a man or woman or family or tribe, whose heart turns away this day

[16]As a corrective to this notion which if over emphasised leads to irresponsibility and despair, the Bible also insists upon the responsibility of the individual, cf Deut 7, 9-10; 24, 16; Jer 31, 29; Ezek 14, 12 and in particular Ezek 18. Doubtless this latter aspect was more strongly developed by Jeremias and Ezekiel, but we must beware of two false conclusions: either that there was no notion of individual responsibility before their time, or that this new emphasis wholly replaced the idea of corporate responsibility, cf J. de Fraine, S.J., 'Individu et Société dans la Religion de l'Ancien Testament', *Biblica* 1952, pp. 324-355 and 445-475.

from the Lord our God to go and serve the gods of those nations; lest there be among you a root bearing poisonous and bitter fruit, one who, when he hears the words of this sworn covenant, blesses himself in his heart, saying : 'I shall be safe, though I walk in the stubbornness of my heart. *This would lead to the sweeping away of moist and dry alike*' (Deut 29, 18-19).

The One and the Many in the New Testament

The notion we have been trying to explain is a fundamental concept of the Old Testament, and without it God's revelation cannot be appreciated. Nor can the Psalms be understood and their true character as prayers realised. But the Christian has no need to acquire this concept as though it were something foreign to his outlook. The Christian has no need to force himself to cultivate an Israelite mentality in order to use the Psalter as his prayerbook. Whether he realise it or not, the very same concept is fundamental to the New Testament also; and this ought to cause no surprise, since there is no more separation between Old and New Testament than there is between the flower and its stem. This is not to say that no progress has occurred, for the stem is not the flower. The coming of Christ is the flowering of the stem, and a tremendous transformation has occurred. But it has been a homogeneous and an organic growth, and there the same fundamental concepts are to be found, easily discernible in spite of the development.

This development presents the paradoxical appearance of a reversal : God began to make Himself known by choosing a group, and this group is the person whom God chose, more fundamentally than the individuals belonging to the group. Israel was as it were the first and primary object of God's choice, and it was primarily within Israel that He saw and loved and cherished the individual Israelites. But in the end, God sent his Only-begotten Son, and it is in the single individual

22

person Jesus Christ that He is well pleased. As Jacob's name was changed to Israel, so, one might imagine, Israel's name was finally changed to Jesus the Christ, and the new Israel is born as a group, by reason of its association with this one individual. The primary object of God's choice now stands revealed as one individual and He sees and loves the group in association with that one individual.

This reversal must necessarily bring with it certain differences of expression: but the fundamental concept of a mysterious relationship between the one and the many remains. Previously it was a relationship between the one corporate person Israel and the many individual Israelites; now it is the equally mysterious relationship between the one individual person Christ, and the many Christians who are one corporate person, or as St Paul says: 'One body in Christ'.

In St Paul's thought Christ himself is not a corporate person as Israel was.[17] When he writes: 'As the body is one, and has many limbs, yet all the limbs of the body, though many, are one body, so also Christ' (1 Cor 12, 12), he does not mean that Christ *is* an entity made up of many. There were two Israels: the individual person who was the son of Rebecca, and the corporate person who was the child brought by God out of Egypt. But there are not two Christs. St Paul means here that Christ 'has' many Christians as closely bound to him as a body has limbs. In other words the name Christ is not used in the same way as the name Israel is used.

But the degree of unity between Christ and Christians is so close that St Paul must make use of the very same concept. The expressing of our salvation through Christ relies com-

[17]This is strongly maintained by L. Cerfaux, particularly in *La théologie de l'église suivant saint Paul*, Paris 1948. He has been attacked on this point by Th. Zapelena in *Verbum Domini* 1959, pp. 78-95 and 162-170, cf J. Havet, 'La doctrine paulinienne du "Corps du Christ", essai de mise au point', in *Litterature et théologie pauliniennes*, Bruges 1960, pp. 185-216. But in spite of considerable obscurity and some exaggeration Cerfaux's main contention is convincing.

pletely on it. According to St Paul we all have suffered by the action of Adam, and we have all been saved by the salvation of Christ: 'As through one man sin entered the world and through sin death, and thus death reached all men, for[18] all sinned. . . . If by one man's fault the multitude died, how much the more did God's grace and the gift conferred by the grace of one man Jesus Christ overflow to the multitude . . . Thus, as the fault of one man brought condemnation to all, so did the work of justice of one man procure life-giving justification for all' (Rom 5, 12-19).

It would be a mistake to think that St Paul is saying here no more than that Christ 'earned' something which is then shared out among mankind, without the latter having any part whatsoever in the earning of it. It would be equally wrong to think that mankind had no part whatsoever in the sin of Adam, though it must suffer the consequences. The truth is rather that mankind is so closely united to Adam that the action of the latter is in some mysterious way the action of the former, and Christ's action is the action of all those who are united to him through Baptism. To emphasise this point St Paul tells us that in Baptism we died with Christ (Rom 6, 8) and were buried with him (Rom 6,4). 'One man died for all; therefore all died' (2 Cor 5, 14). And just as we died in Christ's death, so too we rose from the dead along with him: 'But God, who is rich in mercy, out of the great love with which He loved us, even when we were dead through our trespasses, made us alive together with Christ (by grace you have been saved), and raised us up with him, and made us sit with him in the heavenly places in Christ Jesus' (Eph 2, 4-6). Paul can say: 'I have been crucified with Christ; it is no longer I who live, but Christ who lives in me' (Gal 2, 20). Just as the book of Deuteronomy tells the Israelites of the seventh century how they were slaves in Egypt, and how God delivered them and brought them to the Promised Land, so too Paul can tell

[18]The meaning of ἐφ' ᾧ is disputed.

24

the Christians of Colossae: 'You were buried with him in Baptism, in which you were also raised with him through faith in the working of God, who raised him from the dead' (Col 2, 12). Just as the Israelite inherited by circumcision the experience of Israel, to such a degree that five hundred years after the Exodus he could be said to have been brought out of Egypt, so the Christian inherits by Baptism the experience of Christ, to such a degree that he is said to have died, to have been buried and to have been raised to life.

The same mysterious concept of a profound union between the one and the many lies at the root of all the human language employed by God throughout His revealing of Himself. In spite of the differences arising from the primacy of the one individual Christ, in contrast to the primacy of the corporate person Israel, the solidarity, the unity and the community of experience within God's chosen people remain the same. And though Paul himself may never have spoken of the 'corporate person' Christ, the Church certainly does, and has done so from a very early time. In order to express the unity of life and the common sharing in the experience of the one man Jesus Christ, she speaks of the 'mystical body' of Christ, which we may term the 'corporate person' Christ: the new and the true Israel: the 'Israel of God' (Gal 6, 16).

Possible Objection

We have been studying a phenomenon which for want of a better name we have called the concept of corporate personality. This is a phenomenon of *expression*: a group is *spoken of* as though it were one person, with personal actions and personal sufferings. We have laid considerable stress on its importance, and we maintain that it has significant consequences. But there is perhaps an uneasy feeling that too much emphasis is being put upon particular turns of speech, and exaggerated conclusions are being drawn from them.

After all, it might be objected, this notion of corporate

personality is found everywhere and at all times, though in varying degrees. We are all familiar with the expression 'the brotherhood of man'; we all know that the family, the nation and a multitude of societies all constitute in some degree corporate persons. Shakespeare can write : 'England hath long been mad and scarr'd herself' (Rich III, V5 23) or 'France, hast thou yet more blood to cast away' (K John II 1 334) without demanding any extraordinary powers of understanding from his hearers. We are familiar with the idea that the crime of one man can bring disgrace upon the whole family. We know that in certain regions the vendetta is practised, and the family considers it a sacred duty to revenge an insult offered to one of its members. This sense of solidarity is now much weakened in our western civilisation, but it is strong elsewhere. The following comment for instance, on the outlook of the Nyakyusa tribes in Tanganyika reads like an explanation of Israelite solidarity : 'Kinsmen were members of one another in an immediate and material sense, so much so that the actions or omissions of a grandfather or cousin—still more a father or brother—were held to bring sickness and death upon one. And in a lesser degree men who were fellow members of a village or chiefdom were mystically one. The conception of individual moral responsibility was clearly there ... Nevertheless the individual tended to be merged in his lineage and treated in the ritual not as a person in his own right but as a representative of his group. Just as kinsmen were responsible before the courts for the debts of one of their lineage, and village-mates for the adultery of one of their members, so it was thought that supernatural punishment might fall, not on the wrongdoer himself, but on one of his family or even a neighbour.'[19]

This notion of corporate personality was in no way proper to Israel; it was a prominent feature of Egyptian and Assyro-Babylonian thought, leading, according to Misch to the curi-

[19]Monica Wilson, *The Listener,* Nov. 1, 1956, pp. 692-3.

ously impersonal autobiography which reminds us of the lamentation psalms: 'Unexpectedly numerous are the autobiographical documents which we find among the ancient civilized peoples of the Middle East, particularly those of the Egyptian and Assyro-Babylonian civilizations. . . . But in all this abundance of material there is an infinite poverty of individual character. In all these documents we scarcely ever find any personal touch. They conform to one settled pattern. Their large measure of uniformity marks them as the product of established usages and of traditional forms of self-presentation. Thus before the growth of a sense of individuality we meet with a stereotyped or, so to speak, collective kind of autobiography. These examples are the earliest we have, and they extend back into the second and third millennium B.C.'[20] Within the Bible itself it is not only Israel that is a corporate person. The same mode of expression is used of Edom (Num 20, 18), and other nations and cities: Babylon the virgin (Is 47, 1), Egypt the virgin daughter (Jer 46,11), daughter Dibon (i.e., Moab, Jer 48, 18), Sodom, younger sister of Juda (Ezek 16, 4) or Ninive the prostitute (Nah 3, 5).

The same may be said of the language Paul uses. The image of the body and its limbs had been used to describe the corporate entity which is the city with its many citizens.[21] Is not the attribution of Christ's death and resurrection to all Christians simply an emphatic way of saying that Christians benefit from this death and resurrection? Is it not therefore an exaggeration to stress the turn of phrase and maintain that all Christians have in some way died and risen again?

The answer might perhaps be in the affirmative, if any better way of expressing the supernatural truth could be substituted. Other ways of expressing the truth have in fact been found, but none better, nor any indeed as good. The problem resolves itself into one aspect of that vast mystery: God's

[20]*A History of Autobiography in Antiquity,* London 1950, I, p. 19.
[21]cf John A. T. Robinson, *The Body,* London 1952, p. 59, ftn. 1.

revelation to mankind; it is the mystery of the divine word becoming human. God must use human language and human concepts. The notion of corporate personality is a universal human concept, and God makes use of it. The expressing of it cannot be dismissed as mere metaphor. There is in any case an underlying truth to every metaphor, but 'mere metaphor' is in practice a disparaging expression which implies that the truth is less than its expression would imply. But the attribution of a corporate personality to Israel implies a truth far transcending its expression. It is a deficient way of expressing God's thought in regard to His chosen people. But it is nevertheless the way God elected to express His thought. The use of the same concept in reference to other nations, and the universality of such a concept do not affect the issue at all, because it is not the notion as such with which we are concerned. We have been trying to acquire a clearer idea of how God regarded Israel, and not how Israel regarded either herself apart from God, or other nations. The fact that she regarded other nations as closely knit unities is neither surprising nor significant. The fact that, if she had been capable of purely secular thought completely divorced from God, she would still have regarded herself as a 'corporate person' is equally beside the point. In actual fact God chose to express the supernatural truth of her relationship with Him, and of her supernatural essence, by means of this human notion. And we must make use of the same notion to approach the supernatural truth it attempts to express.

We stress the expressions of her corporate personality, and refuse to dismiss them as mere figures of speech, not because we are unaware of their inadequacy nor insensitive to their metaphorical character, but because we realise that human language cannot be otherwise when used as the vehicle of divine revelation. The sacred authors themselves realised that there was something of the metaphorical in such expressions, and this shows through sometimes, though rarely: 'The Lord thy God carried thee *as a man carries his son*' (Deut 1, 31; cf 8, 5). But the same author would have rejected any such conclusion as: Therefore Israel is not really God's son. God's statement to Israel: 'Thou are My son' is a statement of a relationship between Himself and Israel which is a reality transcending every possible way of expressing it in human language, but it is not falsified by the terms God used. The sacred authors are making use of the well known natural phenomenon of corporate personality to speak analogically of a fundamental truth of faith.

The Notion of 'Corporate Personality' and the Psalms

Belief in the oneness of Israel before God's sight, and of the individual's inclusion within this greater whole was bound to have a profound effect upon Israel's prayer. Since the primary relationship was that between Israel the corporate person and God, the psalms were sung primarily by Israel, and whether the voices were many or few, there was always a vivid realisation of the fact that it was Israel who was speaking. The individual Israelite could not make use of the Psalms without the realisation that he had the duty of praising God, and the right to invoke God's mercy, only insofar as he belonged to Israel.

In a certain sense therefore there was no such thing as 'private' prayer. When we use this expression we refer to that conversation between God and the individual which recognises no need of any intermediary, nor of any prior condition to be fulfilled. The creature speaks to His Creator, directly and independently of anyone else. This is of course as impossible for the Christian as it was for the Israelite, but we nevertheless act as though such prayer were possible for us—such is the excess of our individualism. No such private prayer existed for the Israelite, and there is therefore not one single psalm which does not demand at least tacitly the preliminary realisation of the psalmist's solidarity with Israel.

29

But is this tantamount to saying that no psalm is wholly concerned with the needs of the single individual? If we read the psalms our first reaction will certainly be to deny this. There are very many psalms which are worded in the first person singular. If we read Ps 6 for instance, there seems no reason for understanding it as anything else but the prayer of an individual man who is sick, and begs God for restoration to health : 'Be gracious to me, O Lord, for I am languishing . . . Turn, O Lord, save my life.' (vv. 2. 4). The psalmist of Ps 38 is similarly in the greatest distress : 'My wounds grow foul and fester . . . Lord, all my longing is known to thee . . . Do not forsake me, O Lord!' (vv. 5. 9. 21). The enemies of the psalmist in Ps 41 are saying : 'A deadly thing has fastened upon him; he will not rise again from where he lies.' (v. 8). The psalmist of Ps 88 has been 'afflicted and close to death from my youth up', shunned by lover and friend, and therefore : 'I, O Lord, cry to thee; in the morning my prayer comes before thee' (vv. 15. 13).

These psalms, and many similar ones appear to be the private prayers of individuals in distress. We have others which seem equally individual : 'The Lord is my shepherd' for instance (Ps 23). There seems no reason to suppose that the speaker is any other than the individual expressing his gratitude and confidence in God : 'Even though I walk through the valley of the shadow of death, I fear no evil; for thou art with me . . . I shall dwell in the house of the Lord for ever' (vv. 4. 6). In Ps 30 we have joy and gratitude for some favour received, compelling the psalmist to praise God : 'O Lord my God, I cried to thee for help, and thou has healed me. O Lord, thou hast brought up my soul from Sheol, restored me to life from among those gone down to the Pit' (vv. 2-3). God is praised in Ps 92 because 'Thou hast exalted my horn like that of the wild ox . . . My eyes have seen the downfall of my enemies' (vv. 10-11).

When therefore we read these psalms couched in the first

30

person singular there seems at first sight no reason to doubt that they were written by, and destined for the individual Israelite. But on the other hand, we have already seen how language could be used of the corporate Israel which at first sight seems to indicate one individual. Is it not possible that the 'I' of so many psalms, in spite of the language used, is not one individual but the whole person Israel? There is no doubt about its possibility, and when we read in Ps 129 : 'Sorely have they afflicted me from my youth, let Israel now say, Sorely have they afflicted me from my youth, yet they have not prevailed against me', we must grant that in this case at least, it is a certainty. Moreover we find in a number of psalms that the singular alternates with the plural in a way which shows at least that the psalmist does not regard himself as isolated from the rest of Israel. In Ps 106 we read : 'Remember me, O Lord, when thou showest favour to thy people ... that I may rejoice in the gladness of thy nation' (vv. 4-5), words which point the distinction between the individual and the totality, but which also show clearly that the psalmist regards his blessing as coming through God's blessing of Israel, and there is no incongruity about the change to the plural : 'Save us, O Lord our God, and gather us from among the nations' (v. 47). Ps 40 begins: 'I waited patiently for the Lord', and the psalmist goes on to speak of the great favours God has done for him, favours which he has reported to the community: 'I have told the glad news of deliverance in the great congregation' (v 9), because all Israel is concerned with the favours shown to her members. For that same reason the psalmist in Ps 69 prays: 'Let not those who hope in thee be put to shame through me, O Lord God of hosts; let not those who seek thee be brought to dishonour through me, O God of Israel.... Let the oppressed see it and be glad; you who seek God let your hearts revive. For the Lord hears the needy ... For God will save Sion, and rebuild the cities of Juda, and his servants shall dwell there and possess

31

it' (vv. 6. 32-3. 35). The psalmist may be one individual, but he is profoundly conscious of his solidarity with Israel. Similarly the psalmist in Ps 116 promises: 'I will pay my vows to the Lord in the presence of all his people, in the courts of the house of the Lord, in your midst O Jerusalem' (vv. 18-19).

There are equally significant examples in which the psalm is couched for the most part in the plural, and yet the speaker occasionally uses the singular. Ps 44 is clearly the lamentation of Israel in her sufferings: 'Nay, for Thy sake we are slain all the day long, and accounted as sheep for the slaughter' (v. 22). But in that same psalm we have 'Thou art *my* king and *my* God' (v. 4). 'For not in *my* bow do I trust, nor can *my* sword save me' (v. 6). 'Thou hast made us a byword among the nations, a laughingstock among the peoples. All day long *my* disgrace is before me' (vv. 14-15). In two consecutive verses Ps 85 has: 'Show us thy steadfast love O Lord, and grant us thy salvation. Let *me* hear what God the Lord will speak, for He will speak peace to His people' (vv. 7-8). The remnant of Israel in exile 'by the waters of Babylon' asks: 'How shall we sing the Lord's song in a foreign land?', and then immediately vows: 'If *I* forget thee O Jerusalem, let *my* right hand wither! Let *my* tongue cleave to the roof of my mouth, if *I* do not remember thee' (Ps 137, 4-6).

It is therefore true to say that the psalmist is never isolated in his prayer from Israel. We would conclude this from the fundamental principle we have been considering, but the words of the psalms are a further witness to it. And herein lies the explanation of so many seeming exaggerations which are apt to disconcert us. This question of exaggeration is admittedly a delicate one, since we must allow for poetical language, and for the exaggerations to which we are all prone, especially when under duress. But when, for instance, the psalmist in Ps 57 gives this promise: 'I will praise thee O Lord, among the peoples; I will sing praises to thee among the nations' (v. 9), we rightly feel that it is Israel whom he is committing to the task of making God known throughout the world. When the psalmist in Ps 66 invites the world to praise God for what he has done for them, and promises: 'I will come into thy house with burnt offerings ... with the smoke of the sacrifice of rams ... bulls and goats' (vv. 13-5), he is surely speaking of the liturgical worship of all Israel. When the psalmist describes his sufferings, we cannot help but feel sometimes that they surpass the afflictions of any one individual. In Ps 22 for example: 'Many bulls encompass me, strong bulls of Bashan surround me, etc.,' (cf vv. 12-21), we have a description of the persecution of Israel, rather than of any one individual. It is true that this same psalm gives us another example of a distinction between the psalmist and the group: 'From thee comes my praise in the great congregation; my vows I will pay before those who fear him' (v. 25), but it ends with the claim that posterity will serve the psalmist, and people yet unborn shall proclaim his deliverance. The fact is that God's deliverance of Israel is often the subject of praise in the midst of Israel herself, recounted by one of her number, for the edification and encouragement of his brethren. When the psalmist in Ps 69 complains that 'More in number than the hairs of my head are those who hate me without cause' (v. 4) we may feel that this is not simply poetical exaggeration, in spite of the fact that here once more we have a distinction made between the psalmist and the rest: 'I have become a stranger to my brethren, an alien to my mother's sons' (v. 8). There is no reason to think that the individuals who formed the whole Israel, were in practice any nearer to the ideal of unity, wherein all had but a single mind and heart, than are the members of the new Israel today. But when the psalmist urges God to punish his enemies: 'May their camp be a desolation, let no one dwell in their tents ... Add to them punishment on punishment, may they have no acquittal' (v. 27), we can be confident from the very language, that he is referring to the godless nations which persecuted Israel, and destroyed the cities of Judah, for whose rebuilding the same psalmist so earnestly prays (v. 35).

The oscillation between singular and plural shows that the concept of solidarity with Israel is present in the psalms, as indeed we would expect. In fact it is difficult to accept the point of view of those who would demand explicit evidence before allowing that any particular psalm couched in the first person singular has communal overtones. And yet this latter opinion is maintained by scholars of deservedly high repute. For instance Gunkel-Begrich states: 'The collective explanation of the 'I' in the psalms constitutes one of the grossest errors that exegesis of the Psalter could make.'[22] Without doubt the question is a most controversial one, and it would be rash to claim that any solution chosen is quite obviously the correct one. But one cannot escape the feeling that the distinction between individual and group has been exaggerated. The alternative interpretations of the 'I' of these psalms are not simply either the individual, strictly 'private' Israelite, or of Israel personified. Examples quoted above in which the psalmist distinguishes himself from the community are sufficient to show that the alternatives are less clear-cut. In other words, the 'I' of these psalms may often, and perhaps always except in clear instances such as Ps 129, be an individual. But such an individual is conscious of his representative role, either because he holds an official position or simply because he is part of Israel as a body. The real question is not whether the 'I' signifies one or many, but whether the 'I' ever signifies an individual who is praying without any advertence to his solidarity with Israel.[23]

[22]Quoted by De Fraine, *op. cit.* p. 186.

[23]cf Stephen Neill, *Christian Faith To-day,* London 1955: 'It was rather from the experience of the nation than from that of the indi-

This I doubt very much. I doubt it even in those psalms which are the prayers of a sick man, and which are commonly regarded as the clearest examples of the isolated prayer of the individual, concerned exclusively with his own distress (cf Pss 6, 38, 41, 88). It is important to remember that since Israel is a person, then Israel too can be said to be sick and wounded. Isaias uses such language of all Israel: 'Why will you be smitten, that you continue to rebel? The whole head is sick, and the whole heart faint. From the sole of the foot even to the head, there is no soundness in it, but bruises and sores and bleeding wounds; they are not pressed out, or bound up, or softened with oil' (1, 5-6). It is difficult to accept that vividly personal details in these psalms could not on that account refer to the whole Israel, after reading chapter 16 of Ezekiel, where the birth and rearing of this person Israel, is described in obstetrical detail: 'As for your birth, on the day you were born your navel string was not cut, nor were you washed with water to cleanse you, nor rubbed with salt, nor swathed with bands' (v. 4). Israel's experience at the hand of God is analogous to that of the individual at the hand of his chastiser or his surgeon: 'Come, let us return to the Lord; for He has torn, that He may heal us; He has stricken, and He will bind us up. After two days He will revive us; on the third day He will raise us up, that we may live before him' (Os 6, 2). The constantly recurring image of the 'raising up' of Israel is

vidual that the Israelite inferred the nature of the divine dealings with man. The span of one man's life is too short, and the event often too perverse or too paradoxical, to serve as a basis for general understanding. It is on the larger canvas of the rise and fall of nations that tendencies appear and moral judgements seem to be confirmed by experience. There is, indeed, in some of the highest expressions of Old Testament faith, a curious blending of the individual and the national, and such rapid transitions from singular to collective that it is sometimes hard to tell whether the prophet or psalmist is generalizing from his own experience, or whether he is speaking as the personification of the nation.' (pp. 86-7) borrowed from the parallel of restoration to health of the sick man. There is no reason why the language of sickness should be an obstacle to the collective overtones of such psalms.

Lastly we may reasonably consider that the psalms, whatever their origin, were collected and preserved as part of the Sacred Scriptures, to form primarily and directly the prayer of the community. In other words we must face the possibility that there exist psalms which in the first place were composed by talented individuals to meet their own private circumstances without any reference to the whole Israel, but which were preserved and included in the Scriptures, not solely nor even primarily to provide less talented individuals in the same circumstances with prayers to meet their own particular situation, but to provide the community with prayers in time of Israel's sickness and distress.

This is not meant to imply that the individual was given no consideration whatsoever, in the liturgical worship of Israel. We are indeed amazingly ignorant, in spite of the lengthy regulations concerning such aspects of liturgical worship as the sacrifices, of what precise form liturgical worship took. But in the Book of Leviticus many sacrifices are prescribed for individual cases: 'When *any man* of you brings an offering ...' (1, 2). Yet it follows from the very fact that these were liturgical offerings made in the Temple, that no individual's offering was purely private, without significance for Israel as a whole. It is noteworthy that the Old Testament preserves very little evidence of 'private' prayer, before the late Jewish period. At this time when much of the Wisdom literature made its appearance it would seem certain that psalms were composed for private devotion and unconnected with the Temple cult, in praise of wisdom and of the Law (cf Sir 14, 20-15, 8; 17, 25-18, 14; Dan 2, 20-23; 9, 4-19; 1 Mac 3, 50-3). But Eissfeldt's judgement 'that a really thoroughgoing proof of the existence of religious poetry detached from the cult, called a "spiritual" poetry, cannot be established"[24] seems correct for the earlier periods. Unfortunately therefore the question cannot be altogether separated from that of the dates of the psalms, a question which will never, it appears, be answered with satisfaction. But it seems just to say that there is reason to link up the psalms with the cultus,[25] and therefore to maintain that they have always at least overtones which reflect the solidarity of all Israel in its prayer, unless there are evident signs in particular

[24]According to Aage Bentzen, *Introduction to the Old Testament,* 2nd edit., Copenhagen MCMLII, I, p. 165.

[25]The relationship between the Psalms and the Cultus is another vexed question. There are many, following Mowinckel, who would link practically every psalm with the cultus: 'the psalms were originally ritual poems' (Bentzen, *op. cit.* II, p. 170). Others strongly oppose this view. Thus Tournay for example writes: 'The psalms directly composed in view of a liturgical act are thus less numerous than has sometimes been supposed; it is true that several have been adapted later.' (*Les Psaumes—Bible de Jérusalem,* 2nd edit. Paris 1955, p. 36). Opposition to any considerable relationship between the Psalms and the Cultus may be part of the exaggerated reaction against the emphasis, perhaps somewhat excessive, put upon the influence of liturgical celebration such as the hypothetical New Year Festival, by the Scandinavian School of exegesis. It may also be due to some reluctance to admit the strong influence of Babylonian and Egyptian religious literature on Israel. It seems somewhat ironical that opposition to the cultic setting for the psalms should force Catholic commentators to date many psalms much later than tradition does. It is worth noting also, how many psalms are admitted by such opponents to have cultic connections. Tournay for example admits cultic references in 20, 4; 26, 6; 27, 6; 66, 13; 81, 4; 116, 17; 134; 135, 2. He assigns 81, 95, 134, 118 to the Feast of Tabernacles; 114 to the Pasch and 113-118, the liturgical Hallel. According to him the following were sung in the precincts of the Temple: 20; 26; 48; 65; 118; 134; 135; others 'could be' the same: 23; 29; 63; 92. In others there are exhortations to enter the sanctuary: 76; 95; 96; 100. Pss 24, 68 and 132 seem to have been sung in processions; in others, whilst the psalmist is not in the Temple, he is turned towards it: 28, 2; 143, 6 cf 44, 21; 141, 2; 5, 8; 99, 5. 9; 138, 2 and in the following, promises to pay his vows: 22, 26; 27, 6; 54, 8; 56, 13; 61, 9. In addition, Tournay quotes many examples of psalms which were not originally written in view of the liturgy, but subse-

cases, that they are the product of the Sages, i.e., originating from the same circles of writers who gave us the Wisdom literature: two clear examples are to be found in Pss 1 and 119.

We conclude therefore that the psalms of the Psalter have either by reason of their composition or by reason of their preservation, a communal reference, and that with the exception of the later 'wisdom' psalms, none are purely individual, without any reference to Israel as the first object of God's choice and love. There is sufficient evidence to make this conclusion highly probable, though one cannot claim certainty. The conclusion has been reached on objective evidence, but there is no intention of hiding the fact that the attempt has been made for a practical purpose.

There is no evidence to show whether the Israelites made use of the Psalter as a whole in their liturgical and synagogal worship. In other words we do not know whether the healthy Israelite recited the lamentations of the sick. Christians who make the Psalter their prayerbook do so, and I am thinking in particular of those who use the Breviary. How can the Christian recite such psalms when he is not in a like situa-

---

quently retouched for that purpose. But in practice it is not always clear that they have been retouched. He himself says that 'it will always be hazardous to wish to isolate in the Hebrew text the elements labelled primitive' (p. 38). It is difficult to see why one ought to conclude that 'the place and influence of the liturgy on the Psalter seem to have been less than one might think at first sight.' He goes on to say: 'The majority of Psalms betray weightier preoccupations.' But how precisely does the presence of 'weighty preoccupations' show a non-cultic background? Is this simply an a priori judgement that formal, liturgical worship never shows a sense of urgency, such as is found in 'private prayer'? One might reply with Mowinckel: 'Such a point of view (speaking of Gunkel) is due to an inherited failure to appreciate the constructive part played by the cultus in the life of society, and an over-emphasis upon the opposition between what is regarded as purely formal religion and that which appears to be a more personal type.' (cf *The Old Testament and Modern Study*, edit. H. H. Rowley, Oxford 1951, p. 190).

tion? How can he declare : 'My wounds grow foul and fester because of my foolishness, I am utterly bowed down and prostrate. . . . My friends and companions stand aloof from my plague, and my kinsmen stand afar off' (Ps 38, 5-6. 11)? One solution has been to allegorise : we are all sinners, wounded by the darts of the devil, festering with moral corruptions, our wretchedness causing horror to the angels and the saints. Such allegorising, venerable though it is in the Church, does not satisfy the modern mind, and in the end is a wearisome and an unconvincing method.

Our study of the foundations of Israel's prayer provides us with another solution, both reliable and satisfying. In objective fact this difficulty could not face the Israelite because he was profoundly conscious of his solidarity with the whole Israel. That same solidarity exists for the Christian if he will school himself to realise it in his prayer. St Paul tells us : 'The eye cannot say to the hand, "I have no need of you", nor again the head to the feet, "I have no need of you.". . . But God has so adjusted the body, giving the greater honour to the inferior part, that there may be no discord in the body, but that the members may have the same care for one another. If one member suffers, all suffer together; if one member is honoured, all rejoice together. Now you are the body of Christ and individually members of it' (1 Cor 12, 21. 24-7). Here is the only solid foundation on which the Psalter can become the Christian's prayerbook. It is a solid foundation, for it is the condition on which the Psalter was given us as the inspired prayer of God's chosen people. It is the foundation which will truly transform our prayer, for it will lead us to realise as never before, that we are all one body, depending one on another under the leadership of Christ our head, whom the Father hears always (cf John 11, 42). In this age of exaggerated individualism it demands a great sacrifice : no less than a laying aside of our own personal anxieties and our own

39

personal needs, and indeed our own personal joys and gratitude. In using the psalms as our prayers we must never lose sight of the truth that we are part of the whole Church, the Israel of God, which simultaneously suffers with the suffering Christ, and triumphs joyfully with Christ risen from the dead and victorious over evil.

Chapter II

The Basic Pattern of the Psalms

The Psalms are Stereotyped

Anyone who has read through the Psalter will have felt that one psalm is very similar to another, so similar in fact, that the reading of them can be very monotonous. The psalms are written according to a limited number of patterns, to which on the whole they conform quite rigidly. This fact has been increasingly realised and all studies of the Psalms are now based on the principle that they can be classified according to the particular pattern on which they were composed.[1]

The psalms therefore are commonly grouped according to their literary form, and these groups are usually given such labels as Hymns, Collective Lamentations, Collective Thanksgivings, Individual Lamentations, Individual Thanksgivings, Royal Psalms, Psalms of Confidence, Didactic Psalms and so on. Contrary to what is often implied this classification is never made purely on the grounds of literary form, since it is impossible to abstract completely from the content, and when we

---

[1]In this respect the Psalm Studies of H. Gunkel were epoch making, and all subsequent writers on the Psalms are greatly in his debt, particularly with regard to his final work, edited by J. Begrich after Gunkel's death: *Einleitung in die Psalmen,* Göttingen 1933. Cf S. Mowinckel, 'Psalm Criticism between 1900 and 1935', *Vetus Testamentum* V, (1955), p. 13ff; A. R. Johnson, 'The Psalms', in H. H. Rowley (edit.), *The Old Testament and Modern Study,* Oxford 1951; Hans-Joachim Kraus, *Psalmen,* Neukirchen 1960, p. xxxvii.

consider more specifically the limited and stereotyped content of the Psalms, we are led to the conclusion that basically there are only two types of psalm: the song of praise, and the lamentation.[2] This seems to be altogether too sweeping a simplification, and it must be admitted that there are some psalms, notably the didactic psalms such as Pss 1 and 119, which do not really fit into either of the two classes. But apart from very rare exceptions, such a simplification will stand the test, provided that we realise that both these types include various elements, any one of which may form the sole theme of an entire psalm. We are about to consider the elements of these two types, but by way of illustrating the present point we may refer to Ps 23, which appears to be neither a lamentation nor a song of praise, and which might therefore seem to be outside the two categories which, we claim, share between them the whole Psalter. But Ps 23 is an expression of confidence in Yahweh and as such it is a more lengthy development of one of the elements of the lamentation. On these grounds it would be included in the latter category.

It is this combination of literary form and content which leads to the conclusion that basically there are only two types of Psalm, the song of praise and the lamentation. And this conclusion is of considerable importance for a proper appreciation of the psalms. Israel's prayer has basically only two aspects: lamentation in the face of trials and sufferings, and the praise of God Who has done wonderful deeds on her behalf. Israel's prayer moves incessantly backwards and forwards between these two ideas, sometimes concentrating wholly on the one or the other, but more often than not including both, though with varying emphasis. Thus an appreciation of what is meant by praise and lamentation will be a great help towards understanding the whole Psalter.

[2]cf Claus Westermann, *Das Loben Gottes in den Psalmen,* Göttingen 1954. This chapter owes much to this valuable book.

Though we would rank praise before lamentation since it is the more noble, the logical ordering of these two concepts is the reverse: made by trials and distress to realise her own insufficiency and her need for a more powerful help than she herself is capable of providing, Israel turns to God in tearful supplication. When God has come to her rescue she sings His praises in joyful gratitude.

> They surrounded me on every side,
>> and there was no one to help me;
> I looked for the assistance of men,
>> and there was none.
> Then I remembered Thy mercy, O Lord,
>> and Thy work from of Old, . . .
> And I sent up my supplication from the earth,
>> and prayed for deliverance from death . . .
> My prayer was heard,
>> for Thou didst save me from destruction
>> and rescue me from an evil plight.
> Therefore I will proclaim Thee and praise Thee,
>> and I will bless the name of the Lord.
>
> (Sir 51, 7-12)

This is in its most simple form the whole prayer of Israel. It is in essence the universal form of prayer, to be found wherever man recognises the existence of God. Yet there is a subtle and an important difference between this and the manner of praying which is instinctive to us, who belong to a different epoch and a different civilisation.

Regrettably it would seem to be an inescapable fact that in normal circumstances many people feel neither need nor desire to establish any contact between themselves and God. Even though they have made no formal denial of God's existence, and even though they would protest, if challenged, that they believed there was a God, they never pray. But in time of distress a difference is often seen. When faced with danger which seriously threatens them or when sufferings arise out of a situation they are powerless to escape, they are frequently moved to cry out for help: O God, help me, O God save me from this! The first words many people have ever addressed to God have been forced from their lips by suffering. Their first prayer has been a cry of distress. More likely than not they add to this cry of distress the promise that they will in future live better lives, worship God, perhaps 'go to church'. They strengthen their plea with something resembling a bargain: 'O God, if you rescue me, then I will worship you in the future.' If their plea is granted they would, we trust, thank God and fulfil their promise.

This down-to-earth view of the phenomenon of prayer may well be offensive to people who are deeply conscious of a close relationship between themselves and God, and in whose lives prayer plays an important part. But it is substantiated by the experience of the irreligious. Pious people may resent the suggestion that man's first and instinctive approach to God is in supplication rather than in praise, and that self-interest rather than God's glory is the more powerful stimulant to prayer. But this view of prayer is not only based on experience; it rests in fact on a very sound principle. Man must first know himself, before he is led to look about him for his maker, and it is precisely when he is forced to realise his own insufficiency that he is prepared to approach in supplication one greater than himself and greater than the most powerful man on earth. Moreover this is the logical sequence followed by God in the revelation of Himself. He first appears as the saviour of the Hebrews who are suffering under the cruel yoke of the Egyptian Pharaoh. He is the answer to their prayer for release from slavery, and it is because of this that He then stands revealed as God, the all powerful conqueror of the might of Pharaoh, and God who has chosen and loves Israel. Because He has heard with compassion their lamentation He becomes the object of their praise. Similarly the child born to the Virgin Mary is first and foremost Jesus, that is the supreme revelation that God is the saviour of His people.[3] It is only after and as a result of Christ's redemption that he is seen as the fitting object of our praise.

It is not surprising therefore that all the psalms should belong to the categories of either lamentation or praise or both. Indeed these two literary categories are ideologically two parts of the one whole: man's instinctive address to God consists of a lamentation in face of distress, followed by a promise of praise if God rescue him from his trouble, and lastly the fulfilment of this promise when he praises God for having come to his rescue. The Israelite's view of prayer therefore, corresponds to our own experience. And yet there is a subtle distinction: the terms lamentation and praise seem vaguely unnatural. We would more readily label prayer when viewed in its crude simplicity as petition and thanksgiving: 'O God please save me', and 'O God, I thank you for saving me!' Israel's prayer is lamentation and praise whilst ours is petition and thanksgiving, and the difference in terminology is significant. The reason why we have chosen the former and less familiar terms with which to sum up Israelite prayer is that they are a more accurate description of the contents of the psalms. The idea of lamentation does of course include that of petition, whilst praise includes thanksgiving. But lamentation and praise are wider terms, and in both cases there is a difference, though the distinction between praise and thanksgiving needs more careful consideration than that between lamentation and petition.

Lamentation rather than Petition

In many psalms we find a detailed description of the sufferings being endured by the psalmist. Thus for instance, in Ps 6

[3]Mt 1, 21. The word Jesus is the Greek form of the Hebrew Joshuah, a common name since the successor of Moses cf Ex 17, 9, and meaning 'Yahweh is salvation.'

he declares: 'I am weary with my moaning; every night I flood my bed with tears; I drench my couch with my weeping. My eye wastes away because of grief, it grows weak because of all my foes' (vv. 6-7). In Ps 17 we have a description of the persecution the psalmist is suffering at the hands of his enemies:[4] 'They close their hearts to pity; with their mouths they speak arrogantly. They track me down; now they surround me; they set their eyes to cast me to the ground. They are like a lion eager to tear, as a young lion lurking in ambush' (vv. 10-12). The same theme is developed at great length in Ps 22, 6-8. 12-18; 35, 11-16. 19-21. In Ps 38 we read a particularly harrowing description of the psalmist's sufferings: 'My wounds grow foul and fester because of my foolishness, I am utterly bowed down and prostrate; all the day I go about mourning. For my loins are filled with burning, and there is no soundness in my flesh. I am utterly spent and crushed; I groan because of the tumult of my heart' (cf vv. 3-20). Similar examples are to be found in Pss 41, 6-10; 55, 3b-6; 57, 5. 7. Practically the whole of Psalms 69, 88 and 102 are devoted to lament, as well as Pss 60, 1-6; 74, 3b-9; 79, 1-4; and there are many more examples.

This description of trials and sufferings, which we term the lament, is the most characteristic and prominent feature of the first type of psalm, and this is the reason why it is given the name Lamentation, namely those psalms in which the most prominent element, but not the only one, is the lament. In these psalms God's attention is drawn to the plight of the psalmist by his bewailing his sufferings at considerable length. Now this may strike us as a show of self-pity. It would, however, be shortsighted to adopt such an attitude. In the first place we must undoubtedly allow for a profound difference of temperament between the ancient semitic poet and ourselves. Jeremias for instance provides us with an example of how violently even a prophet of God could complain about his suf-

[4]The question of the psalmists' enemies calls for special consideration.

ferings (cf ch. 11-20). But we ought not to let any tempera-
mental revulsion blind us to the deeper truth which gives rise
to such laments. The psalmist realises his utter helplessness
and his complete dependence on God. Wisely he does not credit
himself even with the strength to 'keep a stiff upper lip' in face
of trials, and so he gives full rein to his lament as the expression
of his belief that no human aid can avail him anything. These
laments may be compared with penitential practices such as the
wearing of sackcloth, the sprinkling of ashes on the head, the
fasting and self-inflicted scourgings which many people now
find repulsive and ostentatious. Penitential practices and
laments are simply two ways, often combined, of expressing
vividly and convincingly the sufferer's wretchedness and his
need of God's merciful help.[5]

If we raise the question of our duty to suffer without complaining, with patience and even with joy, as proof that these
laments are 'unchristian' we are simply confusing the issue.
It is true that we must suffer without complaining, when our
complaints would be addressed to men, for they would be
implicitly suggesting that God Our Father does not take sufficient care of us, and that we need to turn to others for help
and sympathy. The psalmists' laments are addressed to God
Himself, and this makes all the difference. The psalmist
recognises that only God can give him the sympathy and the
help he needs; the detailed description of his sufferings only
emphasises the more his complete dependence upon God and
increases his confidence that God in His great love and compassion will not resist his plea.

But in any case it is a great mistake to consider the lament
in isolation from the expressions of confidence which invariably
accompany it. These two important elements of the lamentation must not be separated from one another, for if this is done,
the lament will inevitably give a false impression. The psalmist

[5]cf T. Worden, 'The Remission of Sins—II', *Scripture* 1957, pp. 117-
122.

does not merely bewail his misery; he also declares his complete trust in God, and this declaration of confidence is astonishing in its strength. The psalmist's enemies are numerous and powerful, 'But thou, O Lord, art a shield about me, my glory, and the lifter of my head. I cry aloud to the Lord, and He answers me from His holy hill. I lie down and sleep; I wake again, for the Lord sustains me. I am not afraid of ten thousands of people who have set themselves against me round about' (3, 3-6). Such unshakable confidence is founded upon the belief that God has chosen Israel, and that He is unchangeable in His loving kindness towards her: 'Rise up, come to our help! Deliver us for the sake of Thy steadfast love!' (44, 26). God will not, He cannot allow His chosen one to be destroyed: 'But for Thee, O Lord, do I wait; It is Thou, O Lord my God, Who wilt answer' (38, 15). Sometimes God is slow to answer, and the psalmist cries out 'How long, O God, is the foe to scoff? Is the enemy to revile Thy name for ever? Why dost Thou hold back Thy hand, why dost Thou keep Thy right hand in Thy bosom?' Yet the exasperation of the psalmist must not be mistaken for despair, for there can be no grounds for despair: God is both willing and able to rescue His people: 'Yet God my king is from of old, working salvation in the midst of the earth. Thou didst divide the sea by Thy might; . . . Thou hast fixed all the bounds of the earth . . . Do not deliver the soul of Thy dove to the wild beasts; do not forget the life of Thy poor for ever. Have regard for Thy covenant (cf Ps 74, 10-20). When the psalmist asks 'Wilt Thou be angry with us for ever?' (85, 5) he knows in spite of his impatience for deliverance that such a thing is impossible and so he adds 'Surely His salvation is at hand for those who fear Him, that glory may dwell in our land' (Ps 85, 9). The psalmist awaits with humble trust the hour of God's intervention: 'To Thee I life up my eyes, O Thou Who art enthroned in the heavens. Behold, as the eyes of servants look to the hand of their master, as the eyes of a maid to the hand of her mistress, so our eyes look to the Lord our God, till He have mercy upon us' (Ps 123, 1-2). When the psalmist recalls all the occasions in the past when God has come to the rescue, he cannot despair since God is not as men are, fickle and changeable : 'I remember the days of old, I meditate on all that Thou hast done; I muse on what Thy hands have wrought. I stretch out my hands to Thee; my soul thirsts for Thee like a parched land' (Ps 143, 5-6). The avowal of confidence is so important an element in the lamentation psalms, that it is sometimes enlarged into the whole psalm, and not one word of lament remains: cf Pss 11; 16; 23; 62; 121; 125; 131.

In some of the lamentation psalms there is not merely an avowal of confidence in God, but a statement that the psalmist has already been heard, cf 6, 9-11; 22, 22; 28, 6; 31, 22-3; 28, 7. The abruptness of the transition from lament to this conviction that God has already granted the psalmist's request is so startling that it has evoked many explanations, none of which indeed is entirely convincing. The most probable one is that which suggests that when the psalm was used in the liturgical worship of the temple, a priestly oracle intervened between the lament and the statement that the prayer has been heard, but that this oracle has not been preserved within the psalm since it did not belong to it.[6] But whatever be the true explanation of this detail in some of the lamentation psalms, we cannot help but be astonished at the degree of confidence which it expresses. If we were inclined to take scandal at the psalmist's indulgence in lament, we cannot but regard his confidence in God with astonishment and envy, and be ashamed at the contrast between his prayer and ours.

His lament and the avowal of his confidence in God are the major parts of his prayer. That element which we are inclined

[6]cf Kraus, *op. cit.* p. xlix f. Examples of the oracle may possibly be preserved in Pss 2, 7-8; 12, 6; 21, 9-31; 27, 14?; 32, 8ff; 35, 3; Is 49, 25; Os 14, 5-9. Cf Aage Bentzen, *Introduction to the Old Testament* I, Copenhagen MCMLII, pp. 158-9. J. W. Wevers rejects this explanation, in 'A Study in the Form Criticism of Individual Complaint Psalms', *Vetus Testamentum* VI, (1956), pp. 81-2.

to regard as the essential of prayer, namely the petition, has only a minor place. Nevertheless the lamentation does include both an introductory cry for help, and a petition. These psalms regularly begin with a plea in very general terms: 'Give ear to my words, O Lord; give heed to my groaning. Hearken to the sound of my cry, my King and my God, for to Thee do I pray' (Ps 5, 1-2). 'O Lord, my God, in Thee do I take refuge; save me from all my pursuers, and deliver me' (Ps 7, 1; cf 17, 1; 31, 2-4; 70, 2). But after the lament proper they usually contain a further petition, either that God should listen, that He should come to the rescue or that He should destroy the cause of the psalmist's sufferings. Thus : 'Arise O Lord! Deliver me, O my God! For Thou dost smite all my enemies on the cheek, Thou dost break the teeth of the wicked' (Ps 3, 7). 'Make them bear their guilt, O God; let them fall by their own counsels; because of their many transgressions cast them out, for they have rebelled against Thee' (Ps 5, 10; cf 6, 5; 7, 7-10; 31, 10. 16-19). But it is surprising how general these petitions remain. They are always couched in terms which are applicable to many different circumstances, and in this regard they are vastly different from the petitions we address to God. The psalmist leaves to God the task of deciding what specific help will be best for him, in contrast to our petitions which state much more precisely what we require of God, and which therefore must be qualified by some such condition as 'If thou seest it to be good for me'.

To sum up our consideration of this first class of psalm we may say that by Lamentation Psalm we mean that type of psalm whose most important elements are a description of the distress which the psalmist is enduring, an avowal of his confidence in God's readiness to come to his assistance, and a petition for that assistance, couched in general terms. These psalms are the equivalent of our petition prayers, but they are clearly very different, and if our aim is to make the Psalter our prayer-book, we must face this fact quite loyally.

On the one hand we must overcome our feeling that to lament our sufferings is wrong, even when that lament is addressed to God. On the other hand we must be willing to sacrifice the specific character of our petitions. To achieve the former we must realise that we are in fact declaring our desperate need of God's help, without which we are doomed, and we are implicitly stating our belief that God cannot remain indifferent to our plight. In order willingly to sacrifice the specific character of our petitions we must convince ourselves that God knows what is best for us, and that we ought to leave ourselves in His care without trying to dictate the precise way in which He ought to take care of us. If we achieve both these attitudes we shall have acquired a new trust in God which will measure up to the acts of faith which are so strongly expressed in these psalms. Finally, if we keep in mind the corporate mentality with which these psalms were written, and our obligation to look beyond our individual selves to the whole body of Christ we will have little difficulty in making these lamentations a genuine expression of our prayer. We may have neither sufferings nor trials in our own individual lives which justify the harrowing laments of the psalmists, but without any doubt the body of Christ suffers grievously in many parts of the world, in hospitals and in prisons, in loneliness and dereliction, in poverty and famine. We are not tempted to dictate to God precisely how He ought to save us from these evils, for we do not know the remedies. But believing that 'If one member suffers, all suffer together' (1 Cor 12, 26) the intensity of the psalmist's plea will not sound hollow on our lips. And though our own individual confidence in God is so often weak and fainthearted, there is abundant evidence to show that the body of Christ has never faltered through two thousand years of hardship and persecution. Generosity and forgetfulness of self is the necessary condition for making the Psalter come alive as our prayerbook, and nowhere is this more true than in the lamentation psalms, which form so large a part of it.

The second basic division of the Psalter is into songs of praise and, once more, we apply the term praise to these psalms because it is the most accurate description of their contents. But most of us do not have a very clear idea of what is meant by praise. The notion of thanksgiving is much more adapted to our mentality, and in fact the psalms here referred to, are generally classed as 'Thanksgiving Psalms'. But this is not an accurate description, for thanksgiving is not exactly synonymous with praise, and the latter is a more correct description than the former.

What difference is there, to our way of thinking, between praise and thanksgiving? Without any doubt they are closely related, and this explains why the translation 'I thank thee because . . .' fits in well enough, although the sense is more fully rendered by 'I praise thee that . . .' Praise includes the notion of thanksgiving, but it is a considerably wider concept, and when we narrow it down to the latter, we lose something of the genuine sense of these psalms, and indeed we misunderstand them quite radically.

Perhaps the difference between the two ideas can be illustrated by pointing to a universal phenomenon in young children. By some strange psychological process they gradually abandon praise in favour of thanksgiving, as they grow older and more sophisticated. Young children are notoriously slow to express their thanks, and the social convention of saying 'Thank you' whenever anything is given, has to be imposed upon them by dint of constant correction and encouragement. It certainly does not come naturally! On the other hand young children are most eager to tell others of what they have been given. With complete spontaneity, and with what we would term naïvety, they will tell anyone willing to listen, what their mother has given them, what their father has made for them, how good, kind, clever, rich even, their parents and their relations and friends are. Praise comes to them so much more

52

naturally and spontaneously than thanks. It is only when the child's praise has been received with coldness, indifference or even hostility, when in fact it has been labelled as boasting, something regarded as bad, that the child reluctantly abandons his practice of praising his benefactors, and becoming a wiser and a more sophisticated person, he begins to murmur his thanks so much more readily. His benefactor to whom he addresses his thanks is evidently much more disposed to listen to what he has to say, than those to whom his praise of the benefactor had been addressed. To praise he has need of an audience which is not forthcoming; but to thank he needs only the benefactor. There are only two parties needed for thanksgiving; praise requires three: the benefactor, the one benefitted and the one to be impressed and delighted by the benefaction. The last is not easy to find, in a society so individualistic as ours, where we are pre-occupied by our own advantage, either as the benefactor duly appreciated, or the recipient of benefaction, but where we tend to consider that generosity shown towards others, in no way concerns or profits us. St Paul's statement that 'If one member is honoured, all rejoice together' (1 Cor 12, 26) seems singularly unrealistic.

The Israelites, like the child, were less sophisticated in this regard than we are, for they did not thank people as we do, but they were generous in their praise. In the Old Testament we have many vivid descriptions of relationships between individuals, described with a wealth of detail, and including many conversational exchanges: yet we find no example of one man saying 'thank you' to another, as we might have expected. If for instance we read the story of Abraham's finding a wife for Isaac (Gen 24), a story which by common consent is one of the most vivid narratives in the Old Testament, we find that Abraham's servant addresses no word of thanks to Rebecca for her great kindness. Instead 'The man bowed his head and worshipped the Lord, and said "Blessed be the Lord, the God of my master Abraham" ' (v. 27). Jacob had been kindly received

53

by the Egyptian Pharaoh, and at the close of the audience 'Jacob blessed Pharaoh, and went out from the presence of Pharaoh' (Gen 47, 10)—he had similarly 'blessed' Pharaoh, when he had first been ushered into his presence (Gen 47, 7). Another example of a highly circumstantial narrative is the story of David's escape from Saul with the help of his friend Jonathan (1 Sam 20). David must surely be grateful for this help, and indeed we read that on taking leave of Jonathan 'they kissed one another and wept with one another' (v. 41), but there is no mention of David expressing his thanks. Again, David had cause to be grateful to Abigail, for she had dissuaded him from taking vengeance on Nabal (1 Sam 25, 23ff). But instead of expressing his thanks he said: 'Blessed be the Lord, the God of Israel, who sent you this day to meet me! Blessed be your discretion, and blessed be you, who have kept me this day from bloodguilt!' (vv. 32-4). When David grants Joab's request that Absolom should be brought back home, 'Joab fell on his face to the ground and did obeisance, and blessed the king' (2 Sam 14,22). In gratitude for the gift of a servant, David does not express his thanks when he takes leave of his friend Barzillai, but 'the king kissed Barzillai and blessed him' (2 Sam 19, 39). Even the famous story of Solomon's judgment concerning the dispute between the two harlots (1 Kgs 3, 16-28) does not end with the profuse thanks of the genuine mother of the infant. Instead Israel 'stood in awe of the king, because they perceived that the wisdom of God was in him' (v. 28).

The Blessing

The absence of any mention of one man thanking another may prove nothing, but it is certainly rather odd and unexpected. Where we would expect some such a phrase as 'then he thanked him' we find 'then he blessed him'. Instead of expressing their thanks, the Israelites were accustomed to pronounce a blessing. This occupied the place which we would allot to thanksgiving, though pronouncing a blessing was not restricted to such a moment, as we have seen from the example of Jacob and the Pharaoh.[7] Yet it might be thought that 'to bless' is simply a synonym for 'to thank'. This is not so.

The blessing, in origin,[8] is that power given by one man to another, and usually to his eldest son, whereby the latter becomes more 'alive', stronger and more prosperous. A man has the power to hand on the life force by procreation, and because of this, he was considered to possess the transmittable power of a good, strong and prosperous life. This is in essence the blessing, considered to be a thing, as real and substantial as food or gold or weapons. This power was handed on by certain actions, most commonly by a touch such as the laying of the hand upon the head of the recipient. We have an example of this when Joseph blesses Ephraim and Manasseh (Gen 48, 14). But it could be handed on simply by pronouncing certain words, for the word was powerful, and could bring into existence the thing to which it referred: 'When an Israelite pronounces blessings on another, then these are not empty though kindly wishes for the future. . . . No distinction is made between the word and the matter described.'[9] A blessing was a real power, the source of life and prosperity. Consequently a man who in actual fact was powerful and prosperous must be termed a blessed man: there could be no other explanation. Every man indeed was blessed insofar as he possessed life, but the explanation of why certain men were superior to the rest

[7]In fact it was so frequent, that 'to bless' is sometimes no more than 'to greet'. The common greeting, itself a blessing, was *Shalom*: Prosperity!

[8]cf J. Pedersen, *Israel, Its life and Culture I-II*, Copenhagen 1926, pp. 182-212. In this book, which is a classic among Old Testament studies, the difference between what might be called the Semitic philosophy, and Israelite theology is not always clearly shown, and is consequently misleading to the reader not sufficiently aware of this necessary distinction.

[9]J. Pedersen, *op. cit.* pp. 167-8. Cf Beyer, in *Theologisches Wörterbuch zum neuen Testament,* II, p. 752.

was that they possessed a greater blessing: they were particularly blessed.

This way of regarding man's strength and prosperity in terms of the blessing received from a source outside himself, is far older than Israel, being a fundamental concept of the Semite from as early a time as we have records.[10] Naturally enough such a concept was retained by God's people: it was a part of the Semitic 'philosophy', a way of thinking and expressing one's thoughts about certain facts of reality. But on the other hand this concept was profoundly modified by revelation. Since Israel regarded Yahweh as alone God, and their supreme Lord, they recognised that the blessing belonged ultimately to Him, as the sole source of life and prosperity. The old way of speaking about the blessing persisted, but always with the realisation that God was ultimately the sole source of blessing. This is clearly shown in the story of Isaac giving the blessing to Jacob (Gen 27). It is obvious from the expressions used that the blessing is something which Isaac possesses and which he wishes to give to his eldest son, now that he is about to die. It is the eldest son's birthright, the most precious gift that Isaac can bestow, and once given, it cannot be taken back and given a second time. But it is to be noted on the other hand how clearly Isaac realises that he is only giving the blessing by God's leave; and he realises too that the blessing itself is really God's power, not his own: 'May God give you of the dew of Heaven.' (v. 28). The same truth is equally emphasised when Jacob blesses his sons; it is 'By the God of your father who will help you.' (Gen 49, 25 cf Gen 48, 15ff).

It is said in Sir 3, 9 that 'A father's blessing strengthens the houses of the children', but there is no suggestion that the father's blessing has any power independently of God. It is always realised that the blessing only has power insofar as God concurs in it, and as it were pronounces the blessing by the lips of the father. Some indeed may be more sure of God's

[10]cf Beyer, art. cit. p. 752.

56

concurrence than others, for such persons as the father, the priest (cf Num 6, 22-7) and the king (cf 2 Sam 6, 18; 1 Kgs 8, 14. 55) are appointed specifically to act as God's spokesmen in the pronouncing of the blessing. But every man may hope for God's support, and may therefore claim to possess and impart the blessing to others. But always it must be remembered that whilst the ancient and pre-Israelite concept of the blessing remains, as far as language is concerned, there is no real trace of the magical, something which had been its essential element. As though to emphasise this, the Old Testament frequently speaks of the blessing being pronounced by God in person (cf Gen 1, 22. 28; 2, 3; 39, 5; Ps 128, 8). This is so frequent that when we read, for instance, 'The Lord blessed Abraham in every way' (Gen 24, 19) we do not advert to the fact that strictly speaking it means simply that the Lord pronounced the richest of blessings over Abraham. Unconsciously adopting the Semitic attitude regarding the efficacity of the pronouncement, we understand the saying as meaning that the Lord did very many good things for Abraham. God's blessing and God's enriching action become identical, such is the power of God's word: it is no sooner said than done.

Blessing in return for favour

Therefore instead of merely expressing his thanks, the Israelite gave his benefactor a blessing which was a real and substantial gift in return. But what could he give God Himself in return for His gifts? If he ought to bless his human benefactor, then all the more ought he to bless God the giver of all good things. But how could he bless God? Yahweh was not like the gods of the Egyptians and Babylonians whose life-force was strengthened or weakened by the diligence or remissness with which their devotees blessed them.[11] The Israelite blessed

[11]cf Beyer, art. cit. p. 756. The same notion is found in the Roman belief concerning the harmony between the spheres and the earth: 'There must be a *correspondence;* heaven and earth are counterparts,

God both because this was a part of the regular stock-in-trade of semitic religious practice, and by analogy with the blessing of human benefactors. But the meaning must of necessity be different. Just as the strong and prosperous man is blessed, namely in enjoyment of the blessing given him by God, so too God is blessed because He is in full and perfect possession of the blessing, as its very source. So, when the Israelite blesses God he does not give God the blessing, but recognises that God is infinitely blessed. When he blesses God he *declares* that God is so to speak full of blessing, and the spring from which all blessing flows. When for instance Abraham's servant 'blessed the Lord, the God of my father Abraham, who has led me by the right way' (Gen 24, 48), he declared that God was the source and the giver of the blessing, namely the power whereby he had discovered Rebecca (cf Deut 8, 10; Jud 5, 2. 9; Tob 12, 6; Pss 16, 7; 34, 1; 66, 20). This is something more than what we mean by thanking God. It is an acknowledgment or 'confession' of what God is, as well as what He has done.

The Proclamation

This analogous meaning of to bless becomes, when God is the object, synonymous with confessing or professing or praising God.[12] Since the Israelite blessed rather than thanked when

and what happens above must be reproduced below, in accordance with the incessant exchange of inter-reacting molecules and effluvia between the two. For it was believed that the heavenly bodies were nourished by emanations from earth, and it seemed equally reasonable to suppose that emanations also proceeded in the opposite direction and profoundly influenced earth—and the human beings who dwelt thereon.' Michael Grant, *The World of Rome*, London 1960, p. 136.

[12] A study of the Septuagint supports this. Its regular translation of *berek* to bless, is εὐλογεῖν ('to eulogise'). But they twice (Is 12, 1; 38, 19) use this same translation for another Hebrew verb, *hôdah*, regularly translated by ἐξομολογεῖν to confess or profess. The latter word is in turn sometimes (1 Chr 23, 30; 2 Chr 5, 13; 23, 12) used to translate a third Hebrew word, *hillel*, regularly translated by to praise. This latter represents on one occasion *berek* (Ps 99, 4).

he had received something from one of his fellow men, he 'blessed', or 'confessed' or praised God when he had been the recipient of the divine favour. In other words he proclaimed what God had done, and what God is, and this proclamation is destined for others to hear. The very concept of proclaiming or praising includes the idea of an audience. When for instance Hannah sings her praise of God (1 Sam 2, 1-10) for taking away the reproach of her sterility, she directly addresses those who stand listening (v. 3). The purpose of the proclamation of God's deed is to make Him known and appreciated, so that His praise may be sung by an ever widening circle of worshippers: 'Let thy saints and all thy creatures bless thee; let all thy angels and thy chosen people bless thee for ever.' (Tob 8, 15). According to Job the man whom God has relieved of his sufferings 'sings before men' of his deliverance (cf Job 33, 27; cf Pss 34, 2; 44, 1. 8). No audience may in fact be present, but this does not make the singing of God's praises impossible. Jonas for example is represented[13] as doing so in the belly of the big fish (2, 1-9) where his song is heard only by God. But it is nevertheless a proclamation of what God has done for him: 'I called to the Lord, out of my distress, and He answered me.' This is why the introduction to this psalm must strike us as odd when it is translated as 'Then Jonah *prayed to* the Lord His God',[14] for the psalm is not a *prayer to God* : *it is a proclamation about God, it is a song in praise of God*.

This is nonetheless true because the song in question not only speaks of God, but also addresses Him. The verse following the opening one just quoted reads: 'Out of the belly of Sheol I cried, and *Thou* didst hear my voice', and the rest of

Moreover the noun αἴνεσις is frequently used as the translation of the Hebrew noun *tôdah*, from the root *hôdah*. All these verbs have the same basic sense when God is the object, namely of 'speaking well' about Him.

[13]Commentators consider that this psalm is a later insertion.

[14]*Revised Standard Version.*

the song is couched in the same form until its last line: 'Deliverance belongs to the Lord'. Having in fact no human audience Jonah directly addresses His one listener, the same God whose praises he is singing. Hannah does the same, even though she is represented as in fact having a human audience: 'There is none holy like the Lord, there is none beside *Thee*, there is no rock like *our* God' (1 Sam 2,2). Since God is always listening, then in any song of praise the singer may turn to him and address Him directly. But it still remains a proclamation *concerning* God; its purpose is still the same, namely to make known God's wonderful deeds and His wonderful self. It may perhaps be thought that in the absence of a human audience songs of praise lose all point—and indeed this may be partly the explanation of why they are now so often spoken of as songs of thanksgiving. Clearly the proclamation when only God hears it, is not intended to increase God's knowledge of Himself, and help Him to realise more clearly how kind and how powerful He is! The intention is rather to show God how fully the singer knows and appreciates Him; and by making this proclamation the singer deepens his own conviction. One might say that the singer is his own audience, and the singing of God's praises gives him a deeper appreciation of the truths he has been proclaiming. 'Praising', 'extolling', 'magnifying' God, or 'giving glory' to God are all expressions for telling oneself and/or others how great God is, so that oneself and/or others may come to a deeper knowledge of Him. To do this is to fulfil the purpose for which God chose a people for Himself: to reveal Himself, or make Himself known to the world He had created.

The Psalms of Praise

Another way of describing the action of blessing God, and a much more common way in the psalms, is to speak of 'proclaiming' God. The translators of the Septuagint certainly thought that these two words, bless and proclaim, were more or less synonymous, when God was the object, for they occasionally translate the latter by the word εὐλογεῖν which is their normal translation for the Hebrew word to bless.[15] The Hebrew word which we translate as proclaim is *hôdah,* and it is very often translated as to thank. But this is inaccurate, and we must spend a little time in showing this.

One of the best known features of Hebrew poetry is parallelism, namely the expression of one idea by two or more parallel statements. When therefore we are in doubt about the meaning of a word, we can often resolve our doubt by considering other, better understood expressions, which are used as parallel statements of the same idea. Now many words are used in the psalms in such a way that we may conclude that they are true parallels with this word *hôdah.* There is, for instance the word *zamar* (Pass 7, 18; 18, 50; 33, 2; 92, 2; 108, 4; 138, 1), and this means to sing. There is *sabah* (106, 47), *ranan* (33, 2) and *hillel* (33, 2) which mean to rejoice. But none of these are particularly helpful in determining the exact meaning of *hôdah,* since we could sing and rejoice equally when proclaiming God as when thanking Him. But other parallel verbs are much more informative: *sipper* (9, 2; 26, 7; 75, 1; 79, 13; 88, 12), which means to recount or recite; *higgîd* (30, 10; 92, 2) which means to announce or proclaim; *'amar* (107, 1; 118, 1) and *malal* (106, 2) which mean to say; *qara'* (105, 1) which means to recite; *hizkin* (6, 6) to recall; *hodîa'* (105, 1) to make known; *berek* (100, 5) to bless, and *hikbîd* (86, 12; 99, 3) to glorify. All these verbs suggest a public proclamation of what has happened. They all suggest the giving of information to others, and this impression is confirmed if we examine the contexts in which they are used. Here are three examples, in which the disputed word is left untranslated so that we may infer its meaning from the parallel expressions:

> (I will) *'ôdeh* Yahweh with all my heart,
> I will recount all Thy wonders. (Ps 9, 2)

[15] cf footnote 12.

Will dust *yôdah* Thee?
Will it announce Thy fidelity? (Ps 30, 10)
Hôdû Yahweh,
Call out His name,
Make known among the nations His deeds. (Ps 105,1)

When we further examine in what this proclamation or announcement or recital consists, we see clearly that it is not what we would call an expression of thanks, but rather a eulogy of God, destined to impress others. For instance in Ps 9, the psalmist first of all declares his intention: 'I shall proclaim Thee,[16] O Yahweh, with all my heart: I shall recount all Thy wonderful deeds: I shall rejoice and exult about Thee: I shall sing Thy name, O Highest!' The psalmist therefore intends to proclaim what God has done for him, and this is the proclamation: 'When my enemies turned back, they became helpless, and perished before Thee.' In other words the psalmist makes his profession of faith that his deliverance from his enemies has been the work of God. This proclamation is enlarged and emphasised, and then he is led from this particular example to profess his belief in God's unending and universal power to establish justice upon the earth. Such a profession of faith ought to be made by all Israel: 'Sing of Yahweh Who dwells on Sion, publish among the nations his actions, (namely) that[17] He, the

[16]Reading *'odᵉka* with the Greek, and cf Pss 86, 12; 138, 1. The fact that *hôdah* is sometimes followed by the direct accusative, and at other times by the preposition *le* makes no difference to the point of discussion: compare for example Pss 122, 4 and 142, 8; notice the use of *le* after *gaddel* in Ps 34, 14.

[17]*kî* is frequently mistranslated as 'because', when it is being used simply to introduce direct speech (cf the similar uses of ὅτι). This is clearest in Ps 118, 2-4. 10; 136 *passim*. In Ps 49, 17-19 the first three *kî* may be translated 'because' but the fourth certainly cannot be, 'because' even after *hôdah*, e.g., Ps 118, la; *kî tôb, but even here it is* possible that it should be translated simply as 'that He is good' or and this last follows *hôdah*. It may sometimes have the meaning 'Truly He is good', since this was a common liturgical exclamation

avenger of bloodshed remembered them: He did not forget the cry of the poor. Yahweh took pity on me; He saw my wretchedness, lifting me up, raising from death's gates, in order that I might recount all Thy praises at Daughter Sion's gates, and jump for joy at Thy rescuing.' God has defeated the enemies of the psalmist, and by so doing 'Yahweh has made Himself known; He has executed judgment.' This is not in fact the end of the psalm, for it continues with a lament, until the final profession of God's glory, in 10, 16-18; but it is sufficient to illustrate the declaratory character of these praise psalms.

We have another example in Ps 118, where the invitation to praise God is addressed to all Israel, and then to each of the three 'orders': the house of Israel, the house of Aaron and those who fear Yahweh, namely the proselytes.[18] Israel is commanded to proclaim God, and the proclamation is immediately given: 'Truly His kindness is everlasting.' And each of the three orders of Israelite is commanded to say this—'Let the house of Israel say . . .' The formula given here is a common liturgical proclamation, which for instance is found in Ps 136 after every sentence of a litany of the wonderful deeds of God. This is equivalent to proclaiming the *name* of Yahweh (Pss 106, 47; 122, 4; 142, 8), for the name is that by which God is made known to men, and He is made known through His actions in rescuing and protecting Israel, and in creating heaven and earth. His name is as it were written across heaven and earth for they bear His imprint: 'How glorious is Thy name on the whole earth, Thou who hast affixed[19] the proclamation of Thyself upon the heavens' (Ps 8, 2; cf 97, 6). In practice therefore, to proclaim the name of Yahweh is to announce what He has

---

(cf 118, 10). In Ps 139, 14 the meaning 'because' after *hôdah* is determined by *'al kî*. For the use of *kî* as the introduction of the direct speech after a *verbum dicendi* cf P. Joüon, *Grammaire de l'Hébreu biblique*, Rome 1923, s. 157c.

[18] cf Kraus, op. cit. p. 789.

[19] cf Kraus, op cit. p. 65.

done; it is to proclaim His 'holy remembrance', a word used in the psalms as a synonym for the name (Pss 30, 5; 97, 12). It is to bless His name (Ps 100, 5) and glorify it (Pss 86, 12; 99, 3).

The presence of an audience, which is an integral part of the concept of proclamation, is often explicitly indicated, and this in turn confirms our interpretation of the word *hôdah*.[20] Ps 22 is a lamentation followed by a song of praise, the two being joined by the astonishingly abrupt declaration: 'Thou hast heard me!' (v. 22). The song of praise (vv. 23-32) begins with the psalmist clarifying what he intends to do because God has heard him: 'I will recite Thy name to my brethren, in the midst of the assembly I will praise Thee. O you who fear Yahweh, praise Him! All the seed of Jacob glorify Him! Reverence Him, all the seed of Israel! ... Thou art my praise, in the great assembly, I will fulfil my vows in the presence of those who fear Him' (vv. 23-4, 26). Here is the audience for the psalmist's proclamation concerning Yahweh's kindness: his brethren, namely his fellow Israelites who make up the assembly or 'church' gathered together at the Temple (cf Ps 35, 18), the 'great assembly' such as was to be found there on the important feastdays. The whole of Israel is invited to hear what Yahweh has done, so that their faith may be increased, their confidence strengthened and above all so that they too may praise and glorify God, echoing themselves this proclamation, that Yahweh does not despise the wretched nor turn a deaf ear to their cries (cf v. 25). This proclamation serves as yet one more example, one more compelling proof of Yahweh's kindness towards them. All the poor and the helpless benefit from what God has done for the psalmist in hearing his plea. They receive new encouragement, new strength, which is symbolised by their eat-

[20]Other examples where *hôdah* must mean 'proclaim' and cannot mean 'thank' are Pss 45, 18; 71, 22; 89, 6. In Ps 32, 5 the verb is used of a confession of sins.

64

ing of the offering[21] which the psalmist brings when he makes his proclamation (v. 27). They must join with the psalmist in praising Yahweh: 'May your hearts live for ever!' (v. 27).

The proclamation therefore is intended first for the brethren, that is for Israel, and it is for their benefit, that their faith and their trust may be strengthened. But it is also for God's benefit, insofar as Israel, strengthened in faith and overjoyed at this display of God's love, will praise and proclaim Him with new enthusiasm. Even the Gentiles will benefit, for the proclamation will reach their ears too. 'All the ends of the earth will remember and turn to Yahweh; all the clans of the nations will bow down before Him' (v. 28). Every mortal man will recognise that Yahweh is alone God; to generations yet unborn will be repeated the psalmist's proclamation of God's action. In his joyful enthusiasm therefore, the psalmist sees his proclamation as the means of making Yahweh known to the whole world: such is the purpose of the song of praise.

We have another example in Ps 34, 3 where we are told that the poor will hear the proclamation and rejoice. In other words the wretched and helpless, who can hope for nothing from men, will be heartened to hear how God has answered the plea of the psalmist who was wretched and helpless like themselves, and how He delivered him: 'This poor man called out, and Yahweh heard, and rescued him from all his trials' (v. 7). 'Yahweh saves his servants' lives and no one who trusts in Him shall be found guilty' (v. 23).

In Ps 138 the psalmist is determined to make his proclamation of Yahweh's kindness and fidelity 'in the presence of the gods'. He intends, in other words, to proclaim the superiority

[21]cf Kraus, op. cit. p. 183. The reference here may well be to the *tôdah* or sacrifice of praise, which was one of the sacrifices of communion (cf Lev 7, 12-15; 22, 29-30), the victim being shared between God, the priest and the offerer. The latter ate his share, joined by his family and other invited guests, and this meal must take place on the day the offering was made. Cf R. De Vaux, *Les Institutions de l'Ancien Testament* II, Paris 1960, pp. 294-5.

of Yahweh, even to the so-called gods of whom the heathens boast, since he is convinced that Yahweh is supreme: 'There is no one among the gods like Thee, O Lord, nor any works like Thine!' (Ps 86, 8; cf 96, 4). This is a challenge to all the powers at work in this world : 'Bow down before Him, all you gods!' (Ps 97, 7). Moreover, the psalmist's proclamation of how powerful Yahweh's word is (cf v. 2) will lead all the kings of the earth to proclaim Yahweh, and sing of His might: great is Yahweh's glory! (vv. 4-5). The psalmist's proclamation therefore is aimed at making God known even to those who worship other gods and who therefore fail to acknowledge that Yahweh alone is God. The proclamation is made in order to praise God before the world and increase His glory (cf Ps 57, 10).

The principal element in the praise psalms, therefore, is the recital of what God has done, or of what God is. To give such a recital is, as we have seen, to bless or proclaim God. It is also to praise Him, and since this last term is the one best known to us we retain it as the name for this second type of psalm. If the recital consists of what God has done, whether it be on behalf of Israel directly considered as a corporate body, or on behalf of the individual Israelite, or whether it be of God's wonderful works in the world He has created, then we may speak of these as *narrative* praise psalms. If on the other hand the psalm is concerned with proclaiming what God is, namely His attributes such as His goodness, His almighty power, His kindness and fidelity, or His royal dignity, then we may call it a *descriptive* praise psalm. But these two classes of praise psalm are rarely found in complete isolation one from the other, since the proclamation of God's deeds leads logically to the recognition of His attributes, and the former explain the latter. Most of the praise psalms are predominantly narrative in form, and examples of this type are Pss. 34; 65; 66; 78; 92; 104; 105; 136. Examples of descriptive praise psalms may be found in Pss 19; 29; 33; 46; 96-9; 111; 113; 115; 117.

Having considered the difference between thanksgiving and

praise, and having in the process clarified our ideas on what the praise of God really means, it only remains for us to consider whether we can make these praise psalms our genuine prayer. The difficulty arises from that difference between thanksgiving and praise which we pointed out at the beginning: in the former there is a closer and a more exclusive relation between the thanker and the thanked than in the latter, which includes within its concept the presence of the third party, the listener. In other words the degree of intimacy with God seems less in praise than in thanksgiving. The difference might be illustrated as that between reciting the Creed and saying: 'O God I thank Thee for having made me well again.' Most of us would feel that the former is less of a prayer than the latter.

This reaction is widespread when it comes to a comparison in general between liturgical prayer and 'private' prayer. Many devout people feel disturbed at the way in which they are constantly being urged these days to take part in the Mass in a liturgical way. They find that this means in practice that they should make the responses with the rest of the congregation, recite or sing various parts of the Mass, listen to the scriptural readings and so on. As a result they feel that they have had little or no opportunity for their own private prayers. If this reaction is extreme they conclude with the statement that they never said a prayer!

No amount of propaganda on behalf of liturgical worship will solve this difficulty, unless a genuine effort is made to explain and understand what is meant by the worship of God; and the praise of God is the highest expression of this worship. To worship God is to acknowledge and proclaim Him; to express our belief that He alone is our good; that He has given us all we have; that without Him we are nothing. This is not simply a preparation for prayer, not just setting the scene and as it were justifying our decision to pray. It is itself our prayer, if by prayer we mean the worship of God.

If we recited the praise psalms with the genuine intention

of praying and worshipping God, we will be dissatisfied with them only as long as there remains that hankering after a more prominent place for our own individual selves before the throne of God. These psalms are essentially community prayers, and they remain so, whether we recite them alone or with others. Their communal character is part of their very essence, as we have seen when we were discussing the presence of the audience to hear the proclamation of God's glory. These psalms are sung for the benefit of the new Israel, the body of Christ, and through it for the benefit of all mankind. We have a duty to confirm the faith of our brethren, to increase their trust in God, and to fire them with new enthusiasm for the God in whom they trust. And we have the duty of making our God known to those who have not heard of Him. We have also the duty of confirming our own faith, of strengthening our own trust, and of rekindling and fanning the flame of our own enthusiasm for Him Who has chosen us and loved us. Even though we are alone when we recited the psalms of praise we are not without an audience, for we hear our own proclamation and are strengthened and encouraged by it.

The psalms are not indeed the Christian's supreme song of praise. He has one more song of praise to add to those of the Psalter, and one which is infinitely superior to them. He has that song of praise which we call the Holy Eucharist. The Eucharist is the specifically Christian praise psalm. That is precisely what its name means. The word Eucharist does not mean thanksgiving, as is often asserted, but praise[22]. Beginning with

[22]The fact that the Greek word εὐχαριστεῖν and the Latin *gratias agere* mean 'to thank' in later Greek and Latin authors (the former does not appear in the LXX except in the Deuterocanonicals Judith 8, 25; Wis 18,2; 2 Mac 1, 11; 10, 7; 12, 31) is not open to question. But it does not automatically follow that this is the meaning of the words when used in the Christian liturgy, whose language and ideas are derived not from profane authors but from the Bible. Now in the New Testament Greek εὐχαριστεῖν is synonymous with εὐλογεῖν, as can be seen when we compare Mk 6, 41 with 8, 6 (Mt 14, 19 with 15, 36);

Mk 8, 6 with 8, 7; Mk 14, 22 with 14, 23 (Mt 26, 26 with 26, 27); Mk 14, 22 with Lk 22, 19; see also Lk 24, 30. In all these cases there is reference to something Christ did before a meal. Without any doubt the thing referred to is the recitation of the formula, prescribed by Jewish Law. The Jews were most strictly forbidden to eat anything before they had pronounced a formula called a *berakah,* i.e., a blessing (cf Deut 8, 10). All these 'table-blessings' began with the words 'Blessed art thou, Yahweh our God, king of the world', and were completed by various statements concerning God's deeds. Here are some examples taken from the Passover: 'Who created the fruit of the vine'; 'Who has given to Thy people Israel this feast of unleavened bread.... Who sanctifies Israel and the days'; 'Who has made bread to come forth from the earth ... Who has sanctified us through His commandments, and commanded us to eat unleavened bread'; 'Who feeds the whole earth with His good things. We proclaim thee, Yahweh our God, that thou has given to our Fathers as their share of land, the beautiful, good and wide land.' Cf Strack-Billerbeck, *Kommentar zum neuen Testament,* München MCMLVI, p. 41ff. The last example is part of the blessing pronounced over the third cup, which was known as the cup of blessing since it was associated with a more elaborate formula, cf 1 Cor 10,16.

Christ therefore, when he fed the multitudes, at the Last Supper and at Emmaus observed the law by pronouncing the blessing before the meal, and this action is indicated by either εὐλογεῖν or εὐχαριστεῖν the two words being used synonymously (cf also 1 Cor 14, 16). The word therefore means 'to pronounce the blessing' or to utter the praise of God, and this must be its meaning in relation to the Christian sacred meal, which is modelled on its Jewish antecedent. As frequently happened, the first word was made the name of the whole liturgy, and this liturgy originally began with the invitation of the celebrant: Εὐχαριστῶμεν τῷ Κυρίῳ τῷ Θεῷ ἡμῶν   (cf Judith 8, 25) *Gratias agamus Domino Deo nostro,* i.e., Let us *praise* the Lord our God. This is confirmed by other synonyms in the song of praise now called the Preface: *hymnum gloriae canimus, laudant angeli, concelebrant, supplici confessione dicentes, gloriosius praedicare, non cessant clamare, collaudare benedicere et praedicare, debitis magnificare praeconiis.*

There are many other examples in the Latin liturgy where the meaning of *gratias agere* is not 'to thank' but 'to praise': e.g., *Gratias agimus tibi propter magnam gloriam tuam*: we do not *thank* God on account of his glory: we praise Him. The response to *Benedicamus Domino*: Let us bless the Lord, is not 'Thanks be to God,' but 'Praise be to God': *Deo Gratias.* We sing a *Te Deum* in thanksgiving, yet the text of this hymn is concerned with God's praise: *laudamus, confitemur*: it is a hymn *In Gratiarum actione*: in praise.

For synonyms of εὐχαριστεῖν cf H. Schlier, *Der Brief an die* the invocation *Gratias agamus Domino Deo nostro*: Let us praise the Lord our God, in the style of the praise psalms of the Psalter, the celebrant makes a solemn declaration of God's supreme and final and perfect work for our salvation. He has revealed Himself in a new and dazzling light, through the mystery of the Incarnate Word. He has attached the salvation of the human race to the tree of the Cross, so that whence death sprang up, thence life might rise, and he who conquered by the tree, might by the tree also be conquered. He has provided us with our Paschal victim, Christ the true Lamb who has taken away the sins of the world, and by rising has restored our life. It is not surprising that the proclamation of such wonderful deeds leads us to interrupt the narrative praise psalm with the brief description of what God is: Holy, Holy, Holy, whose Glory fills heaven and earth. Then the narrative praise continues, proclaiming how Christ Our Lord, the night before he died, took bread and said: This is my body. The Christian declaration of God's wonderful deeds is accompanied by its offering also, and psalm and offering together constitute the sacrifice of praise,[23] the Eucharist of which the poor will eat and rejoice.

Having in the Eucharist the perfect song of praise we may think that its forerunners in the Psalter are no longer of any use to us. Perhaps we feel that the wonders of God proclaimed in them pale into insignificance in the light of the wonders He worked for us in His Son Jesus Christ. And yet no work of God is too insignificant for our admiration. We must always view the deeds He accomplished for our forefathers, as preparations for

Epheser, Dusseldorf 1958, p. 43. For a consideration of the meaning of 'Eucharist' cf. J. P. Audet, 'Esquisse historique du genre litteraire de la "Benediction" juive et de l'"Eucharistie" chrétienne,' *Revue biblique* 1958, pp. 371-399.

[23] This early title for the Holy Eucharist is borrowed from the LXX translation of *tôdah* cf Lev 7, 2; 2 Chr 29, 31; 33, 16; Pss 50, 14. 23; 107, 22; 116, 17.

the final work He accomplished. When we sing of these deeds we must remind ourselves that something far greater is yet to come, and we will proclaim it when we come to the Eucharist. The Holy Eucharist, the greatest praise psalm of them all, is the climax of our worship. But far from leading us to despise and neglect the other songs of praise, it should make us sing them with all the greater enthusiasm, lest when we arrive at the final song of praise we sing it with coldness and indifference.

We need to sing God's praises at all times, for the audience to which we proclaim God's wonderful works is slow to hear, whether it be ourselves or our brethren, or the nations of the world. In fact this may be the reason why all we have said about the praise psalms seems in the end profoundly unreal. We have maintained that they are essentially proclamations to others. Yet who in all honesty listens to them? Even though we grant that the one who recites them pays some attention to what he is saying, how many of our brethren do so? Dare we ask how much attention the world pays to them? Very few listen to our proclamation that God is good, if we make that proclamation in words alone. In the last analysis we do not make God known by what we say, but by how we act: St Paul admonishes us: 'So, whether you eat or drink, or whatever you do, do all to the glory of God. Give no offence to Jews or to Greeks or to the church of God, just as I try to please all men in everything I do, not seeking my own advantage but that of many, that they may be saved. Be imitators of me, as I am of Christ' (1 Cor 10, 31-11, 1). Our whole life must be a psalm of praise, namely a declaration in action that God has done great things for us, that He is loving and kind, and that we fear no evil for He is with us. But we shall never make this declaration in action unless we have made and continually make it in words also. The two cannot be separated, for our faith and our trust need to be continually strengthened by conviction, if they are to be transformed into action.

The songs of praise, like the lamentation psalms, are profoundly social in their orientation: they are for the benefit of the community and the world, whether the benefit derives from a hearing of what is said, or an experiencing of what is done. This is liturgical prayer, based on a realisation of the community and its needs, and through this prayer we fulfil the purpose God had in creating us, namely 'To the praise of his glorious grace which he freely bestowed on us in the Beloved. . . . We who first hoped in Christ have been destined and appointed to live for the praise of His glory' (Eph 1, 6. 12).

Chapter III

The Redemption of Israel

Psalms 66, 1-12; 78; 105; 106; 114; 135; 136

A number of psalms are concerned with the fundamental revelation of Yahweh as the saviour of Israel, and a consideration of this truth will not only help us to appreciate these psalms, but will make us understand why the Pentateuch, or Torah, or the Law is the most important part of the Old Testament revelation. It will also serve as a more detailed consideration of the basis of Israelite prayer, such as we defined it in the first chapter.

This group of psalms is not homogeneous from the point of view of the two basic literary types discussed in the previous chapter. The majority indeed are songs of praise, but there is also one lamentation, and one didactic psalm, a form which as we have already pointed out cannot be classed, strictly speaking, with either of the two types into which we have divided the Psalter. It is for another reason therefore that we group these psalms together, namely because they have for the most part common material. This material consists in the recital of the wonders which God wrought on behalf of Israel when the latter was established as God's own possession among all the nations of the earth. For this reason these psalms are often referred to as the historical psalms; but this is somewhat unfortunate, since it tends to emphasise what is only a secondary characteristic. It is of far greater importance to realise that these psalms are professions of faith in the basic and essential act of redemption accomplished by God in favour of Israel.

Psalm 66 is sometimes considered as in reality two psalms,

vv. 1-12 being a song of praise concerning the redemption of Israel, and vv. 13-20, a song of praise concerned with God's merciful intervention on behalf of an individual.[1] But there seems to be no compelling reason why this psalm should not be a unity, in which a proclamation of God's loving kindness towards Israel in general is further exemplified by a particular instance of His mercy towards the individual Israelite. In any case we may limit our consideration to the first twelve verses, which are the only justification for this psalm's inclusion in this group. These verses celebrate the crossing of the Red Sea and the Jordan (v. 6), and they emphasise that these acts of salvation are not just events of the distant past, nor of significance to Israel alone. All the 'children of men' are urged to 'come and see the deeds of God' (v. 5). The drying up of the Jordan can still be seen, insofar as it has a lasting significance for the whole world, because it was a particular manifestation of that divine power which operates unceasingly. It is still to be 'seen' as a revelation to the nations of the earth, of the existence of Yahweh Who continually keeps His eyes upon them (v. 7).

Psalm 78 is a long didactic poem. This is clear from the introductory verses, in which the psalmist calls upon Israel whom he addresses in typically sapiential style, as 'my people', to listen to his instruction (*tôrah*), which is a parable (*mashal*) and a mystery (lit. dark sayings: *hidôth*). This introduction reminds us of the introduction to the Book of Proverbs (1, 1-6), but the material which constitutes the instruction given in Ps 78 is not the fruit of human wisdom such as is found in the sapiential books; it is the great historical events, the knowledge of which has been handed down from father to son. Moreover this instruction is meant as a warning 'that they might not be as their fathers, a stubborn and rebellious generation' (v. 8). Consequently great emphasis is laid on the sombre details of the great epic of redemption: the constant ingratitude and

[1] cf Hans-Joachim Kraus, *Psalmen*, Neukirchen 1960, vol. I, p.456.

infidelity of Israel, in spite of Yahweh's unfailing fidelity to His promises. This indeed is the parable and the mystery: that Israel could be so perverse in face of such constant and overwhelming love, and that God could be so patient and so persevering in His determination to save Israel, when He met with such great ingratitude. God did wonderful things for them in Egypt. He divided the Red sea, and led them out of Egypt, and He gave them water in the wilderness. Yet the Israelites complained, and had no confidence in God's power to feed them. He gave them manna and quails, and yet they provoked God to anger. They failed to remember the plagues with which he had overcome the Egyptians on their behalf (vv. 43-51). Yahweh had brought them safely into Canaan and to Mount Sion (v. 54) driving out the occupants of the land He had allotted to them. Yet they provoked Him again, so that He gave them over to the Philistines. He abandoned the northern tribes, and chose Judah, building His sanctuary on Mount Sion and appointing David as shepherd of His people. Thus the psalmist recalls the wonders of God from the Exodus to the establishing of the Davidic dynasty, and the building of the Temple. But he also recalls the constant rebellion of Israel in spite of such demonstrations of love.

Psalm 105 is a long praise psalm, proclaiming the fulfilment of God's promise to Abraham that He would give Canaan as Abraham's inheritance (vv. 8-11). The descendants of Abraham are urged with great insistence (vv. 1-7) to proclaim God's fidelity to His word, and to recite in detail how He accomplished it: how He protected the Patriarchs and their wives as they wandered in Canaan (vv. 12-15); how Joseph went down into Egypt in time of famine and was honoured by the Pharaoh. When Jacob had joined his son in Egypt and his people had greatly increased the Pharaoh had become hostile. But God sent Moses and Aaron, and through them He performed prodigies which terrified the Egyptians. There were the plagues of darkness, of water changed into blood, of frogs, of goats, of hail, of locusts and the killing of the first-born. God then brought His people out of Egypt, after they had robbed the Egyptians of their silver and gold. Surprisingly enough the psalm does not mention the crossing of the Red sea, but we have a description of how God protected and sustained His people in the wilderness. Eventually 'He gave them the lands of the nations'—not only the land of Canaan, but the whole world (cf Deut 11, 24). The very last verse gives this song of praise a didactic feature, for all that God has done for Israel is to the end that they might keep His statutes and observe His laws. This psalm is an excellent example of the liturgical praise, which was a prominent feature of the Temple liturgy. From 1 Chron 16, 8ff we may conclude that the recital of God's redemptive work on behalf of Israel was primarily the duty of the priests and levites. But without doubt this psalm is an example of the songs of praise with which the faithful entered God's presence on the great feasts (cf Ps 95, 2). Above all it emphasises Yahweh's fidelity to the pact He made with Abraham, and His determined efforts to rescue and bless His chosen people. To recall this redemption is to revive Israel's trust in Yahweh, to fill them with joy and to remind them that Yahweh their God is alone God, ruler of all peoples and master of the whole earth.

Psalm 106 is in form very different from the last, although it makes use of the same material. It does indeed open in the style of a praise psalm (vv. 1-2), and this is followed by a sapiential saying (v. 4), but in reality the psalm is a lamentation over the great infidelity of Israel. Convinced that their own sins are linked with the sins of their forefathers (v. 6) Israel laments the ingratitude of God's chosen people, which showed itself from the very beginning. The great deeds of God on behalf of Israel provide the contrast and heighten the disgrace. Israel paid little heed to the wonders God worked for them in Egypt: they were rebellious even at the Red Sea. God's destruction of the Pharaoh's army did evoke Israel's praise (v. 12), but soon afterwards they tempted God in the wilderness (vv. 14-15). They were jealous of Moses and Aaron; Dathan and Abiram revolted (vv. 16-17). Israel worshipped the golden calf (v. 19) and the Baal of Peor (v. 28). In fact they were preserved from complete destruction only by the intercession of Moses (v. 23) and the action of Pinehas the Aaronic priest (v. 30). They angered God at Meribah and failed to execute the law of Herem (v. 34). Instead they allowed themselves to be corrupted by the Canaanites (vv. 35-41). As a result God allowed them to be oppressed. The psalm ends with the plea of Israel suffering the Babylonian exile, scattered among the nations: 'Save us, Yahweh our God.' This psalm is a good example of the lamentations sung in penitential liturgies (cf Zach 7, 1-3), portraying the goodness of God and especially His severity in dealing with sin (cf Rom 11, 22; 1 Cor 10, 11). The same story provides material both for praise and for lamentation precisely because the recalling of God's fidelity to His promises, His justice and His love, immediately arouse the conviction that Israel has for her part been wholly unfaithful and shown the greatest ingratitude.

Psalm 114, wrongly[2] joined by the Septuagint with Psalm 15, is a song of praise which proclaims the power of God displayed when He rescued Israel from Egypt. It does not follow the usual pattern, for there is no introduction with its call to praise. But the proclamation is clear, with its statement that Yahweh, Who made Juda His dwelling-place (a reference either to Jerusalem or to the whole of the land of Judah) is the God before Whom the sea flees and the earth quakes. The historical reference is of course to the crossing of the Red Sea and the Jordan (the two are closely linked in Jos 4, 23f), but Yahweh's power over the sea reminds us that He is the creator of the world Who in the beginning conquered the sea which was the chaos.[3]

Psalm 135 is a song of praise used in the Temple liturgy (vv.

[2]op. cit. vol. II, p. 778.
[3]cf op. cit. vol. II, p. 782.

2. 18-21). The proclamation is concerned with Yahweh's wonderful deeds, both at the creation of the world (vv. 5-7), and when He rescued Israel from Egypt (vv. 8-12). It is on account of this latter part which is the central point of the psalm (v. 4), that we include it in this group of psalms. The details here are few in number: the killing of the first-born (v. 8), a general reference to the plagues (v. 9) and the conquest of Canaan (vv. 10-12). The actual crossing of the Red Sea and of the Jordan is not mentioned.

Psalm 136 is a praise psalm in the form of a litany, giving us an idea of how the people listened to the proclamation of God's wonderful deeds in the Temple liturgy (cf 2 Chron 7, 3. 6) and took an active part by repeatedly declaring that God's loving kindness is unceasing. The proclamation in this psalm is concerned with the creation of the world (vv. 5-9), the rescue of Israel from Egypt (vv. 10-16), the conquest of Canaan (vv. 17-22) and the protection of Israel in the time of the Judges (vv. 23-4). And it is the same Yahweh Who daily feeds them (v. 25).[4]

The Story of the Exodus

All these psalms refer to the wonders God has worked on behalf of Israel, and especially to the time when He chose Israel to be His own special possession and led them out of Egypt, and into the land of Canaan. These deeds are the foundation upon which Israel's faith rests for all time, and they are described at much greater length in the Pentateuch. The Pentateuch, known to the Jews as the Torah or Law, gives us the essential part of the Old Testament revelation, and all the rest of the Old Testament revelation is simply the further development and application of the Torah. For a proper appreciation of these psalms therefore, it is necessary to supplement the brief references we find there, by a reading of the story of the Exodus

[4]It has been suggested that this verse indicates the use of the psalm at a harvest festival, perhaps Tabernacles; but it is unlikely, cf. *op. cit.* Vol. II, pp. 900-901.

as we find it in the Pentateuch, not merely to increase the detail, but more important, to grasp the theological significance of the story of the Exodus, and thereby to appreciate how the recital of this story can form an important part of Israel's prayer.

1. The Covenant with Abraham and God's care for the Patriarchs (Ps 105, 8-15)

The emergence of Israel as God's chosen people must be traced back to God's choice of Abraham. It is true that we usually speak of the Exodus as the all-important act of Divine redemption, and the Old Testament itself speaks of the Exodus as the birthday of Israel. Thus for instance Osee writes: 'When Israel was a child I fell in love with him, and out of Egypt I called My son' (11, 1). The time of Israel's youth was when he came up from the land of Egypt (Os 2, 17). Indeed Osee retains nothing of the patriarchal age except references to Jacob's supplanting of Esau, his wrestling with the angel and his fleeing to Aram where he served seven years for a wife (Os 12, 4-5. 13). Jeremias dates Israel's youth to the same occasion : 'I remember the devotion of thy youth, the love of thy nuptials : thou didst follow me in the wilderness.' (2, 2) Ezechiel is still more explicit : 'The day on which I chose Israel, on which I lifted My hand towards the race of the house of Jacob, I made them realise it in the land of Egypt, and I raised my hand over them and said : "I am Yahweh, your God." That day I raised my hand over them and swore to have them depart from Egypt and to bring them to the land I had chosen for them, where milk and honey flow, the most beautiful of all lands.' (20, 5-6). Moreover we read that it was only at the Exodus that Yahweh revealed Himself, and that they had not known His name Yahweh previously (cf Ex 6, 2f). 'I am Yahweh your God since the land of Egypt' (Os 12, 10; 13, 4; cf Ezech 20, 5).

On the other hand there are many passages which date God's revelation of His name and the choice of Israel from the days of the patriarchs. Thus when God called Abram He said : 'I shall make thee a great people' (Gen 12, 2), and we find this promise repeated (18, 18; 22, 16-18). To Isaac God says 'Stay in this country, I will be with thee and bless thee. For it is to thee and to thy race that I shall give these countries, and I will keep the oath which I made to thy father Abraham' (Gen 26, 3-4). To Jacob the same promise is given in still stronger terms : 'I am with thee and shall keep thee wheresoever thou shalt go; I shall bring thee back to this land, for I shall not abandon thee till I have accomplished what I have promised thee' (28, 15). Moreover God reveals His name to Abraham (Gen 15, 7) and to Isaac (Gen 28, 13). It is noteworthy that these passages belong to the oldest strands of the Pentateuch.[5] But we find examples in post-exilic writings also. Thus in Deutero-Isaias : 'Look at Abraham your father, and Sara who bore you. For there was only he when I called him, but I blessed and multiplied him' (51, 2; cf 41, 8; Mic 7, 20).

The birthday of Israel therefore is on occasion said to be the Exodus and at other times at the choice of Abraham, and both are said to mark the 'election' or the beginnings of the chosen people. An easy solution to this difficulty would be to

[5] The Pentateuch is a composite work in which at least four different strands are discernible, though one, indicated by the letter D, is practically confined to the Book of Deuteronomy. The other three are known as J (Jahvist source), E (Elohist source) and P (Priestly source).
Discussion of the date and provenance of these four elements and the apportioning of the text of the Pentateuch among them is extremely difficult and includes uncertainty and conjecture. Nevertheless the existence of these sources cannot be ignored, and they must be taken into account whenever we are considering the Pentateuchal narratives, both for their general intelligibility and especially for the development of revelation. On the question of the composition of the Pentateuch cf. H. Cazelles, in *Introduction à la Bible,* vol. 1, Tournai 1957, pp. 282-388; P. Grelot, *ibid.* pp. 785-828; A. Clamer, *La Sainte Bible: Genèse,* Paris 1953, pp. 10-57; R. de Vaux, *La Genèse,* Paris 1951, pp. 9-21.

suppose that the promise to Abraham and therefore the patriarchal election is simply a later creation, the result of that urge to root everything in the dim and distant past, just one detail in the creation of an ancestral history. But this is too simple a solution, and it does not fit the facts. The patriarchal stories can no longer be regarded as literary creations composed during the lifetime of historical Israel.[6] They show many traces of authentically ancient tradition, and there is no valid reason for questioning the historical foundation for the story of the election of Abraham. A more reasonable solution follows from noticing that there is a certain difference between the election of Abraham and the election of Israel at the time of the Exodus. It is noteworthy that God does not choose Abraham's descendants to be His people (except in the late source of Gen 17), to serve Him under a special covenant. The covenant God made with Abraham according to the earlier source (Gen 15) was simply the ratifying of God's promise, and no conditions were laid down for Abraham's observance. God's promise is simply that He will make of Abraham a great nation: it is a geneological promise, concerned merely with that special Divine favour of the race and there is nothing which we would call specifically religious about it (cf a similar promise to Agar Gen 16, 10).

Towards a solution of the difficulty therefore, we may first of all say that the election, when referred back to Abraham, differs from the election of Israel at the Exodus in its scope and purpose. But the fact that the promise to Abraham concerns the race as such, suggests a further explanation of this double tradition. It is now widely held that not all the semitic clans which later formed the historical Israel entered Canaan from Egypt under the leadership of Moses and Josue. In particular there are good grounds for thinking that the tribe of Judah entered Canaan independantly, and much earlier than

[6]cf R. de Vaux, 'Les patriarches hébreux et les découvertes modernes', *Revue biblique* 1946, pp. 321-248; 1948, pp. 321-347; 1949, pp. 5-36.

in 1250 B.C., at the Exodus.[7] This may well have been true of other clans. If this historical fact be accepted, then a certain difficulty would be felt with regard to the fundamental belief of Israel, namely that God had chosen the whole Israel. It might be asked when He had chosen Judah for instance. It is in the J tradition of the Pentateuch, commonly thought to be of Judan origin, that we find the promise to Abraham, and it would therefore seem reasonable to suppose that in this promise we have the foundation of the election of those tribes which were not led out of Egypt by Moses. 'What the Old Testament writers wished to say by declaring the election of Israel to date back to the time of Abraham was that it was not merely the tribes that were led out of Egypt by Moses that were chosen of God. The tribes that were akin to them in origin, that worshipped the same God ... were also the elect people. This was not a mere antedating of the election through Moses. It was a recognition of facts ... Abraham's migration was a significant moment in the history of Israel's election, in which the hand of God was legitimately seen.'[8]

For this reason then, the story of the redemption of Israel begins with the patriarchs. After eleven preliminary chapters concerning the beginnings of the world, the Torah really commences its revelation that Israel is God's chosen people with the call of Abraham from Ur of the Chaldees, in order that God might make of him a great nation (Gen 12, 2). When Abraham arrived as a stranger in Canaan, God concluded an alliance with him, making this promise 'To thy posterity I give this land' (Gen 15, 18). This was of the greatest importance, and is the cause of all that followed. It was of such primary importance that two different accounts have come down to us of what took place when this alliance was made (cf Gen 15, 7-18; 17, 1-22). This promise was repeated to Abraham's

[7]H. H. Rowley, *The Biblical Doctrine of Election*, London 1950, p. 27.
[8]*op. cit.* p. 30.

son Isaac (Gen 26, 3-5) and his grandson Jacob (Gen 28, 13-15; 35, 12).

God's promise was that the descendants of the patriarchs would inherit Canaan. But meantime the patriarchs themselves were in Canaan as strangers, wandering from place to place, from Sichem to the vicinity of Bethel, and southwards into the Negeb and as far as Egypt (Gen 12, 6. 8. 9. 10ff). Abram settled for a time at Mambre near Hebron (Gen 13, 18) but the land was in a state of great unrest, with many warring kings (Gen 14). The same was true throughout the patriarchal period, and Abraham, Isaac and Jacob were often in danger (cf Gen 27, 41ff). The Egyptian Pharaoh for instance tried to deprive Abram of his wife Sarai (Gen 12, 10-20); Abimelek, king of Gerar, tried to do the same (Gen 20, 1-18); and a similar story is told of Isaac (Gen 26, 6-11). But God protected them from all these dangers, for He was already implementing His promise. 'He suffered no man to do them wrong, Yea for their sake He reproved kings' (Ps 105, 14). In all these narratives God intervenes personally; He guides the patriarchs, He punishes their enemies; He assists and protects in all sorts of ways. The stories are so constructed as to leave the reader in no doubt that Yahweh is with His chosen ones.

2. The story of Joseph (Ps 105, 16-24)

The next stage in God's plan to implement the promise He had made to the Patriarchs was Joseph's going down into Egypt, for God had decided that Egypt was to be the birthplace of Israel. The story of Joseph is told at great length in Gen 37; 39-48; 50, and without mention of direct intervention on God's part. Yet Joseph recognised that the wicked action of his brothers did in fact serve God's purpose: 'It is to preserve your lives that God sent me in advance of you' (Gen 45, 5; cf 50, 20). And it was God who had established him as 'father for Pharaoh, as master over all his household, as governor in all the land of Egypt' (Gen 45, 8). Joseph had at first suffered imprisonment as the result of false accusation (Gen 39, 7-23), but he had obtained his release and had risen to the position of second in the kingdom thanks to his power of interpreting dreams, a power which had been communicated to him by God (Gen 40, 8) as the Pharaoh himself admits (Gen 41, 39). When therefore a famine threatened the survival of Jacob and his family, they were able to go down into Egypt, and Joseph took care of them (Gen 46). As a result Jacob's descendants greatly increased: 'The descendants of Israel were fruitful and increased greatly; they multiplied and grew exceedingly strong; so that the land was filled with them' (Ex 1, 7). Here is God's promise that Abraham's posterity should grow as numerous as the stars in the sky, becoming a reality. And when this increase aroused the hostility of the Pharaoh (Ex 1, 8-22) the time was ripe for God to take the next and all important step of bringing them out of Egypt into the promised land.

3. The plagues. (Pss 78, 12. 43-51; 105, 26-36; 106, 7; 135, 8-9; 136, 10)

God first of all appointed Moses to act on His behalf, with Aaron as his assistant (Ex 4, 10-17), and through them He performed a number of prodigies: wonderful deeds which struck terror into the Egyptians, and eventually gained the release of the Israelites. These terrifying prodigies which we call the plagues were outstanding evidence both of God's power and of His intention to fulfil His promises; they were striking examples of His love for Israel and of His determination to stop at nothing in order to save His own people. Consequently the stories concerning the plagues were told and retold, with much variety and they featured very prominently in the recital of how God saved Israel, as can be seen in the psalms we are considering, and in the Torah. In Ex 7, 14-12, 33 we find these stories collected and fused together into a series of ten plagues, in the following order: the water turned into blood (Ex 7, 14-25); the swarm of frogs (Ex 7, 26-8, 11); the mosquitoes (Ex 8,

84

12-15); the flies (8, 16-28); the cattle pest (Ex 9, 1-7) the boils (Ex 9, 8-12); the hail (Ex 9, 13-35); the locusts (10, 1-20); the darkness (10, 21-9); and the killing of the first-born (Ex 11-12, 33). This order is not followed in either Ps 78 or Ps 105, though the latter is closer to it, nor do either of them mention all ten plagues. The psalms were not using the Pentateuch in its present form as their source, but similar traditions, whether written or oral, to those which have been embodied in the Pentateuch.

If we examine the Exodus narrative concerning the plagues we see that they are composite stories, embodying details from distinct accounts in such a way that the picture of what actually happened is blurred. To take just one example, it is difficult to obtain a clear picture of what actually took place when the water was turned into blood (Ex 7, 14-25). How much water was actually changed? Was it a bucketfull (cf Ex 4, 9), or the whole Nile, or every drop of water throughout Egypt? And if the latter, how did the Egyptian magicians find water to change into blood? Was it Moses or Aaron who performed the prodigy? Did he strike the river, or stretch out the stick over the water? The literary critic can in fact, discern three different presentations of this incident, which have provided the threads out of which Ex 17, 14-25 has so to speak been woven. But it is much more important for us here to realise the theological importance these narratives of the plagues have. The tendency was to increase the prodigious element, and this for one reason only : to underline and emphasise that these occurrences were due to the direct intervention of God on behalf of Israel. They were divine prodigies, and for that reason alone were they of interest to Israel, and deserving of a place in the Torah which is the divine revelation.

This theological significance is underlined for instance, by the frequently repeated explanation of why God worked these wonders. In the account of the first plague Moses is commanded by God to go and tell Pharaoh on His behalf : 'By this you shall know that I am Yahweh' (Ex 7, 17). The changing of the water into blood is a revelation to the Pharaoh that Yahweh is God, with prodigious power over the natural elements. The second plague will end, in answer to Pharaoh's plea: 'In order that thou mayst know that there is no one like Yahweh our God' (Ex 8, 6). In the story of the third plague the Egyptians recognise in the arrival of swarms of mosquitoes, the 'finger of God' (Ex 8, 15). God punishes the Egyptians with hail 'In order that thou (Pharaoh) mayst know that there is no one like me upon the earth. . . . It is so that thou mayst see My power, and that My name may be proclaimed throughout the whole world' (Ex 9, 14-16). And by this plague Pharaoh is made to admit: 'Yahweh is just; but I and my people are guilty' (Ex 9, 27). Moses then promised to obtain relief, 'In order that thou mayst know that the earth belongs to Yahweh' (Ex 9, 29). God's purpose in performing these prodigies is most explicitly stated at the beginning of the eighth plague: 'That you may tell in the hearing of your son and of your son's son how I have made sport of the Egyptians and what signs I have done among them; that you may know that I am Yahweh' (Ex 10, 1-2). Thus the primary purpose of the plagues, clearly brought out by the way in which the story is written, is the revelation of God, the making known Yahweh as the sole ruler of the world, to the Egyptians and more especially to the sons of Israel.

Another purpose, or rather another aspect of this same purpose, was to win freedom for Israel His people, in order that they might worship Yahweh. God did not rescue His people from Egypt merely to give them independence and release them from oppression. Their freedom was the preliminary condition of their worshipping Yahweh in a fitting way. In the story of the first plague Moses is commanded to tell Pharaoh: 'Yahweh the God of the Hebrews has sent me to thee to tell thee to let My people leave, so that they may serve Me in the wilderness'

(Ex 7, 16). The same is said in respect of the second plague (Ex 7, 26), and it is more precisely defined as the offering of sacrifices to Yahweh (Ex 8, 4). Once more, before the fourth plague, Pharaoh is ordered to 'Let My people leave so that they may serve Me' (Ex 8, 16). When Pharaoh suggests that they offer sacrifices in Egypt Moses refuses. They must go a three day journey into the wilderness, and there offer sacrifices to Yahweh their God, according to His instructions (Ex 8, 21-23). The fifth, seventh and eighth plagues are introduced by the same command to Pharaoh (Ex 9, 1. 13; 10, 3). In the last, Moses and Aaron insist that they must all go, with their families and their cattle, 'For it is a feast of Yahweh for us' (Ex 10, 9). When, in the story of the ninth plague Pharaoh gives them permission to go, but only on condition that they leave their cattle behind, Moses rejects this offer because it destroys the purpose of their departure, namely to serve God by offering sacrifices (Ex 10, 25-6). After the tenth plague Pharaoh finally yields: 'Go away from my people, you and the sons of Israel; go and serve Yahweh, as you said' (Ex 12, 31).

This regularly recurring feature in the stories of the plagues emphasises how important is Israel in God's eyes, and how much He values the worship they give Him. God always speaks of them to the Pharaoh as 'My people', and on several occasions He makes a telling distinction between the Egyptians and the Israelites. Thus in the story of the plague of flies God says: 'I will set apart the land of Goshen, where My people dwell, so that no swarms of flies shall be there; that you may know that I am Yahweh, in the midst of the land' (Ex 8, 18). In the story of the cattle pest we are told that Yahweh will treat the animals belonging to the Israelites differently from those of the Egyptians: not one of the former will perish (Ex 9, 4). When, in the ninth plague God made darkness to descend upon the Egyptians, 'There was light for all the sons of Israel in the places where they lived' (Ex 10, 23). Lastly, when God announced the final and most terrible prodigy, when He Himself would pass through Egypt and all the first-born would die, He promised that no harm would come to the Israelites: 'But against any of the people of Israel, either man or beast, not a dog shall growl; that you may know that Yahweh makes a distinction between the Egyptians and Israel'(Ex 11, 7).

These are the main features of the plague stories which lead us to speak of their theological character. They are features which are beyond the scope of history, and yet are far more important than the historical details of these narratives. It is precisely these features which make the stories so important an element in the proclamation of Israel's redemption, and ensure that the stories of the plagues are preserved at length in the Pentateuch, and are referred to in the group of psalms concerned with Israel's salvation. They are not the only theological features. There is also an attempt to answer a theological difficulty which might possibly occur to the reader of these stories. How was it that Pharaoh could resist the will of God? Why was not one plague sufficient, when it was the manifestation of divine power? The answer lies in the mysterious free-will with which God has endowed all men, and every Israelite knew from his own experience that man can resist the will of God. Hence we are told in regard to six of the plagues, that Pharaoh hardened his heart and refused to listen to God's command (Ex 7, 22; 8, 11. 15. 28; 9, 7. 34). But in the case of the other three unsuccessful plagues we read that Yahweh hardened Pharaoh's heart so that he would not listen (Ex 7, 12; 10, 20. 27). This may seem strange: why did Yahweh frustrate His Own purpose? On the one hand He performed the prodigy to force Pharaoh into obeying His command, and yet, on the other, He hardened Pharaoh's heart so that he would not obey. This anomaly becomes understandable when we realise that the reference to Yahweh's hardening of Pharaoh's heart is a feature taken from other forms of the plagues stories than those in which Pharaoh is said to harden his own heart, and that it is a theological detail, intended to counteract any impression these stories might give, that God is less than almighty, and that He had need, absolutely speaking, to make reiterated efforts in order to overcome Pharaoh. The compiler of these stories made no attempt at a neat reconciliation of human free-will with divine omnipotence; but he is willing to allow the inconsistency, in order to preserve both truths, namely that man has free-will and that God's will is supreme.

Another interesting detail connected with the same theme, and again a detail which features in only one of the three original forms in which these stories were presented, is that of the Egyptian magicians. In the first and second plagues they succeeded in performing the same prodigy (Ex 7, 22; 8, 3). Some readers may find this disconcerting: are the Egyptian gods as powerful as Yahweh? But in the third plague their attempts are unsuccessful (Ex 8, 14), whilst in the sixth they cannot even make the attempt, since they have been themselves struck down (Ex 9, 11). Now we do not know how many plagues featured in this particular tradition, and we do not know whether anything more was heard of these magicians. But what is preserved in the book of Exodus is sufficient for us to point out that this detail of the Egyptian magicians serves the same theological purpose of explaining why a number of plagues was necessary. Yahweh had in fact decided to perform a number of prodigies. In the beginning therefore, His prodigies are equalled by the Egyptian magicians. But He gradually increased their difficulty, so that He outstripped the magicians. God is as it were playing with these men who claim divine powers. He allows them to succeed at the beginning, only to make it clearer how limited their powers are.

A final theological feature of these stories stresses the dignity and the importance of the priesthood. Anyone who has read the stories carefully, will find the references to Aaron somewhat confusing. Frequently he is mentioned by the side of

Moses without being assigned any really active role in the narrative. The historical role played by Aaron during the plagues is confused, but this is of very little importance. Of far greater significance is the role of the Aaronic priesthood in the history of Israel. The priests were the intermediaries between Yahweh and His people, acting on God's behalf. And in order to recall and to strengthen this belief, it was important that Aaron should be associated with Moses, however confused the role he played, in the story of the plagues, which was, as we have seen, an essential element of the story of Israel's redemption.

4. *The Crossing of the Red Sea (Pss 66, 6; 87, 13. 53; 106, 7; 114, 3; 136, 13-15)*

The first wonder which God performed for His people after He had led them out of Egypt, was to enable them to cross the Red Sea,[9] and if we read the narrative of this great event in Ex 13, 17-14, 31 we will see that this also is a theological narrative, written and preserved not for its description of the event, so much as for its contribution to the knowledge of God and of His attitude towards Israel.

As with the whole of the Pentateuch this narrative is a conflation of three different traditional accounts of the crossing of the Red Sea. As a result the precise way in which the prodigy occurred is somewhat obscure. We read that Yahweh aroused a strong east wind, which blew all night and dried up the sea. The Israelites crossed, but the Egyptians pursuing them were caught by the returning water and drowned. Thus Yahweh enables His people to escape by commanding the east wind to come to their assistance. But this account is neither so spectacular nor so flattering to Moses as the alternative description. In this Moses stretched out his hand over the water and the sea was divided in such a way that the water stood up on each side

[9]We retain the traditional name, but the Hebrew is *yam sûph* meaning reed sea.

like a wall. The Israelites passed between these two walls of water, pursued by the Egyptians. And when the whole Egyptian army was on this dry path, Moses raised his hand and the walls caved in, drowning all that were passing between them. In this second and more recent presentation God's power is far more vividly revealed, and it has been developed for this reason. Both narratives reveal God's power as lord of the earth, but this theological truth is emphasised far more in the second narrative, and the existence of these two narratives shows us how the theological truth of Yahweh's mastery over the natural elements was here the primary preoccupation.

But God's dominion over the natural elements is not so important as his victory over the Egyptians. Hence the climax of this story is the destruction of the Egyptian army, with their chariots and cavalry. Egypt was at this time the greatest power in the known world, and so its gods were the most powerful gods of the universe, or so it seemed to those who did not know Yahweh, the God of Israel. The destruction of Pharaoh's army shows that the Egyptian gods are nothing, and that Yahweh is alone God. It is pre-eminently a glorious revelation of Yahweh's almighty power over men and the gods in whom they trust. This was God's purpose: 'I shall harden Pharaoh's heart, and he will pursue them, in order that I may get Myself glory at the expense of Pharaoh and all his army; and the Egyptians shall know that I am Yahweh' (Ex 14, 4; cf 14, 17-18).

But God's glory is at the same time Israel's boast. God did this wonderful deed for their sake. From the moment they left Egypt He took special precautions to protect them (Ex 13, 21-2). They had no cause to fear: they would see the salvation wrought by Yahweh, and Yahweh would fight for them (Ex 14, 13-14). The crossing of the Red Sea, and the destruction of the Egyptian army were for their sake: 'On that day, Yahweh saved Israel from the hands of the Egyptians' (Ex 14, 30). As a result of this wonderful deed 'Israel thus recognised that the powerful hand of Yahweh had weighed down on Egypt; the people feared Yahweh and they trusted in Yahweh and His servant Moses' (Ex 14, 31). For this same purpose, namely a renewal and an increase of reverence and of trust in God, the story of the crossing of the Red Sea was constantly repeated from generation to generation, and the form that repetition took was dictated by this same purpose. Even a passing reference to the crossing of the Red Sea is an act of faith in the omnipotence of God, in His dominion over all the universe, and in His love for His people.

5. *Israel in the wilderness* (Pss 66, 10-12; 78, 14-41; 105, 39-43; 106, 13-33; 114, 8; 136, 16)

The story of Israel's wanderings through the wilderness on her way to the promised land is an important part of the Torah, and in it we read of further wonders worked by God on behalf of His people. But in this story the sombre side of divine revelaion comes into prominence, and that is why this story provides most of the material for Ps 78 which is an admonitory instruction, and for Ps 106 which is a lamentation.

The story of the wandering in the wilderness is told in Exodus 15, 22-18, 27; 32; Num 11-14; 16; 20-5, and it provides the setting for the book of Deuteronomy. God's wonders are all examples of His loving care and protection : thus He sustained His people by providing them with food and drink : He sweetened the bitter water at Marah (Ex 15, 25); He fed them with manna and quails (Ex 16, 4-35; Num 11, 6-9; Deut 8, 3. 16). At Raphidim and at Cades God provided them with water from a rock (Ex 17, 6; Num 20, 1-13). But a shadow is cast over these wonders by the distrust and discontent of Israel : 'The people murmured against Moses saying ' "What shall we drink?" ' (Ex 15, 24), after three days without water; God's prodigious rescue of His people had not produced in them that complete trust which would have driven away all anxiety, even in difficult circumstances. Nor did the sweetening of the bitter water lessen their discontent. Soon they were expressing their regret that they had ever left Egypt, and they were voicing their despair (Ex 16, 3; Num 11, 4-6). Though God provided them with quails and manna, they were just as querulous and untrusting when they lacked water at Raphidim; in face of difficulty they were only too ready to ask 'Is Yahweh among us or not?' (Ex 17, 3-7; cf Num 20, 3-5). God's miraculous provision of water did not increase their confidence, and they were afraid to enter Canaan, in spite of the repeated proof of God's protection : 'Why does Yahweh bring us into this land, to fall by the sword? Our wives and our little ones will become a prey; would it not be better for us to go back to Egypt?' (Num 14, 3). It is not surprising that God should express His indignation at the unending distrust of Israel, and that He should punish them for it (Num 14, 11-24).

Among the most outstanding examples of Israel's infidelity there is the making of the golden calf[10] at Sinai, the revolt of Dathan and Abiram, and the promiscuity of the Israelites with the Moabites. The incident of the golden calf (Ex 32, 1-33, 6) was a flagrant act of disobedience, since Yahweh had forbiden them to make graven images (Ex 20, 4). So early a turning away from the way prescribed for them led Yahweh to speak of Israel as the people of Moses, rather than His Own (Ex 32, 7), and to threaten their extermination. This was only averted by Moses' entreaty, reminding God of the satisfaction which the Egyptians would derive from this failure, and of the promises God had made to Abraham, Isaac and Israel (Ex 32, 12-13).

The revolt led by Dathan and Abiram (Num 16) against the authority of Moses was tantamount to a revolt against Yahweh Himself, and their ingratitude towards Moses for leading them out of Egypt (cf Num 16, 13) was in reality ingratitude towards Yahweh. Again, the promiscuity of the Israelites with the Moabite women (Num 25) led to their taking part in sacri-

[10]The traditional term is perhaps a little misleading: 'egel means a young bull.

fices offered to false gods, and Israel served the local god, Baalpeor. For this betrayal God punished them severely, and was only pacified by the zeal of Phinehas, the Aaronic priest, when he slew the Israelite who had ignored God's warning.

In the story of Israel's wandering in the wilderness lies the explanation of the continued infidelity of Israel throughout her existence, for in every generation Israel proved to be largely unchanged, largely unreformed. In practice the story of Israel's wanderings served the same purpose as does the story of the fall (Gen 3). Christian theology with its more conscious universalism, points to the original sin of the father of the whole human race, in order to explain man's propensity towards evil, and the constant frustration of the divine purpose. But to explain the still more mysterious propensity towards evil in God's own people we may point, along with the psalmist, to the original sins of Israel, a rebellious and a stiff-necked people from the very day God led them out of Egypt. The mere mention of Massa,[11] Meribah,[12] the golden calf, Baalpeor, Phinehas and indeed of manna and water from the rock, are as evocative as is the mention of the tree, the serpent or the forbidden fruit.

The Redemption of Israel

The non-Christian student of ancient history might well entitle this story of the Exodus 'The legendary account of how certain Semitic clans migrated from Egypt to Canaan.' The non-Christian student of the history of Comparative Religion might refer to it as the record of early Jewish beliefs attaching to the migration of certain of their ancestors from Egypt to Canaan. But the Christian, with his firm belief that the Old Testament is part of the inspired revelation of God, must regard this narrative as the story of the Divine redemption of Israel the chosen people. It is the record of the truly objective and

[11]Massah comes from the Hebrew verb *nasah* to tempt or test.
[12]Meribah comes from the Hebrew verb *rîb*: to quarrel or dispute.

special intervention of God in history, on behalf of one particular people.

Our references to the different traditions concerning the Exodus, to the heightening of the prodigy by one tradition compared with another in the account for instance of the crossing of the Red Sea, to the theological significance of such details as the intervention of the Egyptian magicians or the prominence given to Aaron, and even the simple use of the word story in reference to these narratives, have perhaps given the impression that the belief in the Divine redemption of Israel does not rest on objective fact. It would however be most regrettable if such a method, designed to emphasise what is truly the more important aspect, namely the theological character of this narrative, should lead to the denial of the necessary though secondary characteristic of this story, namely its historicity. It is unfortunately a common tendency at the present time to regard any account of a historical event which embodies details which are historically speaking neither verifiable nor feasible as devoid of all historical foundation. This is an absurd exaggeration which if allowed free rein is bound to destroy all divine revelation.

For divine revelation is by definition beyond the scope of history. 'To the modern historian, the action of God is not an "observable phenomenon"; he does not, as a historian, affirm or deny it, he simply cannot find it in strictly "historical" sources. In this he is quite correct; human deeds are recorded by human testimony, divine deeds by divine testimony.'[13] Insofar therefore as the story of the Exodus is the simple narrative of God's redemption of Israel, it must be in a certain sense 'unhistorical' because it relates in impressive language easily grasped by ordinary people, the action of God which is beyond the scope of history. The whole Bible is, in varying degrees, not so much history as theology. It was written and it must be read, not for the purpose of learning what human events took

[13] J. L. McKenzie, *The Two-Edged Sword*, Milwaukee 1956, p. 65.

place at any given time, but of learning how God has acted, and consequently how He acts now, and will act in the future, and thus learning what God is, for it is by His actions that we know Him.

The story of the Exodus therefore is a theological account of certain historical events, and we have already pointed to signs which make it quite clear that the main purpose of this story is to teach with the greatest insistence that God directly intervened on behalf of the Hebrews, and that their exit from Egypt and journey to Canaan was the result of God's direct action; that moreover such a deliverance would never have been obtained but for God's action. But precisely in fulfilling this purpose the historical character of the same story is lessened. It cannot be otherwise, if this purpose is to be achieved in a vivid and simple way. The historical details are bound to become obscure since the narrator must avoid at all costs the impression that these events were ordinary human happenings. As a result, we must admit our ignorance about much of the detail in the story of the Exodus. Precisely how the prodigies occurred, precisely how the Israelites escaped from Egypt, precisely what route they followed in their journey to Canaan, precisely how many they were, and other historical questions must remain largely unanswered since, contrary to what may appear on the surface, the biblical narrative does not aim to satisfy our curiosity on such points. But if as a result of our historical curiosity being left unsatisfied we conclude that there is no historical foundation to the story at all, then we leave a massive historical fact, the lasting existence of a nation, unique in its faith and moral standards, and unparalleled in its power of endurance among all the nations of the world without any reasonable explanation. Having rejected that nation's own explanation of its origin and uniqueness as devoid of historical foundation, the historian ought to supply an historically satisfying alternative.

The failure to do so has not been for lack of trying. It was common enough not very long ago to deny all that the story of the Exodus claims. The presence of any Israelites in Egypt was considered as completely unhistorical. Such details as their being builders' labourers oppressed by harsh task-masters were regarded as romantic fiction. The very existence of Moses was at one time doubted, though Renan granted that it was very probable.[14] But such scepticism is now quite discredited as unhistorical and uncritical. In the first place scientific research has opened up for us a much more accurate knowledge of the history of this period. The migration of people south into Egypt is a well established fact, and documents which are not suspect of being theological tracts help to give an authentic historical ring to biblical narratives. But more important, it is now recognised that the Exodus, which has so profound an effect upon Israelite memory, life and religion must, for that very reason, have some foundation in fact. It is recognised as unrealistic to suppose that so influential an event was in reality no event but the figment of someone's imagination. And the same argument is valid with regard to the existence and work of Moses. He is the greatest figure in Israelite history, and had an enormous effect upon the life of a whole nation. Now it is a fact that in all such cases the decisive figure has been historical, not fictional. As Lods says, speaking simply as an observer of history: 'It is ordinarily by great individuals that are given the decisive impulses in the religious life of peoples, when they rise above the level of cultures which are quite inferior.'[15] It is an historical fact that Israelite belief and moral practice showed a marked superiority to that of other surrounding peoples of the same time. Today then the claim that the human agent of this was initially and outstandingly Moses is completely justified from the historical point of view.

The biblical narratives therefore have a historical and an

[14]cf A. Clamer, *La Sainte Bible: Exode,* Paris 1956, p. 28.

[15]A. Lods, *Israël, dès origines au milieu du VIIIe siècle,* Paris 1952, p. 358, quoted by Clamer, *loc. cit.*

objective basis. They correspond fundamentally to fact, and it is unreasonable to question the historicity of events[16] described in the story of the Exodus unless there are positive reasons for doing so. But it would be disastrous if this were to lead us to the opposite extreme, and one not infrequently to be found among Catholics, of adopting a fundamentalist attitude in defence of the historicity, whilst ignoring the primary purpose and the theological character of these narratives. A fundamentalist defence of the rigid historicity of every detail is not only futile but a gross abuse and a distortion which forces the Scripture into self-contradiction. Whilst for instance, the Exodus narrative gives the clear impression that all Israel was led out of Egypt by Moses, the historian, on evidence provided by the Bible itself to a large extent, would rightly question the historical truth that all twelve tribes had at this period been in Egypt.[17]

[16]Much evidence in support of the historicity of various details is to be found in Werner Keller, *The Bible as History,* London 1956. 'Plagues', we are told, 'are neither improbable nor unusual. Indeed they are part of Egypt's local colour. . . . These things which the Bible describes are still experienced by the Egyptians, as, for example, the "red Nile".' There follows a further explanation of how this occurs. Moreover, 'The "boils". . . . may be the so-called "Nile-heat" or "Nile-itch" . . . "Hailstorms" are extremely rare on the Nile, but they are not unknown. . . . The same is true of sudden "darkness". The Khamsin, also called the Simoon, is a blistering hot wind which whirls up vast masses of sand and drives them before it. They obscure the sun, give it a dull yellowish appearance and turn daylight into darkness.—Only the death of the "first-born" is a plague for which there is no parallel.' (pp. 123-4) Keller discusses the crossing of the Red Sea and ends with the statement: 'The flight from Egypt by way of the sea of reeds is therefore perfectly credible.' (p. 127). Observations in similar vein follow, on the subject of quails (p. 129) and Manna— the secretion of a plant-louse living off the tamarisk (p. 130). This popular book is full of interesting information, but one wonders what its final effect is. The subtitle claims: 'Archaeology confirms the book of books.' But the reader may perhaps wonder as a result of the importance laid upon the 'credibility' of these events, why so 'natural' a record is called 'the book of books'.

[17]cf p. 82, ftn. 7, and R. de Vaux, *Dictionnaire de la Bible, Supplément* vol. IV, col. 735.

If, as another example, we take the chapters on the institution of the Pasch as an account historical in every detail of what took place on that very night, then they are self-contradictory and historically incredible. Still more obvious, the whole of the second half of the book of Exodus is composed of laws, which are all said to be given by God to Moses. Yet an examination makes it quite clear that the same laws are repeated, modified according to different circumstances, many of which could not possibly have obtained at the time of the Exodus.[18] The elaborate construction of the Tabernacle and its furnishings, so closely resembling the Solomonic Temple might reasonably be considered unhistorical, though nothing is historically more certain than that the Israelites had *a* 'tabernacle' during their wanderings through the wilderness.[19] To attribute to Moses the laws in all their detail, and the tabernacle in all the intricacies of its description in the Book of Exodus is historically unsound; from the theological point of view, which is that of the writers, it is no more untrue than for the priest to tell his people, for instance, that Our Lord has commanded us to go to Mass every Sunday.

We may therefore conclude by saying that these narratives are historical in the sense that they are based upon events which actually took place, and which were of such a kind as to support the faith of Israel that God Himself intervened in order to rescue them from Egypt; but that due to the time when they were written,[20] the style of writing then in use, and especially due to their theological purpose, it is extremely difficult accurately to determine the historical events in detail. Whilst Moses, for instance, is not only a historical person, but someone who is historically important, it is impossible to write an historical

[18]On the substantial Mosaic authorship of the Pentateuch cf. A. Clamer, *La Sainte Bible: Genèse,* Paris 1953, pp. 17-20.
[19]cf R. de Vaux, *Les institutions de l'ancien testament* vol. II, Paris 1960, pp. 124-5.
[20]Historiography had not yet made its appearance; it is generally considered to have begun with the Greeks.

biography of him. The Exodus was an historical event: but it is impossible to describe it in detail, with any guarantee of historical accuracy. We must beware of letting our realisation of the theological character of these accounts make us universally sceptical of the historicity of its details. But on the other hand we must not let our modern obsession with historical accuracy force us to claim historical accuracy at the risk of making the texts self-contradictory and ridiculous. Moreover the latter pre-occupation has the infinitely more serious effect of obscuring the purpose for which these accounts were written, and for which we read them. To establish their historical basis is to remove the objection that our Faith is the product of the Israelite imagination. To read them as theological writings in which God's loving concern for His chosen one is described, is to nourish our Faith.

For truly, the story of the Exodus is the proclamation that God redeemed Israel, and that is why it plays an important part in Israelite prayer. I use the word redemption quite deliberately, although it is unsuitable if its etymology is allowed to influence our understanding of it. But I use it because of its unmistakable theological implication. The truth is that even Christians fail to accept the exodus as truly an act of redemption. They are inclined to regard it as nothing more than the type or figure, or foreshadowing of THE redemption. The Fathers have indeed made it abundantly clear that the exodus can be regarded in this way, but it is only safe to do so after we have realised that the exodus was first an act of redemption in its own right, with an objective reality of its own. To speak of the exodus as a foreshadowing without this realisation, is to turn the Israelites into puppets with God the puppet-master, putting them through their paces in a world of make-believe serving no other purpose than to announce in an oblique way what is to follow.

The exodus was a real act of divine redemption, as real as the resurrection of Christ, which itself is the type, the figure, the foreshadowing of our own. The Christian, who can look back from the death and resurrection of Christ over the whole complex action of God whereby He redeemed the world, sees that the exodus was only the first of a series of divine interventions; but this should not rob it of its own reality. The essential Christian profession of faith in brief, is that we have been redeemed through the death and resurrection of Christ. But the act of divine redemption which from God's point of view is one, single and unified process is from the human angle so complex that it must be viewed in its various stages. Every stage in God's plan was ordered towards its climax, and its completion in Christ. The Exodus therefore was part of Christ's redemption of the world even though at that point in time neither Christ nor the universality of the redemption were revealed to men. When St Paul writes that our fathers 'drank from the spiritual rock which followed them, and the rock was Christ' (1 Cor 10, 4) he is reminding his readers of this truth that the exodus was part of Christ's redemption of the world.

We must not deny therefore that the exodus is truly part of the divine act of redemption on the grounds that Christ is our sole redeemer. Nor must we refuse to admit its reality on the grounds that the exodus was only concerned with the things of this world. Many Christians may be tempted to object that at the exodus God simply freed the Israelites from the captivity of Egypt and settled them in Canaan, but that through the death and resurrection of Christ men are freed from sin and hell and given access to heaven : the exodus was concerned merely with men's bodies; the redemption through Christ is the saving of their souls. If such an objection simply implies that the exodus was only the very imperfect beginning of the divine redemption of mankind, then it is perfectly valid. But more likely than not it is meant as a denial of any truly redemptive value in the exodus. If that is so, then the objection is quite false, and arises from certain dichotomies which in their uncompromising distinctions are quite alien to biblical revelation. The distinction for instance between sin and physical evils such as slavery and oppression is not so absolute as is often thought. In fact revelation makes it quite clear that they are intimately connected.[21] Similarly a sharp dichotomy of man into soul and body can easily falsify our understanding of divine revelation which makes it perfectly clear that the object of God's saving love is men, as they exist in reality, whether we describe that reality as animated body or incarnated soul.[22] Even too sharp a distinction between heaven and earth is not without its danger. If we speak of heaven as man's final goal we must remember that it will not be peopled by disembodied spirits; since we believe in the resurrection of the dead we might just as well look forward to the new earth (cf Rom 8, 19; Col 1, 20; Ephes 1, 10; 2 Pet 3, 13; Apoc 21, 1).

All this has been said in an effort to show that the theological reality conveyed by the Exodus is really a redemption, and not merely a figure or a metaphor of it. It is part of the redemption through Christ, and not simply a foreshadowing of it. True, it might well be said that the death and resurrection of Christ is so overwhelming and so perfect that it puts all that went before it into the shade; but no action of God is mere shadow without substance. When we read the gradual unfolding of God's single plan of redemption through Christ we must always keep in mind that there are two sides to the story: God's and man's: God's intervention and man's free association with that intervention. From the latter's point of view the one divine act of redemption was long drawn out, and in many stages, and indeed has always been and will continue to be a partial failure. Moreover we must remember that the divine intervention in this world is both temporal and atemporal: in so far as it is 'in this world', it is datable, and becomes something that

[21]cf T. Worden, 'The Meaning of "Sin" ', *Scripture* 1957, pp. 44-53.
[22]cf O. Cullmann, *Immortalité de l'âme ou résurrection des morts,* Neuchâtel 1956.

happened in the past, whether in 1250 B.C. or 33 A.D.[23] But it is also atemporal, insofar as the action is divine and therefore eternal, enduring and in a sense always happening; it is never past history, but always present and efficacious reality. Lastly we must keep in mind that there are two ways in which God's act of redemption may be called gradual: the revelation of His redeeming action was a gradual one, from the time of the Exodus to the Resurrection of Christ. But this process is now completed, and perfected for all time. Yet God's act of redemption remains gradual when we view it from the standpoint of those redeemed, whose number increases gradually. From this point of view the divine redemption will remain a gradual (and therefore unfinished) action until God brings this period of free choice to an end.

The Lasting Efficacy of the Redemption of Israel

God's purpose in rescuing the Israelites from Egypt was first of all to fulfil His promise to the patriarchs. In this way the election through Abraham and the election of Israel at the Exodus are linked together and made one theological unity, for the latter can be viewed as the fulfilment of the former. Thus in one of the accounts of the call of Moses we already have the forging of this link, since God chooses Moses because, as He says 'I have seen the affliction of *My* people', and He wishes to bring them to the land flowing with milk and honey, which is a reference to the promise made to Isaac (cf Ex 3, 7-8; Gen 27, 27-8). Thus what may seem confusing to the strictly logical mind, namely that God should refer to *His* people before He had brought them out of Egypt in order to make them His people, is clearly understood if we remember the different theological truths to be united. The choice of Abraham was a promise, fulfilled by the Exodus, and this is the constant pattern of God's redemption : each act of

[23]These are probable dates of the Exodus and of the death and resurrection of Christ.

103

redemption is the fulfilment of a previous one, and the latter in relation to what is to follow becomes in its turn a promise or a prophecy. This linking of the two elections by way of the carrying out of a promise, stated in the earliest traditions where it was most necessary,[24] is carried on by the later traditions and retained in the development of Old Testament theology. We have, therefore, in Deut 7, 8 as an explicit statement of the reason for the Exodus : 'It is for love of you, and to keep the oath sworn to your fathers that Yahweh brought you out with a strong hand'. Thus the purpose of the exodus was a truly religious and redemptive purpose, the manifestation of God's fidelity to His promise.

But another purpose of God was to acquire for Himself a people of His very own. 'You have seen what I did to the Egyptians, and how I bore you on eagles' wings and brought you to Myself. Now therefore, if you will obey My voice and keep My covenant, you shall be My own possession among all peoples; for all the earth is Mine, and you shall be to Me a kingdom of priests and a holy nation' (Ex 19, 4-6). God soared aloft like an eagle, looking for its prey, and swooping down He picked up Israel and carried her off to His nest (cf Deut 4, 34; 32, 11). For He wanted Israel as His *segullah*. This word so significant in its implication, is rarely found apart from this context, but its meaning is made quite plain by its use in 1 Chron 29, 3, where it signifies the personal wealth which David gives for the building of the temple, in addition to all that he has been able to supply from the royal treasury (cf Eccles 2, 8; Mal 3, 17). Israel therefore is to be God's private property, His personal treasure, quite apart from all other nations who are His public and official property by virtue of His being creator of the world.

They are to be a kingdom of priests, for the whole people is to be in that close relationship with God which would usually

[24]On the hypothesis, not shared by de Vaux *loc. cit.* in ftn. 17, that the tribe of Judah did not enter Palestine from Egypt.

be associated with the priests alone, and every one of them will minister to Yahweh in a way which would usually befit only the priest.

Consequently they will be a holy nation. The fundamental sense of holy is set apart from ordinary, everyday circumstances for a special purpose, and therefore having a quality of 'separateness'. God is holy because He is separated, above and beyond everyone else. So too His people would be set apart from all the rest for His sake; they would share His separateness, and they would be consecrated to Him. During the trials in the wilderness Moses had pleaded with God : 'If Thy presence will not go with me, do not carry us up from here. For how shall it be known that I have found favour in Thy sight, I and Thy people? Is it not in Thy going with us, so that we are distinct, I and Thy people, from all other people that are upon the face of the earth?' (Ex 33, 15-16).

The redemptive purpose of the Exodus could not be expressed more clearly. The freeing of this people from slavery is not an act of kindness and compassion, but an act which is to serve God's eternal purpose of glorifying Himself through the people He has made His Own. This people, quite insignificant by comparison with Egypt or Assyria or even when compared with the Hittites and the Canaanites, the Edomites and the Moabites, are given the incomparable privilege of being the instrument whereby God will make Himself known to the world, and thereby glorify His name. God will glorify His name, for the world will see the glory of Israel, and will ask : Who is your God? (cf Ex 14, 4. 17. 18; Lev 10, 3; Is 26, 15). To express the same idea by a synonym, God will 'sanctify' His name, for seeing the holiness of Israel, the world will ask why this nation is separated and different from all other nations (cf Lev.10, 3 : Ez 26, 24).[25]

In order that God's purpose may be fulfilled the Exodus must

[25]Compare Mt 6, 9 with Jo 12, 28.

have a redemptive efficacy which is lasting and effective from generation to generation. So lest it be thought that only those who historically speaking were brought out of Egypt, constituted God's chosen people, God made a treaty with Israel, a pact or covenant which ratified and perpetuated God's ownership : by the covenant God bound this people to Himself as closely as the ties of blood bind together members of one family. For in the world of the Exodus covenants were an important element of civilisation, serving to establish the same relationship as that set up by flesh and blood, and thereby ensuring peace and mutual help. The making of these covenants was always accompanied by some ritual act, perhaps the sharing by the parties in the blood of a slaughtered animal, or the sharing in a common meal or even the mingling of their own blood. Whatever the ritual was it signified that the parties to the covenant now shared the same life. The ritual which marked the covenant between Yahweh and Israel, was according to one tradition a common meal (Ex 24, 1-2. 9-12) whilst according to another it was a sharing of the blood of the slaughtered animal (Ex 24, 3-8), for the covenant was proof that there now existed between God and Israel a relationship as close as that of blood. Israel was God's chosen people for ever : the covenant proved it. But the covenant at the same time laid down conditions. If they did not keep these conditions, epitomised in the ten commandments, then they would cease to be God's personal property. They would become useless for His purpose; they would not be separated, and different from all the nations of the world; no one would see their glory and their holiness, and be led to ask Who is their God, and they would become a useless instrument in God's hand.

But provided that they listened to His voice and obeyed His commands set forth in the covenant, they were God's chosen people for ever. We saw in the first chapter how in general every individual Israelite believed that he shared the experi-

ence of Israel as a whole, unaffected by any question of time.[26]
But this is particularly true of the exodus, the fundamental
act of redemption for Israel. As an historical fact the exodus
was something transitory, and a thing of the past. But the faith
of Israel was completely convinced that it was not only the
small group of people of that generation who had been rescued
and made God's personal property. Each succeeding generation was redeemed from Egypt, insofar as each succeeding
generation fulfilled the purpose and reaped the benefit of the
exodus, by becoming God's chosen people with the rights and
the responsibilities laid down in the covenant. This truth of
faith is especially emphasised, as we saw in the first chapter,
by the book of Deuteronomy: 'It is not with our fathers that
Yahweh made this alliance, but with us, us ourselves who are
here today, all alive' (Deut 5, 3; cf 10, 15). And this truth was
to be constantly recalled. Fathers must instruct their children
concerning the great event, and the redemption of the exodus
must be preached continually (cf Deut 6, 7-8. 20-5). This
purpose was accomplished by the reading of the Torah, and the
singing of these psalms which proclaim the divine rescue from
Egypt. But above all it was accomplished by the celebration of
the Pasch.

The Pasch was the efficacious sign of the redemption of
Israel wrought by God at the exodus. It is beyond our scope
here to treat adequately of the complicated origins of this great
feast.[27] There are good grounds for thinking that the ritual was
both pre-Mosaic and pre-Israelite. Many of its details may be
the more satisfactorily explained if we accept that the Pasch
was in origin the spring festival of nomad and pastoral com-
munities, offering to their gods the firstlings of their flocks, and
that the feast of Azymes or unleavened bread with which the
Pasch in the Old Testament is joined, was in origin an analogous

[26] cf pp. 16-19.

[27] cf H. Haag, in *Dictionnaire de la Bible Supplément,* fasc. **XXXIV**
Paris 1960, col. 1119ff.

but independent[28] festival, celebrated by sedentary and agricultural peoples such as the Canaanites.

But whatever the origin of this festival, and the question is not without importance for an understanding of the prescriptions in Ex 12, 1-13, 16, the significant thing here is the use to which God put this feast. He authorised the adoption of these rites by His chosen people, for one particular purpose: the Pasch is 'instituted' as a sacred sign, on the eve of the redemption from Egypt: 'This day shall be for you a memorial, and you shall keep it as a feast to Yahweh.' (Ex 12, 14). It is to be a memorial of the Exodus, the redemption of Israel: 'And when your children say to you: "What do you mean by this service?", you shall say, "It is the sacrifice of Yahweh's passover, for He passed over the houses of the people of Israel in Egypt, when He slew the Egyptians but spared our houses' (Ex 12, 26-7). The Pasch, which in its origin was celebrated in spring because that was the time when new life began, was to be celebrated at that time, as an Israelite feast, not because it was Spring, but because that was the time when Yahweh brought the Israelites out of Egypt (Deut 16, 1. 6).

But the Pasch was not simply a memorial or commemoration of the past: it was an efficacious recalling, which reaffirmed the effect of the Exodus for every generation of Israelites. It was the means whereby succeeding generations of Israelites were associated in a real way with that group who in historical fact had been led out of Egypt: 'Thou shalt eat no leavened bread with it; seven days thou shalt eat it with unleavened bread, the bread of affliction—for thou didst come out of the land of Egypt in hurried flight—that all the days of thy life thou mayst remember the day when thou didst come out of the land of Egypt' (Deut 16, 3; cf Ex 13, 3. 8-10). Because of this efficacious power inherent in the Pasch of reaffirming the unity of all Israelites in the one body of Israel, it could only

[28]There is evidence in the Old Testament that this independence continued for a time even in Israel, cf. H. Haag, art. cit.col. 1132.

be celebrated by those who were circumcised (Ex 12, 48). For the same reason the Israelite who failed to keep the Pasch when impeded by no legitimate reason, was thereby cut off from his people (Num 9, 13). Whilst it would be unreasonable to expect any theological discussion in the Old Testament of the efficacy of this rite comparable to the medieval theological development concerning the *ex opere operato* character of the Christian sacraments, it is nevertheless sufficiently clear that the pasch was the sacrament[29] of the old covenant, a ritual commemoration of the redemption at the exodus which perpetuated the effects of that redemption for Israel, generation after generation. Not surprisingly, it was made more explicit by later Jewish theology. Concerning the Pasch the Mishna states: 'Everyone must consider himself, from generation to generation, as though he himself had come out of Egypt, for it is written (Ex 13, 8): on that day, namely that on which thou dost celebrate the memorial of the exodus from Egypt, explain thus to thy son : It is because the Lord intervened for me, when I came out of Egypt. That is why we owe Him proclamation, praise, blessing, glorification, homage, veneration and adoration, Him Who did for us and for our fathers all these wonders, Who led us from slavery to freedom, from hardship to joy, from affliction to jubilation, from darkness to the great light, and from servitude to redemption. Let us sing before Him : Alleluia !'[30]

The Redemption of Israel and the Christian

These psalms in which the events of the exodus are recited constitute declarations of faith in the revealed truth that it was God Himself Who rescued the Israelites from Egypt, and made Israel His Own private property, with the privileges and

[23]According to St Thomas's description of a sacrament: *signum rememorativum eius quod praecessit* . . . *et demonstrativum eius quod in nobis efficitur* . . . *et prognosticum, id est praenuntiativum, futurae gloriae.* (cf *Sum. Theol.* IIIa, q. LX, art. 3).

[30]Mis. Pes. X, 5, quoted in French by H. Haag, *art. cit.* col. 1140.

the responsibilities that entailed. As such they had an important place in the prayer of Israel. But why does it follow from this that they are also a genuine part of the Christian's prayer? There must be many Christians who feel that the exodus has nothing to do with them. Faced with the strange fact that these psalms do appear in the Church's liturgical prayer, they must try and find some explanation, but it is rarely a satisfactory one. They may borrow the allegorising exegesis of the Fathers, and see these psalms as nothing more than the story of God's redemption of their souls from the slavery of sin, of His provision for their supernatural life while they journey through the wilderness of this world, and of their constant straying from the path of virtue. But in our day most people find allegorising an irksome task, and in the end an unsatisfactory protection against the unwelcome intrusion of Jewish history into their prayer. Alternatively they may have to content themselves with the thought that these psalms do at least extol the power and generosity of God, as do for instance the creation psalms. But they may well feel that God's generosity towards the Jews whilst admirable enough, and providing a terrible lesson in man's ingratitude, can hardly be sufficiently close to their hearts to occupy a prominent place in their prayer.

For many Christians still, the Jews are the people who rejected Our Lord, and there is little more to be said about them.[31] The growing insistence of some Catholic writers on the organic unity between Israel and Christianity, and such seemingly new clichés as 'our forefathers the Israelites' are still regarded either with suspicion as smacking of heresy, or with resentment because they cause new difficulties, or perhaps with indulgence as the latest craze of writers avid for novelties. At the least, they regard them with indifference, because they make no

[31]Strangely enough there are Jews even today who think that antiSemitism is rooted in the charge of deicide brought by Christians against Jews, cf Josef Blinzler, *The Trial of Jesus,* Cork 1959, pp. 4-5.

significant impact upon their belief and practice as Christians. The very existence of the Old Testament as a part of the Sacred Scriptures of the Christian Church is for many a cause of embarrassment rather than the object of pride and gratitude. Whilst Catholics have always defended the Old Testament because it is part of the Bible and therefore inspired, they have rarely felt any inclination to open and read it.

It is not surprising therefore that this deep-seated aversion towards the Old Testament should be unaffected by the quoting of one or two texts from St Paul. Israel and the Jews are for many synonymous terms, and however strongly they abhor anti-Semitism in the modern sense of the word, they feel that their Christianity cannot help but be anti-Jewish and therefore anti-Israelite, at every stage in their history. Events over the past two thousand years can hardly have failed to leave some mark on the European Christian at least, and the history of relations between Christian and Jew makes sad reading. It is the story of a race hated, ostracised and persecuted; sometimes tolerated, at other times massacred; sometimes feared and flattered, at other times openly despised and insulted; but at all times a race regarded as alien and dangerous; and for its own part, a race which has hated Christians and condemned them. The reasons for this horrifying history have never been exclusively religious, nor has blame lain only with the Christians. The popes as recognised heads of medieval Christendom were for the most part the protectors of the Jews. Cecil Roth remarks: 'It is significant that, under papal aegis, the (Jewish) community of Rome, almost alone in the whole of Europe, was enabled to continue its existence undisturbed from classical times down to the present day.'[32] But another

[32]*The Cambridge Medieval History*, col. VII, Cambridge 1932, p. 634. Gregory X wrote in 1272 'Even as it is not allowed to the Jews in their assemblies presumptuously to undertake for themselves more than that which is permitted them by law, even so they ought not to suffer any disadvantage in those (privileges) which have been granted them. Although they persist in their stubbornness rather than to

111

Jewish author writes somewhat differently : 'The Church persecuted Judaism with the despotism of a Diocletian, with all the resources of invention, all the devices of torture and force which had been the painful experience of her own ancestors.'[33] The truth is that papal tolerance was rarely imitated by the popes' subjects, or indeed reflected in ecclesiastical legislation.[34] The frequency of papal interventions to curb the outrages against Jews is sufficient evidence that secular Christian rulers and the mass of their Christian subjects refused the guidance of their spiritual leaders. What Baeck falsely attributes to the church can unfortunately be said of many Christian rulers. And the more ignorant were often roused to action by an unscrupulous play upon their religious emotions by those whose hatred of the Jews was inspired by political or economic reasons. The scurrilous story for instance, that the Jews at Passover were accustomed to murder a Christian child in order to use his blood in the making of unleavened bread led to many Holy Week riots and murders.[35] The entire Jewish population of

recognize the words of their prophets and the mysteries of the Scriptures, and thus arrive at a knowledge of Christian faith and salvation; nevertheless, inasmuch as they have made an appeal for our protection and help, we therefore admit their petition and offer them the shield of our protection through the clemency of Christian piety. In so doing we follow in the footsteps of our predecessors of blessed memory, the popes of Rome—Calixtus, Eugene, Alexander, Clement, Celestine, Innocent and Honorius.' He goes on to forbid Christians forcibly to baptise Jews, or to seize, imprison, wound, torture, mutilate, kill or inflict violence, or rob them of their money. They are not to be disturbed during the celebration of their festivals. 'The testimony of Christians against Jews shall not be valid unless there is among these Christians some Jew who is there for the purpose of offering testimony.' cf James Bruce Ross and Mary Martin McLaughlin (edit), *The Portable Medieval Reader*, New York 1949, pp. 170-171.

[33]Leo Baeck, *The Essence of Judaism*, London 1936, p. 265.

[34]Roth instances the 3rd and 4th Lateran Councils, cf. *op. cit.* p. 642.

[35]'Since it happens occasionally that some Christians lose their Christian children, the Jews are accused by their enemies of secretly carrying off and killing these same Christian children and of making

Belitz was burned alive in 1243 for the alleged desecration of the consecrated host.[36] Even the Good Friday liturgy served in the popular mind to justify the Christian's hatred of the Jew, for the solemn intercession *pro perfidis Iudaeis* was misunderstood as a reference to Jewish treachery.[37]

This long and unhappy experience of the Christian church can hardly have failed to leave a scar. But the barrier of hatred and mistrust which divided the Christian from the Jew did not

sacrifices of the heart and blood of these very children. It happens, too, that the parents of these children, or some other Christian enemies of these Jews, secretly hide these very children in order that they may be able to extort from them a certain amount of money by redeeming them from their straits. . . . And most falsely do these Christians claim that the Jews have secretly and furtively carried away these children and killed them, and that the Jews offer sacrifice from the heart and the blood of these children, since their law in this matter precisely and expressly forbids Jews to sacrifice, eat, or drink the blood, or to eat the flesh of animals having claws. This has been demonstrated many times at our court by Jews converted to the Christian faith: nevertheless very many Jews are often seized and detained unjustly because of this. We decree, therefore, that Christians need not be obeyed against Jews in a case or situation of this type, and we order that Jews seized under such a silly pretext be freed from imprisonment, and that they shall not be arrested henceforth on such a miserable pretext, unless—which we do not believe—they be caught in the commission of the crime.' Gregory X, cf James Bruce Ross and Mary Martin McLaughlin, *op. cit.* p. 172.

[36]cf Roth, *op. cit.* p. 642. As recently as 1913 a Jew was on trial in Russia, charged with ritual murder. This was the occasion of an exchange of letters between Lord Rothschild and Cardinal Merry del Val which pays tribute to the efforts made by various popes to protect the Jews, cf *The Tablet,* Nov. 1st 1913, pp. 690-692.

[37]The words *perfidi* and *perfidia* in this liturgical text mean unbelieving and unbelief, cf Eric Peterson, 'Perfidia Judaica', in *Ephemerides liturgicae* 1936, pp. 296-311: John M. Oesterreicher, 'Pro perfidis Judaeis' in *Theological Studies* 1947, pp. 80-96. In the new *Ordo Hebdomadae Sanctae* the words are omitted. The peculiar absence of *flectamus genua* before the prayer had also caused speculation and popular explanations of this discrepancy were generally anti-Jewish. The genuflection has now been restored in line with the other prayers of this solemn intercession.

first appear in the Middle Ages. Its foundations were laid at the very time when the foundations of the Church were being laid. In the middle of the second century the heretic Marcion made a determined bid to convince Christians that the God worshipped by the Jews was no more than a lower demiurge, and that in consequence the Old Testament was not worthy to have a place in the Holy Scriptures of the Church.[38] A contemporary writer stated : 'For He (the Lord) declared that circumcision was not of the flesh, but they transgressed because an evil angel deluded them.'[39] We can go back to the very first century, for there are many passages in the New Testament itself, which may be, and have in fact often been quoted to demonstrate the anti-Jewish character of Christianity. Was it not the Jews who were responsible for Christ's death? The blame could not be limited to Pilate or the Sanhedrin : it rested with the Jewish people as St Matthew's gospel emphasises : 'Now the chief priests and the elders persuaded the crowds to ask for Barabbas and destroy Jesus. . . . They *all* said, Let him be crucified' (Mt 27, 20. 22). When Pilate protested his innocence, '*all the people* answered, His blood be on us and on our children' (Mt 27, 25). This was the climax of Jewish opposition to Christ throughout his public ministry, an opposition which St John's gospel emphatically attributes to the Jewish people,[40] in contrast to the Synoptics where the Scribes and Pharisees are named as Christ's opponents. The language of the gospels is sufficiently familiar to the Christian for him to react instinctively against the suggestion that his religion is in any way Jewish : and for him the Old Testament is Jewish.

For him too the mention of the Old Testament evokes a confused memory of the Jewish law, with its unending regulations on many peculiar subjects : its manifold animal sacrifices, its

[38]cf J. N. D. Kelly, *Early Christian Doctrines,* London 1960, p. 57.

[39]*The Epistle of Barnabas* IX, *Ante-Nicene Christian Library* vol. 1, Edinburgh 1868, p. 114.

[40]cf Leonhard Goppelt, *Christentum und Judentum,* 1954, p. 251.

dietary laws, its strange ideas on ritual purity, its recognition of slavery and divorce, and its insistence on circumcision. But all this was decisively rejected by Christianity. Is it not true to say that St Paul is little short of abusive in his references to the law? 'By the works of the law shall no one be justified' (Gal 2, 16). 'All who rely on works of the law are under a curse' (Gal 3, 10). 'If it had not been for the law, I should not have known sin' (Rom 7, 7). 'The very commandment which promised life proved to be death to me' (Rom 7, 10). At best the law was a guardian and tutor, useful for a time but to be discarded when childhood was over (cf Gal 3, 24-5); 4, 1-7). The old covenant may be compared to the child of the slave woman Agar, whilst the new is child of the free woman Sarah, born of God's promise (cf Gal 4, 21-31).

It is easy to quote texts such as these to show that the Mosaic law is of no significance for Christianity, and it is equally easy to draw the conclusion that the events of the Old Testament are of no real importance for us: if the Mosaic law has been abrogated, then the exodus which prepared for the giving of the law on Sinai has no place in Christian faith except that of a type of figure or foreshadowing of what was to come. If circumcision no longer counts for anything (cf Gal 5, 6; 6, 15), then neither does God's choice of Israel as His Own private possession, of which circumcision was the sign. The Christian's belittling if not open rejection of the Old Testament, which in the ignorant may have no better explanation than that it is considered to be Jewish and therefore opposed to Christ, can it would seem, be provided with solid reasons from the New Testament, and appear to the better informed as an essential part of Christian teaching.

But the question of the relationship between the Old and New Testaments, and between Israel and Christianity, is not answered so easily, and the quoting of those texts which seem to resolve the question to the detriment of the Old Testament is a particularly clear example of the dangers lurking in text hunting. All the writings of the New Testament, and particularly St Paul's epistles to the Galatians and the Romans must be read against the background of the crisis which the church was experiencing at the time they were written, and not as a series of lapidary pronouncements without need of qualification in the light of what preoccupied both writer and reader. It is not easy for us to acquire a clear and accurate picture of that background, since the New Testament takes it for granted and makes little explicit reference to it. But there is sufficient evidence to show that the infant church had to face a crisis of terrifying dimensions, within the first two decades of its existence.

Perhaps this is seen most clearly in the Epistle to the Galatians. St Paul is obviously filled with anxiety about the future of this community, made up of people whom he had converted to Christianity from paganism. He had received the disquieting news that certain individuals were disturbing and unsettling the Galatians (5, 10. 12), by preaching to them a gospel different from that which Paul has preached to them (1, 6). They were insisting that if the Galatians did not accept circumcision and observe the Mosaic law, they could not be sharers in the salvation announced by the gospel. Thus they were attempting to shut them out from the community of the saints into which Paul had admitted them, so that the Galatians would be forced to come to these false brethren and plead for circumcision at the hands of their new evangelists (cf 4, 17). When the Galatians had protested, as well they might, that Paul had made no mention of the necessity of circumcision and the observing of the Mosaic law which this epitomised, these perverters of the gospel (1, 7) had had the audacity to calm their disquiet by suggesting that Paul had not been in possession of the true gospel when he had visited Galatia: at that time he had learned the gospel from unreliable teachers who had rejected the Mosaic law. But now, after visiting Jerusalem and there receiving instruction from the brethren, Paul was better informed and would bear out their teaching.[41] Had he not been zealous for the law (cf 1, 13-14)?

Perhaps we are astonished to find that such a thing could happen within the infant church? Perhaps we still find it hard to believe? Our scepticism will hardly survive a reading of St Paul's second epistle to the Corinthians. Any notion of the church growing up as a community of saints in perfect peace and harmony, without rivalry or hostility, without bickering and difference of opinion is wildly inaccurate. The church in Corinth for instance was torn by factions and jealousy, and Paul is clearly being driven frantic by his anxiety for its survival in the truth of the gospel. Here too, as in Galatia, there are 'false apostles, deceitful operators, disguising themselves as apostles of Christ' but in reality servants of Satan (2 Cor 11, 13; cf v. 15). They too, are preaching a gospel contrary to that which Paul had preached; but far from any pretence that Paul is on their side, they reject his authority and add personal abuse for good measure: Paul is a weak man and a poor speaker (10, 11; 11, 6), out to make money (cf 11, 8-9), a fool (11, 16), crafty and deceitful (12, 16). These super-apostles, as Paul sarcastically calls them, are corrupting the faith of the Corinthian church, and we can be reasonably sure that their erroneous teaching is similar to that being preached

[41]Whether the Judaizers did claim Paul's name or not may be questioned, and it is not commonly stated. But it would seem the best way of explaining certain features in the Epistle to the Galatians: Paul's strong protestation that he did not receive the gospel from men (1, 1. 12); nor that he went immediately to Jerusalem (1, 17). He swears that when eventually he did go to Jerusalem he saw only Cephas and James, and no other apostles (1, 19-20). The Judean churches knew nothing of his teaching (1, 22. 23). When Paul went up to Jerusalem fourteen years later and expounded his gospel, it was only to the 'notables' lest he waste his time (2, 2). Paul did not yield to the 'false brethren' though they gained access to him by subterfuge and tried to make him readopt the law (2, 4). All this seems to be a rejection of a claim made by brethren from Jerusalem, that they have given him further instruction in the gospel.

in Galatia, since they are boasting of the fact that they are Hebrews, Israelites, descendants of Abraham as well as servants of Christ (cf 1, 22-3).

The Roman church is not free of dissenters who oppose the doctrine which they have been taught (Rom 16, 17-20) and Paul must warn the Philippians: 'Look out for the dogs, look out for the evildoers, look out for those who mutilate the flesh' (Phil 3, 2). The same false teachers are obviously at work here also, urging the necessity of circumcision.

But let us not be misled by Paul's vehemence into thinking that these teachers were both wicked and stupid to a degree that is almost beyond belief. Let us try to realise how they could teach such a doctrine, not to excuse their error, but to enter as far as is possible into the situation and really feel the tension. The apostles and disciples, like Christ himself, had grown up to love and serve God within the Jewish law, and their very piety and zeal for the kindgom of God was due initially to the faithful observance over many years of that law which they rightly believed came from God. They had learned much from Christ, but not that they should repudiate the law. He had told them: 'Think not that I have come to abolish the law and the prophets; I have come not to abolish them but to fulfil them. For truly, I say to you, till heaven and earth pass away, not an iota, not a dot, will pass from the law until all is accomplished. Whoever then relaxes one of the least of these commandments and teaches men so, shall be called least in the kingdom of heaven; but he who does them and teaches them shall be called great in the kingdom of heaven' (Mt 5, 17-19). If scholars still find it difficult to explain what exactly 'fulfil' means here, are we right to expect more of the first disciples, to whom Christ said: 'I have yet many things to say to you, but you cannot bear them now. When the Spirit of truth comes, he will guide you into all the truth' (John 16, 12)? We know from the history of the church's doctrine that the Holy Spirit did not cram their minds with the explicit knowledge of all the implication of Christ's teaching. Moreover he had also said to them : 'The scribes and the Pharisees sit on Moses' seat; so practise and observe whatever they tell you, but not what they do' (Mt 23, 2-3). Ought we then to be surprised that even after the coming of the Holy Spirit at Pentecost, Peter and John should go up to the temple at the hour of prayer, and that the whole christian community could be described as 'day by day attending the temple together' (Acts 3, 1; 2, 46)?

The first converts were all Jews, many of them priests and Pharisees (Acts 6, 7; 15, 5), and the Christian community in Jerusalem was that *Jewish* community which followed a new 'way' (Acts 9, 2; 18, 25f; 19, 9. 23; 22, 4; 24, 14. 22) by acknowledging that Jesus, whom God had raised from the dead, was the Messiah. Hence it is not difficult to appreciate what a burning question the continued observance of the law was, and how difficult it was to answer this question. It was not long before the question was raised, for although the Jerusalem community was Jewish, some were Palestinian Jews whilst others belonged to the diaspora, namely those who were natives of Hellenist cities outside Palestine. The latter were already, by force of circumstances, more aware of the problem of the Gentiles than the former,[42] and it was they who first fell foul of the Jewish authorities. One of their number named Stephen was accused of speaking 'blasphemous words against Moses and God', and of declaring that 'this Jesus of Nazareth will destroy this place (the temple) and will change the customs[43] which Moses delivered to us' (Acts 6, 11. 14). Stephen died a martyr for Jesus Christ, and those of the Christian community who were hellenist had to flee from Jerusalem[44] (Acts 8, 1).

[42]The Jews of the Diaspora were very zealous in making proselytes, cf A. Tricot, *Introduction à la Bible* II, Paris 1959, p. 101.

[43] τάξθη, a word used in reference to the liturgical laws and Jewish customs cf Lk 1, 9; 2, 42; Jo 19, 40; circumcision is included, in Acts 15, 1.

[44]Though Luke tells us that only the apostles remained in Jerusalem,

The apostles revered Stephen as a martyr, but did they necessarily understand the full implications of what he had said, or indeed did they necessarily judge it prudent to have spoken in that way? All we know is that when Peter baptised Cornelius and his household, he had been fortified by a vision in which God had warned him not to consider Cornelius unclean, and had witnessed the descent of the Holy Spirit on them whilst he was still speaking.[45] Even so there seems to be a note of hesitancy about Peter's question : 'Can any one forbid water for baptising these people who have received the Holy Spirit just as we have?' (Acts 10, 47). It was something so momentous, this baptising of the uncircumcised, that when Peter returned to Jerusalem he must answer to the community : 'Why did you go to uncircumcised men and eat with them?' (Acts 11, 3). His answer silenced them, 'and they glorified God, saying "Then to the Gentiles also God has granted repentance unto life"' (Acts 11, 18).

Yet not every doubt was resolved, nor every pious member of the Jerusalem community satisfied. According to St Matthew's gospel Christ himself had forbidden the twelve to preach to the Gentiles : 'Go nowhere among the Gentiles and enter no town of the Samaritans, but go rather to the lost sheep of Israel' (Mt 10, 5-6). Of his own mission Christ had declared : 'I was sent only to the lost sheep of the house of Israel', and he had seemed reluctant to help the Canaanite woman because she belonged to the Gentiles who, compared with the House of Israel, were as dogs under the master's table, shown particular favour if they were allowed to eat the scraps that fell from it (cf Mt 15, 21-8). Our Lord's warning 'Do not give dogs what is holy; and do not throw your pearls before swine, lest they

there are good reasons for thinking that this includes the Judeo-Christian community, cf Ernst Haenchen, *Die Apostelgeschichte,* Göttingen 1956, p. 256.

[45]Moreover Cornelius was not wholly gentile in the religious sense, cf Acts 10, 2.

trample them underfoot, and turn to attack you' (Mt 7, 6) may have seemed to many disciples a warning not to preach the gospel to the Gentiles. It is therefore far from surprising that even Peter hesitated at Antioch, when 'certain men came from James' and objected to his associating with Gentiles (cf Gal 2, 11-14). The difficulty was considerable, and clearly there was no easy solution. But the activities of Paul among the Gentiles made them face it. The Christian community therefore met together in solemn assembly at Jerusalem to avert the growing crisis, for 'some believers who belonged to the party of the Pharisees rose up and said "It is necessary to circumcise them, and to charge them to keep the law of Moses" ' (Acts 15, 5). The council's decision was to the contrary, though they commanded the Gentiles 'to abstain from the pollutions of idols, and from illicit unions[46] and from what is strangled and from blood' (Acts 15, 20), realising that the time was not yet ripe for completely abandoning the Jewish marriage and dietary laws. Paul saw this point, when the Jerusalem community reminded him of 'how many thousands there are among the Jews of those who have believed; they are all zealous for the law' (Acts 21, 20). For the same reason he consented to circumcise Timothy (Acts 16, 3).

In view of the caution of the leaders of the church in Jerusalem, it is not difficult to understand why there were many other Jewish Christians, less cautious and with less understanding of the Christian revelation, who were spurred on by their zeal for the law to preach the necessity of circumcision. It was these unfortunate people who regarded Paul as a heretic, and tried to correct his gospel to the Gentiles. Coming in many cases no doubt from Jerusalem, after having had contact if not with Christ himself, then with his apostles and closest disciples they could claim an authority which to many seemed greater

[46]This seems to be the correct sense of πορνεία here, namely matrimonial unions contracted contrary to Lev. 18, whatever the word may mean in Mt 5, 32; 19, 9.

than Paul's, a man who had not known Christ in the flesh (2 Cor 5, 16); a man who, they claimed, was trying to win favour with these Gentiles by excusing them from circumcision, something they found repulsive (Gal 1, 10); and a man who was preaching freedom from the law which would surely lead to the licence to which the Gentiles were accustomed : immorality, impurity, licentiousness and so on (cf Gal 5, 16-21).

Such was the crisis. But if our attempt to recreate the urgency of the situation has shown too great indulgence towards those who were preaching false doctrine, let us recall the vehemence with which St Paul attacks them. No term of abuse is too strong! They are perverters, disturbers, dogs and servants of Satan. Their boasting so exasperates him that he indulges in it himself, in spite of its foolishness (2 Cor 11, 1-12, 13). We can gauge his anger against those who demand circumcision when he cries : 'I wish those who unsettle you would mutilate themselves'[47] (Gal 5, 12). 'Their end will correspond to their deeds' (2 Cor 11, 15). Thus abuse is directed not so much at the false teachers as at their false teaching, and so Paul seeks to discredit that teaching by every means in his power. In these circumstances circumcision and the Mosaic law must be discredited at all costs, and so his vituperative rhetoric is aimed at them with all the force he can muster. There was no more powerful weapon than the Old Testament itself, for the prophets had constantly upbraided the Israelites for their complacency in the observing of the law whilst all the time they were displeasing to God. Texts had already been gathered for this purpose before Paul wrote his epistle to the Romans, and

[47]'There is possibly a tacit reference to the emasculation of the priests of Cybele, with which the Galatians would doubtless be familiar, and, quite possibly, in the apostle's mind,. at least, though he could hardly have expected his Galatian readers to think of it, to the language of Deut 23, 1.' Ernest de Witt Burton, *The Epistle to the Galatians,* International Critical Commentary, Edinburgh 1921, p. 289.

his extensive use of them there is to some extent dictated by this Christian practice.[48]

Paul's vehemence is demanded by the circumstances, and if we forget this and fail to take into consideration his rhetorical style we shall misunderstand his remarks about circumcision, the law and by implication the meritorous value of good works.[49] We shall wrongly quote texts as isolated and unqualified pronouncements—as we did above, and fail to understand the far more subtle teaching he gives us in the epistle to the Romans, admittedly so difficult to interpret.

Here he teaches that the observance of the Mosaic law must come to an end, not for any absolute reason, but because its continuation is in the concrete circumstances a denial of the gospel that we are justified, uniquely and wholly through faith in Christ. Jewish converts were so conditioned in their belief that justification came through the observance of the law, that any retention of the latter meant in practice the retaining of the belief that accompanied it, and consequently it usurped the unique place of Christ.

The Mosaic law had been given to Israel by God as the means whereby they should realise His design of making them His own personal property and a holy nation (cf Ex 19, 5-6). As we have seen the law laid down the conditions to be fulfilled in order that God's purpose guaranteed in His covenant might be effected. It was the detailed elaboration of the condition he imposed when He said: 'If you will obey my voice and keep my covenant' (Ex 19, 5). That many in Israel had failed to obey His voice was not the fault of the law (cf Rom 2, 18), though in fact the giving of the law had made sin clear (Rom 6, 20; 7, 7), since it had shown clearly what God demanded

---

[48]cf L. Cerfaux, *La Théologie de l'Église suivant saint Paul*, 2e édit. Paris 1948, pp. 35-8.

[49]The well-known contrast between *Romans* and *James* with its theme: 'Faith without works is dead' (2, 26) cannot be understood unless the restricted purpose of *Romans* be duly appreciated.

and what He forbade. But the law was the God-given means whereby the Israelites had been able to fulfil God's purpose and therefore attain justification, if they wished.

Most had not wished to do so. They had failed, not only because they had been too weak to observe the law, the flesh lusting against the spirit (Rom 7, 13-25), but also because they had become blind to the truth that even the observance of the law demands faith if it is to bring with it justification (cf Rom 9, 32). God's promise that they would be His own people if they obeyed His voice, had obscured the truth that they could only be His people because He had freely chosen them: 'It was not because you were more in number than any other people that the Lord set His love upon you and chose you, for you were the fewest of all peoples; but it is because the Lord loves you, and is keeping the oath which He swore to your fathers' (Deut 7, 7-8). God had not sworn to make Abraham into a great nation because Abraham had observed the law: it was a sheer gift on God's part, unearned by Abraham. Nor did Abraham 'earn' justification by observing the law from that day forth, since the law had not been given. He was justified because he believed in God's promise.

The Jews did not, in practice, believe in God's promises: they saw no need, because they were of the opinion that their observance of the law assured them of justification as of right, not free promise. Misunderstanding God's fidelity to His promises as a juridical obligation from which He was powerless to escape, they no longer *hoped* for Justification, since they already *saw* it as something attainable by their own efforts. Thus they were without faith, and they had no hope (Rom 8, 24). They could not have understood Our Lord's admonition: 'So you also, when you have done all that is commanded you, say "We are unworthy servants; we have only done what was our duty" ' (Lk 17, 10).[50]

[50]The rabbis gave a similar warning, cf J. Schmid, *Das Evangelium nach Lukas,* Regensburg 1955, p. 271.

The law therefore had failed as the divinely appointed means of justification because it had been observed wrongly, without faith and with the presumption that it established a strict right to the fulfilment of God's promises. Because of this failure God in a last supreme effort, to speak very humanly, had sent His only begotten Son (Rom 11, 11-12. 15. 30). At the Exodus God had said: 'If you will hear my voice. . . .' and He had spoken through Moses. At the transfiguration of Christ, and in the presence of Moses and Elias God said: 'This is my beloved Son, with whom I am well pleased; hear him' (Mt 17, 5). The law and Christ may be compared as two divinely given means through which God's people were to realise their vocation. From the human point of view they are two successive means, both originating from God, but the latter to be substituted for the former because the law had in fact failed, and had demonstrated the need of a more potent means. Both means, the law and Christ were at man's free disposal, and therefore neither were irresistible: Paul's cry, 'I only knew sin by the law' (Rom 7, 7) may be paralleled by Our Lord's saying: 'If I had not come, they would not have sinned' (John 15, 22).

But from God's point of view, as He contemplates the one single divine action of saving mankind, the law is so to speak part of Christ, for Christ is the only means whereby all men from the beginning to the end can be saved. The law was the first sign of Christ's coming (cf Rom 10, 4), the first sound of God's word which, falling on deaf ears, increased to the volume of the word made flesh. When Christ said 'I am the way and the truth and the life' (John 14, 6) he was saying: I am the law. There are not, and never have been two divinely appointed means whereby mankind may be saved, for only the word of God can reveal what God wants of us, and the word of God is essentially one and not many. Christ is not another law, but the fulfilment of the law, just as the first faint sounds of the one who calls from a distance, belong to the same voice which sounds so clearly in our ears when he has come close to us.

In spite of the urgency of the situation and the pressing need Paul has to show the futility of further observance of the law, he must admit that the law is not of itself against the promises of God, and that it is indeed the source of knowledge of God's will (Rom 2, 18), the embodiment of knowledge and truth (Rom 2, 20). Nor does he seek to overthrow the law. He claims that in reality he is upholding it (Rom 3, 31). 'So the law is holy, and the commandment is holy and just and good' (Rom 7, 12). Of itself it is spiritual (Rom 7, 14). 'I delight', Paul asserts, 'in the law of God in my inmost self' (Rom 7, 22). It is not the law in itself which is powerless, but the law weakened by the flesh (Rom 8, 3). The fleshly observance of the law, such as was the Jews', and such as it would inevitably continue to be in Paul's day, would result in the Christian convert's regarding Christ as a means of salvation *along with* the law, and this would be to deny the ultimate revelation of God in Christ, whilst at the same time robbing the law of its efficacy.[51] For the law never had any efficacy apart from Christ (Rom 8, 3-4). 'We ourselves, who are Jews by birth and not Gentile sinners, yet who know that a man is not justified by works of the law but through faith in Christ Jesus, even we have believed in Christ Jesus in order to be justified by faith in Christ, and not by works of the law, because by works of the law shall no one be justified' (Gal 2, 15-16).

[51] It must be remembered that once this crisis was overcome the law was in its essentials readopted by the Church, as the practical guide for the life of God's Israel. The decalogue, which was the core of the Mosaic law, remains the revealed source of Christian conduct, because it has an eternal validity. But its observance is now the practical demonstration of our faith in Christ, and the strength which enables us to keep the law now flows through Christ. It is often forgotten that the decalogue is the divinely revealed basis of morality, and not a 'natural' law. Moreover the attempt has often been made to reject the decalogue on the grounds that it is not Christian. This is a question currently debated in the Anglican Church, cf letters in *The Times* of Jan. 31st; Feb. 4th & 10th., 1961.

With vehemence and passion, and not without exaggeration and incoherence,[52] Paul rejected the law, because it had been so misused that it had become useless for the attaining of God's purpose; and because God in His mercy had given us Christ in its place. But it would be fatal to think that in rejecting the means,[53] Paul rejected the end God intended. God has given us another and an incomparably better means, not to a new end[54] but to the same end : 'that in Christ Jesus the blessing of Abraham might come upon the Gentiles, that we might receive the promise of the Spirit through faith' (Gal 3, 14). God has in mind for us Christians the very same purpose He had in mind from the moment He called Abraham : 'If you are Christ's then you are Abraham's offspring, heirs according to promise' (Gal 3, 29). Nothing is more striking than that it should be Paul who insists on this truth : Paul, the bitter enemy of the Judaizers is yet able to retain his faith in God's unwavering purpose to redeem Israel, that through Israel the whole world may come to know that He alone is God (cf Sir 36, 3-5). Paul's is the great mind which even in the heat and confusion of the battle could distinguish between the means to the end and the end itself. He saw clearly that the law had been what Christ now is : the revelation of God and the means whereby man is justified, for both the law and Christ are the word of God. Man cannot be justified unless God speaks to him, in order that he may come to the true knowledge of what God is and what God requires of him. Or to say the same thing in different words, man can never of himself possess the wisdom

[52]cf L. Cerfaux *op. cit.* p. 30, ftn. 1; 46, ftn. 3; pp. 50-54.

[53]And it would be well to remember that the Canon of the Christian faith includes the Epistle of James.

[54]Such expressions as *new* testament, *new* man, *new* creation, do not contradict this, for throughout the Scriptures there is not an adequate distinction between 'new', 'renewed', 'restored' (and one may add 'spiritualised'): all are applied to the fulfilment of God's designs in each of the stages which lie in the future from the speaker's point of view. cf L. Cerfaux, *op. cit.* pp. 44-47.

to fulfil God's design in his regard, unless wisdom be given to him by God. God's wisdom, God's word, God's law and God's son gradually stand revealed as synonymous. Before the incarnation the law was the word and the wisdom of God as far as this world could grasp it: 'He (God) found the whole way to knowledge and gave her to Jacob His servant and to Israel whom He loved. Afterward she appeared upon earth and lived among men. She is the book of the commandments of God, and the law that endures for ever. All who hold her fast will live, and those who forsake her will die. Turn, O Jacob, and take her; walk toward the shining of her light. Do not give your glory to another, or your advantages to an alien people. Happy are we, O Israel, for we know what is pleasing to God' (Bar 3, 36-4, 4). But Israel did not heed this exhortation. The word of God, in which was life and light for men, came to its own home, and its own people received it not (cf John 1, 4. 11). So the word became flesh and dwelt among us in the person of Jesus Christ. All therefore that the author of Baruch has said of God's wisdom can now be said of Jesus Christ: he has appeared upon earth and lived among men. He is the book of the commandments of God, and the law that endures for ever. All who hold him fast will live, and those who forsake him will die. Turn, O Jacob, and take him; walk toward the shining of his light! To continue to cling to the law and to reject Christ, is to continue to strain the ear for the faint sound of God's voice when He is already by our side desiring to speak to us. God's graciousness towards us now stands revealed in all its overwhelming generosity, and the means of our salvation now stands revealed in all its truth: 'For the law was given through Moses; grace and truth came through Jesus Christ' (John 1, 17).

Christ therefore replaces the Mosaic Law as the revelation of God's will and as the means whereby God will fulfil His purpose. But he does not replace that purpose, and he does not nullify God's promises. God's purpose remains the same and His promises are still valid. God still works towards the forming of the one people who will be separated and holy and hence will manifest God to the world. Israel God's chosen people must continue and must grow to the full enjoyment of God's promises in its regard. If God had abandoned Israel He would have admitted defeat and been shown incapable of accomplishing the task He had set Himself to do. But the word of God cannot fail, 'for the gifts and the call of God are irrevocable' (Rom 11, 29).

But did not the word of God fail, and did not God revoke His call, when the Jews rejected Christ? St Paul, in spite of the urgency of his attack on those who still clung to the law knew that this could not be. 'But it is not as though the word of God had failed' (Rom 9, 6). No one surely has ever been more strongly tempted than he, to say that all God had promised to Israel was now cancelled. Yet what a disaster it would have been if he had yielded! Is God like a man, inconstant and unreliable, promising great things, but in face of difficulty and failure disowning His word? God's unwavering fidelity to His word is the foundation of all our hopes. The word of God cannot have failed. But the rejection of Christ by his kinsmen by race shows Paul that 'Not all who are descended from Israel belong to Israel, and not all are children of Abraham because they are his descendants. . . . It is not the children of the flesh who are the children of God, but the children of the promise are reckoned as descendants' (Rom 9, 6-8). Israel according to the flesh and Israel the object of God's promises had been too frequently identified, in spite of the constant warnings of the prophets.[55] The Jews had thought it sufficient to retort: 'We are children of Abraham' (John 8, 33) when they were told they did not enjoy the freedom of the sons of God. But in fact they were not children of Abraham though they were of his stock by physical descent. The time had come to make it clear that

[55]cf the texts quoted by St Paul in Rom 3, 9-18; 9, 25-26. 29. 33; 10, 19-21; 11, 8-10; 15, 9-12. 21.

race means nothing: 'There is neither Jew nor Greek, there is neither slave nor free, there is neither male nor female; for you are all one in Christ Jesus. And if you are Christ's, then you are Abraham's offspring, heirs according to promise' (Gal 3, 28-9).

Precisely as Christians we are Abraham's offspring and the object of God's promise. For the most part we are not Jews by race, but because we are Christians we are Israelites, namely heirs to the promises first made to Abraham, but inherited by Israel alone of Abraham's children (cf Rom 9, 10-13). God has not rejected Abraham in favour of us; God has not grown tired of Israel his first-born and disowned him. Rather, in His generosity He has enabled us to gain admittance into the family of Abraham. He has graciously deigned to number us in Israel. How then could we possibly think that God's love for Israel matters nothing to us? How could we consider that all God has done for Israel in no way concerns us? St Paul warns Christians who are Gentile by race against this attitude. We must always remember that we have been grafted into the stock of Israel. Without the stock the branches are dead (cf Rom 11, 17-24).

We are Israel, not according to race, not that part of Israel which was hardened (Rom 11, 25) and which failed to obtain what it sought (Rom 11, 7), but Israel God's chosen people and the object of His promises: we are the Israel of God (Gal 6, 16). Now it is precisely with the Israel of God that the Scriptures of the Old Testament are concerned. The Scriptures are never interested in Israel as a race, comparable to Moabites or Edomites or Canaanites. They are only concerned with Israel insofar as it belongs to God. Israel in its self-sufficiency is of no significance, but Israel as the child of God and the object of His choice is the most significant thing in the world, because God will be known to the world through His people Israel. Our vocation is to be Israel as God intends Israel to be. Our justification and our salvation lies in Israel. True, we are no

130

longer required to accept circumcision, because God has made His voice to be heard in Christ, and our faith in Christ makes us part of the Israel of God as did circumcision in former time. No longer is it required of us to observe the Mosaic law, because it is through Christ that we continue as God's Israel. 'Our hope is not through Moses nor through the law' Justin Martyr said to the Jew Trypho, 'or there would be no difference between you and ourselves; but I have read that there should hereafter be a final law, and covenant more mighty than all others, which every one who hopes for the inheritance of God should henceforth observe. The law given at Horeb has become obsolete, and was for you Jews only, but the one of which I speak is for all men alike. A new law passed upon a law abrogates that which is old, and in like manner does a subsequent covenant anul a former one. An everlasting and perfect law, and a faithful covenant, is given to us, even Christ, after which there shall be no other law, or ordinance, or command.'[56] We have a new law, but our hope is still centred in the inheritance of God. That is not new. So Justin concludes : 'He (Christ) is in truth that new law and that new covenant, and the expectation of those who, from all nations, have awaited the blessings of God. For we who have been brought to God through this Christ who was crucified, are the true spiritual Israel, and the race of Juda, Jacob, Isaac and Abraham, who in uncircumcision received a testimony and a blessing from God for his faith, and was named the father of many nations.'[57]

In proclaiming God's love for Israel therefore, we proclaim God's eternal love for us. In recounting God's wonderful deeds on behalf of Israel, we recount God's wonderful deeds on behalf of us. In reminding ourselves of God's promises to Israel, we remind ourselves of God's promises to us. The psalms which narrate God's choice of Abraham, His protection of the Patri-

[56]*Dialogue with Trypho,* § 11, quoted from *The Works now extant of S. Justin The Martyr,* Oxford MDCCCLXI, p. 84.
[57]*ibid.,* p. 85.

131

archs, His conquest of Egypt on behalf of Israel, His leading Israel across the Red Sea and His patience in the wilderness, are the recital of God's unwavering love for us. The climax of that love came when God sent His only-begotten son, and this is always present to our minds when we sing these psalms. But no gesture on the part of Him who loves us is without its delight and its comfort. Experience teaches us that we are fickle, and that we cannot be too often reminded of God's love for us if we are not to lose our trust in Him. God has, absolutely speaking, only one word to say to us, and that word is Christ. But just as that one divine word had to be spoken through many actions before it became flesh, so now we may fail to comprehend all that the Word made flesh really signifies, unless we recall the actions which preceded it. In so many different ways God has proved His love for us. We ought not to be indifferent to His slightest gesture.

CHAPTER IV

Yahweh the Conqueror of Israel's Enemies

Pss 44; 60; 74; 79; 80; 83; 85; 123; 126; 137

The psalms of this group are all lamentations, sung by the community in face of grave calamity, and for the most part they conform to the stereotyped and easily recognisable pattern which we have already outlined.[1] After an introductory cry for help there is the lament, and this is followed by an avowal of confidence in God's saving mercy, and a petition for the speedy accomplishing of their salvation. There are of course certain variations to be found : thus some psalms begin with the praise of God (Pss 44, 1-9; 85, 2-4; 126, 1-3), whilst others end with the promise of praise (79, 13; 80, 19), and there are divine oracles in Pss 60, 8-10; 85, 9-14. But on the whole these psalms are remarkably homogeneous.

It is clear from the laments that the community is suffering the effects of grave disasters, caused by the successful attacks of Israel's enemies. They are humiliated by the scorn of neighbouring peoples, and their abject condition is a reflection upon God, for their enemies taunt them with His helplessness. It would seem that Yahweh has abandoned them (cf Ps 44, 10-17), and hence the indignant cry : 'Awake ! Why sleepest Thou, Yahweh? Arouse Thyself, cast us not off for ever. Wherefore hidest Thou Thy face, and forgettest our affliction and our oppression? For our soul is bowed down to the dust; our belly cleaveth unto the earth. Arise for our help, and redeem us for Thy mercy's sake' (Ps 44, 24-7).

[1] cf pp. 45-51.

And yet it cannot be true that God has abandoned Israel for ever. When at the beginning He had led them into the Promised Land, had He not defeated their enemies? No nation had been allowed to stand in their way. Although so few in number, had they not crushed their enemies because Yahweh had fought with them? He had driven out the nations so that He might plant the vine which He had brought from Egypt (Ps 80, 9). He had been victorious over Midian, over Sisera and Jabin, Oreb and Seb, Sebah and Salmuna who had threatened to dispossess God's people (Ps 83, 10-13). Since God was steadfast and unchanging in His love for Israel and since His might had not lessened, He must now repeat His victories over the enemies of Israel : 'Render unto our neighbours sevenfold in their bosoms' (Ps 79, 12). 'Pour out Thy wrath upon the nations that know Thee not' (Ps 79, 6). 'O My God, make them like the whirling dust; as stubble before the wind. . . . So pursue them with Thy tempest, and affright them with Thy storm' (Ps 83, 14-16).

The Historical Disasters

There were a number of occasions in Israel's history when they suffered defeat at the hands of their enemies, and when the ensuing suffering and degradation could well have called forth the laments in these psalms. There was for instance the onslaught of Assyria and its local allies, which ended in the destruction of Samaria and the deportation of many Israelites belonging to the northern tribes. Only a very brief reference is made to this disaster in the Books of Kings : Salmanasar king of Assyria captured king Osea of Israel, and besieged Samaria for three years; when the city fell to his son Sargon II in 721 B.C. the Israelites were deported to Assyria (2 Kgs 17, 3-6). The compiler of the Books of Kings is more anxious to explain how such a disaster could have happened, and he gives as the reason the fact that the Israelites of the northern kingdom had aped the ways of the Canaanites even in their religious

134

practices, and had failed to observe the law of God such as it is found in Deuteronomy (2 Kgs 7, 7-23. 34-41). But the brevity of the notice in 2 Kings does not hide the fact that it was a grievous calamity, and according to the Annals of Sargon 27,290 Israelites were taken into exile.[2]

But a far greater catastrophe occurred over a century later, when the Babylonians conquered the southern kingdom of Juda. In 597 Nabuchodonosor punished Joachim of Juda for his attempts to obtain help from Egypt, by pillaging the temple and taking him into exile with ten thousand of his more notable citizens. Ten years later the Babylonians besieged Jerusalem and in 586 captured it, destroying the temple and taking into exile Sedecias and many of the citizens of Jerusalem. Others fled to Egypt, and Jerusalem was ruled by a foreign governor living in Samaria (cf 2 Kgs 24, 1-25, 26). The enormity of this disaster can scarcely be exaggerated : not without reason did it seem to be the complete rejection by God of Israel His chosen people (cf 2 Kgs 23, 27). The Davidic dynasty whose throne, according to God's promise through the prophet Nathan was firm for ever (2 Sam 7, 16) had been completely overthrown; Jerusalem, the city which God had chosen and in particular the temple which was His dwelling-place, lay in ruins. The land was plundered by the Edomites, Israel's inveterate enemy. It is therefore not difficult to understand how in such circumstances the agonising question could be asked: 'Hast Thou cast us off for ever?'

The last major trial the Jews had to endure came much later, when in the second century B.C. the Syrian Antiochus Epiphanes made a determined bid to hellenise them. This was a direct attack upon their religion, and those who were faithful to the law were called upon to suffer death for their faith. In 169B.C. Antiochus plundered the temple. Two years later Jerusalem was pillaged and many were taken prisoner, while the

[2]Quoted in A. Robert et A. Feuillet, *Introduction à la Bible* I, 1957, p. 236, ftn. 1.

temple was profaned by the setting up there of the abomination of desolation (1 Mac 1, 54). The author of 1 Maccabees tells us that 'Israel mourned deeply in every community, rulers and elders groaned, maidens and young men became faint, the beauty of the women faded. Every bridegroom took up the lament; she who sat in the bridal chamber was mourning. Even the land shook for its inhabitants, and all the house of Jacob was clothed with shame' (1 Mac 1, 25-8).

These were the three major catastrophes which befell the Israelites. But there were also lesser defeats which might nevertheless be the occasion for lamentation. Judah was invaded by Sennacherib in 701 B.C., during the reign of Ezechias and some of its fortress towns captured (2 Kgs 18, 13). Sennacherib urged the people to transfer their loyalty from Ezechias to himself: 'Do not listen to Ezechias when he misleads you by saying: Yahweh will deliver us! Has any of the gods of the nations ever delivered his land out of the hand of the king of Assyria? Where are the gods of Hamath and Arpad? Where are the gods of Sepharvaim, Hena, and Ivvah? Have they delivered Samaria out of my hand? Who among all the gods of the countries have delivered their countries out of my hand, that Yahweh should deliver Jerusalem out of my hand?' (2 Kgs 18, 32-5). The situation was certainly grave enough for lamentation, and actually Ezechias went into the temple and recited a lamentation which is very similar to these psalms (2 Kgs 19, 14-19).

In view of the fact that these psalms are clearly connected with historical disasters it is surprising that it proves impossible to link them with certainty to one or other of the catastrophes we have just mentioned. Yet an examination of the commentaries shows a great variety of opinion on this question.[3] Psalm 44 for instance has been linked by commentators with the Maccabean period, the post-exilic, the exilic and even with the

[3]cf for instance the discussion concerning the historical reference of these psalms in Hans-Joachim Kraus, *Psalmen,* I pp. LVI-LXI, and at each psalm.

ninth century, when Moabites and Ammonites threatened Jerusalem, and king Josaphat along with his people went to the temple to lament the impending disaster (2 Chron 20, 3-19). The truth is that the wording of the psalm is sufficiently vague and general to enable a case to be made for any of these opinions. 'Thou hast scattered us among the nations' (v. 12b) is the nearest we get to a positive indication, which might link the psalm with the Babylonian exile. Yet even this reference is not decisive since it could be explained by the Assyrian exile or the dispersal of the Jews during the Maccabean war.

It is also extremely difficult to give the historical occasion of Psalm 60, in spite of the reference to Gilead, Manasses, Ephraim, Juda, Moab, Edom and Philistia. The psalm itself is unfortunately obscure.[4] In v. 11 we read 'Who will bring me to the fortified city? Who will lead me to Edom?' But does this refer to a journey in flight or to a military expedition against Edom? In favour of the first interpretation there is in v. 6, if amended,[5] a plea for a sign or a banner which will enable the Israelites to flee from the bow. In favour of the second, we have in v. 14 'Through God we shall do valiantly; for He it is that will tread down our adversaries.' If the first interpretation is correct the historical reference is probably to the Babylonian destruction of Jerusalem, after which some of the Israelites fled into Edom (Obad 14; Jer 40, 11). If the second, then it may be to a campaign against Edom such as that led by Joram in the ninth century (2 Kgs 8, 20-2), and which was unsuccessful. But vv. 8-9 cause a further difficulty if as seems probable, they imply the occupation by the enemy of Shechem, Succoth, Gilead, Manasses, Ephraim and Judah. This could only be understandable after the fall of both Samaria and Jerusalem. All things considered the psalm probably refers to the situation during the Babylonian exile when the whole of the promised land seemed lost to Yahweh, and when Moab, Edom and

---

[4]vv. 7-14 are also found in Ps 108, 7-14.
[5]Reading *tenah* instead of *natattah*, cf Kraus, *op. cit.*, I, p. 426.

Philistia were no longer vassal states. The oracle (vv. 8-10 or 11?) is a statement that in spite of appearances Yahweh is still the warrior, fully armed and with undiminished authority over His vassals. And this authority He will soon reassert.

In Psalm 74, where to make matters worse the text is very corrupt, great stress is laid on the length of time that has elapsed since the disaster without the longed for restoration taking place. Yahweh is asked: 'Why hast thou cast us off for ever?', and the ruins are said to be 'perpetual'. The disaster has involved the wanton destruction of the temple and, it would seem, its desecration by the setting up of the enemy's standards there. This last detail suggests the profanation of of the temple by Antiochus Epiphanes and this impression is strengthened by a reference to the burning down of 'all the meeting places of God in the land' (v. 8; cf 1 Mac 2, 7; 4, 38; 2 Mac 5, 16). On the other hand the length of time during which the temple remained desolate does not suit the Maccabean period, but rather the period of the Babylonian exile, between 586 and 515. Ezechiel had referred to the lack of prophets as does this psalm (Ez 7, 26; Lam 2, 9), and Nabuchodonosor had burned the temple, and broken the bronze pillars and the Sea (2 Kgs 25, 9. 13-17).

In psalm 79 the particular reference is to the defiling of the temple and the holy city by the bloodshed and the unburied dead. It is quoted in 1 Mac 7, 17 with reference to the treachery of Bacchides. But this fact hardly indicates that the historical reference of Ps 79 must be the Maccabean tragedy. It is more likely to be the destruction of Jerusalem in 586.

Psalm 80 possesses no clear reference to any of the historical catastrophes we have described, although the mention of Ephraim, Benjamin and Manasses (v. 3) may indicate the threat to the northern kingdom by Assyria. Possibly the time is that of Josias (cf v. 18?) when there was a renewed hope for the restoration of unity among the twelve tribes.

138

In Psalm 83 there is indeed an abundance of historical reference. The enemies threatening God's people are Edom, Ishmael, Hagar, Gebal, Ammon, Amalek, Philistia, Tyre and Assyria. In other words there is a conspiracy of all Israel's hostile neighbours backed by the great power of Assyria, and they are planning nothing less than the annihilation of Israel. It is to be noted that the lamentation is concerned with the threat, not with an actual attack, and although there is a surprisingly similar list of enemies in 1 Mac 5 (with of course the exception of Assyria), it would seem that reference is made here to none of the historical disasters, but rather to a period of grave anxiety preceding one of them. The mention of Assyria may be simply for good measure, in order poetically to emphasise the critical danger that God's people faces. This is probably the explanation of the very complete list of enemies. But when this state of anxiety obtained is impossible to decide.

In Psalm 85 the lament is unusually moderate in tone. The community stands in need of God's help, but no reference is made to any specific sufferings. The fact that the psalm opens with a reference to the return from captivity leads us to suppose that the historical situation is that of the years after 538, when the returned exiles suffered hardship and disillusion during their efforts to restore Jerusalem and rebuild the temple (cf Is 56-66; Esd 3, 12; Agg 2, 3). The same can be said for Ps 126 where there is also the undertone of disappointment and disillusion.

The lament of Ps 123 is caused by the contempt of Israel's oppressors. There is no other detail in this short psalm which can help towards deciding the historical situation, and clearly this is too vague to be of any real assistance. The exile is a suitable period to choose.

The opening line of Ps 137 'By the rivers of Babylon, there we sat' is the most precise historical reference in the Psalter, for clearly the psalmist is looking back on the Babylonian exile. But it is impossible to say how long after this the psalm was written.

The Use of these Psalms in Israel

The vagueness of the historical references, so frustrating to those who want to determine the historical occasion for which these psalms were written, is not without significance. It is a fairly clear indication of how unimportant the precise historical situation is when we are trying to appreciate these psalms. They have been preserved not because of their significance as historical records, but because they have been continually in use over a long period, during which the particular historical situation might be different, and at times when the original historical situations have become vague memories. They have provided the text for liturgical celebrations for which there was a perennial need within the complex of Israelite worship. There has always been a need for liturgical lamentation, because Israel has never fully enjoyed the perfect peace and prosperity God promised her. She has never been wholly free of suffering and privation, any more than a family has been free of the ravages of death.

Liturgical lamentation has as natural a place in Israel's worship as funeral rites in the life of the family, and the influence of the latter upon liturgical practice is clear. Lamentation was an important part of the funeral rites,[6] as it still is today, among certain nations. In Israel the dead man was lamented by his family, assisted by friends and professional mourners. We read that when Jacob's funeral cortege reached Transjordan 'they made a great and solemn lamentation, and Joseph celebrated for his father mourning rites lasting seven days.' (Gen 50, 10). When so important a person as Samuel or Saul died, we are told that all Israel gathered together and celebrated the mourning rites (1 Sam 25, 1; 28, 3). It was the

[6]cf R. de Vaux, *Les institutions de l'ancien testament* I, 1958, pp. 93-100.

140

task of the professional mourners to assist in the carrying out of the funeral rites and particularly to sing the lamentation which was the principal ceremony. When for instance King Josias died at Megiddo in an attempt to bar the way to Neko King of Egypt, Jeremias composed a lamentation for him, and 'all the male and female singers perform it even today, among their lamentations for Josias. It has become a rule in Israel, and these songs are to be found in the lamentations.' (2 Chron 35, 25). Without doubt the profession of lamentation singer was universally recognised (cf Jer 9, 16), and they possessed a considerable repertoire which was passed down from generation to generation (cf Jer 9, 19). It was highly stylised and stereotyped. The lament for Judas Maccabeus of which we are given only the first line (1 Mac 9, 21) doubtless followed very closely that sung for Saul and Jonathan (2 Sam 1, 19-27).

This universal custom of lamenting the dead, the mourners being clothed in sackcloth, seated in the dust, with ashes on their heads and keeping a fast, was extended to the lamentation for Israel in times of national grief. Already the lament for a King was also a lament for Israel, because the fortunes of Israel were closely bound up with her King. But the prophets extended the use of funeral lamentation to all the various calamities which afflicted Israel, such as a severe drought (Jer 14, 1-8), or a plague of locusts (Joel 1, 2-19), and especially defeat and oppression by her enemies. The best known examples of these are the five lamentations traditionally attributed to Jeremias,[7] which bemoan the desolation of Jerusalem after its destruction by Nabuchodonosor in 586. Liturgical lamentation was in fact held among the ruins of the Temple, for we read of the arrival in Jerusalem after the destruction of the Temple of eighty men, their clothes torn, and their bodies gashed, bringing cereal offerings and incense to present at the temple of Yahweh (Jer 41, 5). Their appearance indicated that they intended to

[7]On the authorship of *Lamentations* cf H. Lusseau, in A. Robert et A. Feuillet, *op. cit.*, I, pp. 677-8.

take part in mourning rites, and these were celebrated annually, as can be seen from the inquiry made by the people of Bethèl: 'Ought I to mourn and fast in the fifth month, as I have done for so many years?'[8] (Zach 7, 3). We do not know in detail what form these liturgical lamentations over the fate of Jerusalem took, for the Bible is strangely lacking in description of how feasts were celebrated. But the book of Joel helps us to some extent. The liturgical celebration of a lament according to this source, was solemnly proclaimed to the people by the sounding of the trumpet, and a fast was imposed (2, 15). All the people gathered at the Temple, where the priests and ministers, clothed in sackcloth sang the lament and bewailed the misfortune that had come upon Israel (1, 13; 2, 17), saying : 'Spare Thy people, Yahweh, and make not Thy heritage a reproach, a byword among the nations. Why should they say among the peoples "Where is their God"?' (2, 17).

Lamentation of Israel's misfortunes was bound to include a plea for restoration, and in this respect it differed from the funeral rites which had served as its model. It is an interesting fact that none of the laments for the dead which are preserved in the Old Testament has any religious characteristics. The best example is David's lament over Saul and Jonathan, in which he recalls the glory they brought to Israel. He praises their valour in battle : swifter than eagles, stronger than lions. He calls for tears over Saul who had clothed Israel's maidens in scarlet, and over Jonathan whose friendship had been dearer than life to him. But there is no mention of their devotion to Yahweh. David's lament over Abner is an expression of regret for his untimely death : 'Should Abner die as a fool dies?' (2 Sam 3, 33). Ezechiel's lament over the princes of Israel, probably Joachaz and Joaqin,[9] extols their valour and bemoans

[8]"This fast in July commemorated the destruction of Jerusalem and the temple in 587. Since rebuilding had begun it seems out of place.' (*Bible de Jérusalem* ad vers.)

[9]cf *Bible de Jérusalem*, p. 1155, ftns. *d*) and *f*).

their fate in highly poetical imagery, but no mention is made of Yahweh's part in their overthrow (Ezech 19, 1-14). These laments are secular songs because Yahweh is God not of the dead but of the living, and contact with the dead resulted in an impurity (cf Lev 21, 1-4) from which the name of God must be protected. The carrying out of the funeral rites and especially the burial of the corpse was a work of piety and a strict obligation. But it could not include any intercession to God on behalf of the dead, because there was for a long time no revelation that God interested Himself in those who had gone down to Sheol.[10] There could be no restoration to life. Even as late as the second century Ben Sirach urges those who seek wisdom to carry out the funeral rites dutifully for the prescribed period, but not to let their grief be excessive, for 'Do not forget, there is no coming back; you do the dead no good, and you injure yourself. . . . When the dead is at rest, let his remembrance cease, and be comforted for him when his spirit has departed' (Sir 38, 21-3).

But whilst Israel suffered calamities akin to death, she could not die, and there could not be an end to the people whom God had chosen.[11] In an excess of grief Amos could lament for Israel as though for one dead: 'The house of Israel is fallen; she will not rise again. The virgin Israel has collapsed on her

[10]cf P. Grelot, 'La révélation du bonheur dans l'ancien testament' in *Lumière et Vie* No. 52, 1961, p. 10, where he refers to Ps 6, 6; 88,6. 11-13; 115, 17; Is 38, 18.

[11]This belief was to prepare the way for the further revelation that the individual Israelite was destined for a true life beyond the grave: 'The living God's rejection cannot be final: His lack of interest in those who are no more is not His last word. One day He will cease to tolerate the existence of Sheol by His side. Slowly, and under pressure of many circumstances, the faithful of the Old Testament become certain that the living God can and will make all things new. Israel's vision of the future reserved for the dead, clarifies little by little. They arrive eventually, almost at the time of his coming who through his own destiny was to give it an incomparable clarity, at the belief in the resurrection.' Robert Martin-Achard, *De la mort à la resurrection d'après l'ancien testament,* 1956, p. 46.

land : there is no one to raise her up' (5, 1-2). But he immediately adds an oracle of God, which reduces this to its true proportions; and however terrible these are, they are not those of the hopelessness of death : 'The city that went forth a thousand, shall have a hundred left, and that which went forth a hundred shall have ten left to the house of Israel' (5, 3). However close Israel is brought to death, she cannot die, and therefore the lamentation over Israel can and must include a plea for her restoration. The funeral dirge, with its excess of grief and its violent sorrow had indeed a great influence upon the communal lamentations over the desolation of Israel, and this is to be borne in mind in our effort to appreciate these psalms. The unrestrained bewailing of Israel's fate may at first be as distasteful to us as the keening of mourners in the funeral rites of people whose temperament and customs differ from our own. Their note of bitter complaint may seem as rebellious as a mother's frenzied outburst because God has taken her son. The cry of 'Why, O God' (Ps 74, 1. 11) and 'How long, O God ?' (Ps 74, 10; 79, 5; 80, 5) are like the sighs and the groans of the mourners, crying Alas! and Woe! But such outbursts of grief are not to be misunderstood by being isolated from their circumstances. Only the onlooker who witnesses the lamentation of the mourner with cold indifference, is shocked at the intemperance of the utterances. From those who realise the greatness of the loss sustained there is nothing but sympathy and understanding. And when grief has run its course, and gives place to a humble and trustful plea for God's mercy, the whole is seen in true perspective.

Yahweh's Honour at Stake

But the true perspective of these communal lamentations can only be seen when we realise the unique relationship which exists between God and Israel. The adversaries whose victories Israel laments are the adversaries of God : 'Shall the enemy blaspheme *Thy name* for ever ?' (Ps 74, 10). God is urged :

144

'Remember this, Yahweh, how the enemy has reproached, and how a base people has blasphemed *Thy name*' (Ps 74, 18). Consequently God is exhorted to defend *Himself*: 'Arise O God, plead *Thine own* cause: remember *Thy* reproach all the day at the hand of the base man. Forget not the voice of *Thine* adversaries, the tumult of those that rise up against *Thee* which ascendeth continually' (Ps 74, 22-3). The enemies of Israel are 'the nations that know Thee not' and 'the kingdoms that call not upon Thy name' (Ps 79, 6), those who ask 'Where is their God?' (Ps 79, 10) in tones which are a reproach against Yahweh (Ps 79, 12). Israel's enemies are those who hate God (Ps 83, 3), those who make a covenant against Him (83, 6) and who refuse to acknowledge that Yahweh alone is the 'Most High over the whole world' (Ps 83, 19).

Perhaps we feel that there is an air of unreality about such a claim. Is this a genuine motive for lamentation or is it not rather an attempt to enlist God's sympathy, by unduly identifying Him with the fortunes of Israel? Is it not simply a hypocritical pretence that the motive for grief is the impugning of God's honour, when in reality it is their own misfortunes which Israel is lamenting? The lamentation does in fact seem equally concerned with the impugning of Israel's honour: 'Thou makest *us* a taunt to our neighbours, a scorn and a derision to them that are round about us. . . . All the day is *my* confusion before me and the shame of *my* face hath covered me' (Ps 44, 14-16; 79, 4; 80, 7). One might object that it is not God's honour but Israel's discomfiture that is their preoccupation: 'Wherefore hidest Thou Thy face, and forgettest *our* affliction and *our* oppression?' (Ps 44, 25). 'Be gracious unto us, Yahweh, be gracious unto us, for we are full sated with contempt. Our soul is full sated, with the scorning of those that are at ease, and with the contempt of the proud oppressors' (Ps 123, 3-4). This, we are inclined to say, paints a very different picture. Moreover this impression of a nation concerned with its own interests rather than with God's, seems to be confirmed by the vindic-

145

tiveness with which they plead for their enemies' overthrow: 'Pour out thy wrath upon the nations that know Thee not, and upon the kingdoms that call not upon Thy name' (Ps 79, 6). 'Render unto our neighbours sevenfold in their bosom' (Ps 79, 12). God is urged to destroy them, as He had once destroyed Midian (cf Jud 7, 19ff), Sisera and Jabin (cf Jud 4, 12ff), and to 'make them like the whirling dust, as stubble before the wind' (Ps 83, 10-19).

Not only do the Israelites seek revenge upon their enemies, under the pretence, it would seem, of zeal for God's honour, but they also associate God with their own desire for vengeance, and represent Him as a war-god, prepared to destroy their enemies as ruthlessly as an Assyrian general at the head of a conquering army. The arrogance of the Israelites in identifying their enemies with God's enemies seems only matched by their presumption in fashioning Yahweh in the likeness of a god who mercilessly destroys his enemies when his anger has been aroused. How can such notions have a place in genuine revelation? And even if we are willing to excuse their presence by labelling them as primitive notions suited to a primitive people, though this satisfies no one, we are still bound to ask how the expression of such sentiments can be allowed a place in *Christian* prayer. Is it not here above all that we meet the 'God of the Old Testament': warlike, violent, jealous and wrathful, Who stands in such great contrast to the 'God of the New Testament', Who is love? Is it not here above all that the Israelite, materialistic and vain, fearful of suffering and resentful of opprobrium, shows himself as so different from the Christian of whom Our Lord said : 'Blessed are you when men revile you and persecute you and utter all kinds of evil against you falsely on my account' (Mt 5, 11)? The Christian has received the command : 'Love your enemies and pray for those who persecute you' (Mt 5, 44; cf 1 John 3, 15). How can the Christian complain : 'Thou makest us a taunt to our neighbours, a scorn and an derision to them that are round about us'

(Ps 44, 14), when he remembers Our Lord's words: 'Blessed are the meek, for they shall inherit the earth' (Mt 5, 5)? How can he urge God to 'render unto our neighbours sevenfold into their bosom, their reproach wherewith they have reproached Thee Yahweh' (Ps 79, 12)? Did not Our Lord say: 'Do not resist one who is evil. But if any one strikes you on the right cheek, turn to him the other also; and if anyone would sue you and take your coat, let him have your cloak as well' (Mt 5, 39-40)?

This is the common Christian attitude[12] towards these psalms, and not only towards these psalms but also towards many parts of the Old Testament in which the Israelites are said to wage war under the protection and even the direct instructions of God. In examining this problem therefore, we are seeking an explanation of something which is found in practically the whole of the Old Testament, and something which raises many difficulties for the Christian reader. The fault lies with the latter. The Christian reader very frequently fails to undertand the true purpose underlying this aspect of the Old Testament. But the very fact that this difficulty is so generally felt warns us beforehand that it is no easy matter to eliminate it. What part does the violent and the vindictive play in divine revelation? It is only one element of course, and all hope of a true understanding is destroyed if we regard the Old Testament as totally lacking in those other qualities of love and forbearance which we more readily associate with the New. Nevertheless it remains an important part and indeed a necessary part of divine revelation. More important, it is also a part of the *New* Testament revelation, and a failure to appreciate this is perhaps the main reason for the Christian's misunderstanding of the vindictiveness of the God of the Old Testament. We must therefore carefully examine the significance of the military activities of Israel, of its destruction without mercy

---

[12]The second century heretic Marcion has had in this regard many followers in spite of the Church's strong condemnation of him.

of all its enemies, of its desire for vengeance, of God's jealousy and His vengeance on Israel's enemies. We must find out what exactly the Scriptures teach us in these narratives which at first sight seem out of place in the revealed word of God. We must, in other words, learn still more about God and His divine purpose, and about Israel in her role as God's chosen people. We shall then see how this facet of divine revelation is continued and developed in the New Testament. It is only when we have done all this that these psalms can be seen as an authentic expression, even today, and contrary to all appearances, of Christian prayer.

The Survival of Israel

It is important first of all to recall the basic propositions on which Scriptural revelation is built. The first one is that the choice of Israel by God constitutes the essential means whereby God has decided to make Himself known to the world. This proposition has already been discussed at length in the previous chapter, but its importance cannot be stressed too much, for it is the starting point of our understanding of everything concerned with Israel and hence of everything we read in the Bible, with the possible exception of the wisdom literature. The Semitic philosopher might go so far as to say that God's existence depends upon the existence of Israel, because for the Semite existence was inextricably bound up with the knowledge or recognition of existence. The ontological existence of the supreme being, the uncaused first principle of all that is, was never the object of Semitic thought. For the Semite a being was identified with its name. The name was that by which the being manifested itself to others, and to be without a name was to be without existence. The Accadic epic of creation, the *Enuma Elish*, opens with the lines:[13] 'When on high the heaven had not been named, Firm ground below had not been

[13]Quoted from James B. Pritchard (edit), *Ancient Near Eastern Texts Relating to the Old Testament*, 1950, pp. 60-61.

148

called by name', as an expression of the primordial void when heaven and earth did not yet exist. Because they were un-named they were not beings, and the poem continues: 'When no gods whatever had been brought into being, uncalled by name, their destinies undetermined': to be 'uncalled by name' is synonymous with 'not brought into being'. The name of a being and therefore the presence of a knower and a pronouncer of that name had in Semitic thought an importance quite un-paralleled in any system of western philosophy, and the way in which this notion is applied to the supreme being is to us quite irrational, since it would demand the existence of the created knower before the uncreated object of his knowledge, if we were to press this to its logical conclusion. But the Semite was not logical, and he was much more influenced by practical experience than by pure reason. To him a thing unknown did not exist, because it made no impact upon his experience. The notion of God existing from eternity but unknown to men and therefore unacknowledged, had in the beginning no signi-ficance.

Hence in the Israelite mind the existence of God depended upon the existence of His chosen people. When God chose Israel, His purpose was that they should invoke His name and proclaim it; they should recognise His existence, know Him for what He is, and bear witness to Him before the peoples of the earth. Not given to philosophy as we know it, the Israel-ites were not greatly concerned with God's existence before the call of Abraham, though the first eleven chapters of Genesis pay some attention to 'the beginning'. Neither did they con-sider the partial recognition He had previously received from the nations who worshipped false gods: with their usual disregard of the degrees between two extremes, they considered these nations simply as those 'who knew Him not'. But they were fully conscious of the supreme importance of Israel's knowing God and of Israel's professing His name. The existence of Israel was of supreme importance; God had so ordained it, and to this day it remains true that upon the existence of Israel depends the knowing and the acknowledging of God as He truly is, by the whole of His creation.

The second basic principle follows from this. It is that the continued physical survival of Israel is essential to God's purpose. The word 'physical' would not be necessary here, if it were not for the fact that there often exists in Christian minds a strangely confused notion about physical or bodily survival. Influenced by that exaggerated dichotomy between soul and body to which reference has already been made,[14] the question of *physical* survival is thought to be unimportant. But any such notion constitutes an insuperable obstacle to solving the problem which faces us here. If the physical survival of Israel is a matter of indifference then the physical means to ensure that survival must remain unintelligible or unacceptable within the context of divine revelation. But the Bible makes it abundantly clear that the physical survival of Israel is of the greatest significance, and any notion to the contrary thereby stands condemned. Such a notion exists, not only because certain philosophical considerations have been allowed to take control of revelation when they were initially called in simply to help, but also because we fail to distinguish the believer's double mode of existence : as a constituent part of the corporate person which is Israel, and as an individual. It is the physical survival of *Israel* that is essential to God's purpose. The physical survival of the individual Israelite is not indeed an entirely separate question,[15] but it must nevertheless be carefully distinguished from that concerned with the physical survival of the corporate person Israel. Much of our objection to these psalms arises from our failure to make this distinction. The identification of Israel's plight with God's, for instance, strikes us as nothing less than arrogance, if we think of Israel in terms of individuals, rather than that as a corporate entity which is the

[14]cf pp. 101-102.
[15]cf *supra* p. 143, ftn. 11.

object of God's choice. Israel as a body clearly understood the dignity and the responsibility conferred on her. She understood that God has in a certain sense made Himself dependant on her, and that it was in God's own interest so to speak, that He should preserve Israel. She believed in her indefectibility because it had been revealed by God. When therefore her survival was threatened she could rightly remind God that He must save her for the sake of His own name. Such a reminder was itself a declaration of faith in the fidelity of God to His promises, and His unswerving adherence to His plan of salvation. It was not arrogance; it did not exclude a deep consciousness of Israel's unworthiness and her infidelities. Disasters which threatened her existence and therefore God's plan, could be acknowledged in spite of the apparent inconsistancy, as coming from the hand of God in punishment for her sins: in Pss 44 and 80 it is God who causes the defeat of Israel, whilst in Pss 74, 79, and 83 the enemies inflict it. Israel must always remain conscious of her indefectibility, for it is essential to God's purpose. When Our Lord promised that the gates of hell would not prevail against his church (Mat 16, 18) he was reiterating a truth of faith which had been a basic principle of divine revelation from the beginning.

The basic principles we have just stated have already been discussed in the previous chapter, for no aspect of the Bible can be understood without them. But a proper understanding of the group of psalms under discussion here, demands a more extended consideration of the significance of Israel's physical existence and survival in God's plan of salvation. It is only when we have examined the way in which Sacred Scripture teaches us how Israel's physical existence is necessary to God, that we shall appreciate the language of these lamentations and particularly the pleas for vengeance and extermination of Israel's enemies, which may at this stage strike us as thoroughly unbecoming of the Christian. It is to be hoped that when we have discovered the true significance these psalms had for Israel

151

before Our Lord's coming, we may realise that they still have the same significance for the Christian. These psalms have been exposed to much allegorising because of their supposed unchristian sentiments. It is indeed true that God's Israel is no longer attacked by Assyria, Edom or Philistia. But their essential significance remains, and there is no need to allegorise them. There is in reality no such short cut to an understanding of them. It requires a painstaking investigation, but this has the advantage of covering much more of the Bible than a few psalms, and making intelligible certain books of the Bible which seem to have very little theological significance.

We must try first, to obtain as clear a realisation as possible of the *historical facts* relating to Israel in Canaan, before we can appreciate the *theology* of Israel's inheriting the promised land. There is a distinction between the history and the theology,[16] which is perhaps not easy to grasp, or rather which is not easily discerned by the casual reader of that part of the Old Testament which was formerly known as the books of the earlier prophets, viz., Josue to 2 Kings. But this distinction gives us the key to a proper understanding of these books, and of the so-called vindictiveness and cruelty of the Old Testament. It is therefore desirable to attempt a reconstruction of the history, though this is very difficult,[17] and to realise as vividly as possible what happened in actual fact. The actual history will stand out in sharp contrast to much that we have

[16]The justification for this distinction should become plain from the consideration of the actual contents of Deuteronomy, Josue and Judges. In order to present this material in a more significant way for the general reader, we assume the legitimacy of the distinction from the outset. But cf *infra* p. 182. For an examination of the sources, dates and characteristics of these books, cf A. Robert et A. Feuillet, *op. cit.*, pp. 367-371; 387-412; F. M. Abel, *Josué* 1950 (*Bible de Jérusalem*); A. Vincent, *Le livre des Juges, le livre de Ruth* 1958 (*Bible de Jérusalem*); *Josué* in the series *Connaître la Bible*, 1960.

[17]Our sources are almost exclusively from the Old Testament itself, and their use for a theological purpose there has made their recognition and historical interpretation complicated.

read in Deuteronomy and Josue, but this contrast will be the stimulus for a new effort at understanding these books, and will, it is hoped, lead to the realisation that the distinction between the history and the theology of Israel in Canaan is both necessary and enlightening, in somewhat the same way as the contrast between Our Lord's conquest of sin and the world by his redeeming death and resurrection, and the history of the church and the world which he redeemed.

The History of Israel in Canaan

The people whom God chose to form Israel lived in a very small region on the south-west coast of the Mediterranean. The land best known as Palestine was at the beginning of their history called Canaan, a narrow corridor of territory between the sea and the Jordan, divided into two by a ridge of hills running its whole length except for the valley of Jizreel which cut across this ridge of hills from Mount Carmel to the Jordan just south of Lake Galilee. It was not a particularly attractive land, nor did it lend itself to occupation by any one united nation. The southern part was arid; the central hill region was cut off from both north and south. Inland from the sand dunes at the sea's edge there was a fertile plain but this soon gave way to the hills, where the ground was poorer; it was better watered on the west than the east side, but only supported those who settled there at the cost of much hard work and no little ingenuity. All things considered it was not a land to arouse enthusiasm except among the nomads of the desert regions to the east and the south, for whom life was far harder. But this land had a unique importance in one respect. It was the bridge which linked north-west Asia and Mesopotamia with Egypt. There was consequently a continuous movement of peoples through it, and many of these settled there. In the thirteenth century B.C. Canaan was occupied by many different groups of people: according to the classical biblical formula 'the Hittites, the Girgashites, the Amorites, the Canaanites, the Perizzites, the

153

Hivites and the Jebusites' (Deut 7, 1; cf Gen 15, 20; Ex 3, 8. 17; 13, 5, etc). This stereotyped list is not of any great interest except as an indication that Canaan was occupied by many groups more or less isolated from one another. We usually refer to these groups generically as Canaanites, but it must be remembered that this is an ethnological and not a political term. The Canaanites were not one united nation. They were Semitic by race and had first settled in this region during the third millennium, and they lived in fortified towns as farmers and merchants. Naturally they lived where it was suitable for the growing of crops and the rearing of cattle, and so the plains and valleys were thickly populated, whilst the hill region was almost unoccupied.

According to the book of Judges the first of the Israelitic tribes to enter this land of Canaan were Judah and Simeon (1, 1-2). They found a place to settle, in the south around Hebron (1, 10), and closely associated with them here were the Calebites (1, 12-15) and the Qenites (1, 6). Later the 'house of Joseph', namely the tribes of Benjamin, Ephraim and Manasses found living space around Bethel in the central hill region (1, 22-6), cut off from the southern region by the Canaanite towns. Manasses settled north of Ephraim, in the region bordering the southern edge of the valley of Jizreel where Canaanite towns such as Bethshan, Taanack, Dor, Ibleam and Megiddo were situated (1, 27-8). Ephraim, more central, settled around Gezer (1, 29). In the hill region north of the valley of Jizreel there was the tribe of Zabulon, around the towns of Kitron and Nahalol (1, 30). To the North-west was the tribe of Asher, in the district of Acco, Sidon, Ahlab, Achijib, Helbah, Aphik and Rehob (1, 31). The tribe of Naphtali, east of Zabulon, inhabited the region along the west side of Lake Chinnereth, in the district around Bethshemesh and Bethanath. The tribe of Issachar is not mentioned but it was closely associated with the northern tribes just named

(Jud 5, 15). The tribe of Dan first tried to settle in the lowlands south-west of Ephraim, but the Canaanites pushed them back into the hill country (1, 34). They later emigrated northwards and settled around Laish (Jud 18).

The Israelitic tribes settled in Canaan therefore, in three separate groups: in the southern hill region and the Negeb were Judah and Simeon; in the central hill region was the house of Joseph, namely (from south to north) Benjamin (cf 2 Sam 19, 21), Ephraim and Manasses; in the northern hill region were (from west to east) Asher, Zabulon, Naphtali and Issachar. Each of these regions was separated from the others: between Juda and Benjamin the hills were broken by a number of valleys, commanded by Canaanite towns such as Gezer, Aijalon, Shaalbim and Jerusalem. The central hill region was cut off from the northern hills by the broad valley of Jizreel, which was effectively controlled by the Canaanites in Taanack, Megiddo and Bethshan. The southern and central tribes occupied land in the hills which had previously been almost unpopulated, and therefore they enjoyed within these narrow limits an independence which their isolation provided. But the northern tribes of Asher and Naphtali, as is clear from the phraseology of Jud 1, 32-3 had to find living space as best they could among the Canaanites. Clearly the so-called occupation was even less thorough here than in the central and southern regions. This is the reason why this northern part of Canaan was known as *Gelil haggoyim* : the district of the Gentiles (cf Is 8, 23), or simply *Gelil* (Galilee : cf 1 Kgs 9, 11; 2 Kgs 15, 29).

Whilst the southern and central hill regions were more effectively occupied by the Israelitic tribes, it is made quite clear in Jud 1 that this occupation was largely limited to that territory into which they could infiltrate without encountering much opposition. We do read of Judah's victory over Adoni-Bezeq (Jud 1, 5-7), probably the same person as Adoni-Sedeq King of Jerusalem (Jos 10, 1),[18] but the statement that Judah captured Jerusalem and destroyed it (v. 8) is contradicted by v. 21, by Jos 15, 63, and especially by 2 Sam 5, 6ff where it is made quite clear that the conquest of Jerusalem was only effected by David, more than two hundred years later. Judah (or rather Caleb cf Jos 15, 13) attacked and defeated the Canaanites of Hebron, but it is not said that he captured the city, still less that he slew all its inhabitants. Whether, therefore, they gained complete possession or simply gained access to Hebron and the right to live alongside the earlier inhabitants must remain doubtful, though by the time of David it was Judah's capital city (2 Sam 2, 1). With regard to Debir the text is more categorical: Othniel, nephew of Caleb took it. Simeon is said to have captured Sepath and there carried out the *herem,* hence its name Horma (v. 17). The text of v. 18 tells us that Judah took Gaza, Ashkelon and Ekron, but these are precisely the cities of the plain which were inhabited by the Philistines, who used iron chariots and whom Judah could not drive out (v. 19). It is not surprising therefore that the Septuagint of v. 18 tells us that Juda did not take Gaza, Ashkelon and Ekron: this is the historical fact.

Hence the history of Judah's and Simeon's settlement in the south shows us two tribes, with the Calebite and Qenite clans joined to them in friendship, settled around and possibly in Hebron and Debir, but cut off from the coastal plain by the Philistines, and from the central region by the Canaanites. With regard to the other tribes, we read that the House of Joseph smote Bethel 'with the edge of the sword' (1, 25); no other city is mentioned as falling into the hands of any of the Israelitic tribes. On the contrary it is clearly stated that they failed to capture the Canaanite towns (cf 1, 27. 29. 30. 31. 33. 35).

The historical picture given by the book of Judges of the so-

[18]cf George F. Moore, *Judges (International Critical Commentary)* 1895, p. 16.

called invasion of Canaan is now becoming clearer. It consisted in a gradual infiltration by semi-nomadic tribes seeking a more sedentary mode of existence. These tribes succeeded in settling only in the hill regions and the southern desert. How long this process took and its chronological sequence can hardly be determined, though every indication points to the settlement of Judah and Simeon in the south having occurred before that of the Joseph tribes in the centre, whilst the northern tribes may have been the last to occupy their territory.

Thus the Israelitic tribes settled in Canaan, a land already occupied by 'the five lords of the Philistines, and all the Canaanites and the Sidonians, and the Hivites who dwelt on Mount Lebanon. . . . So the people of Israel dwelt among the Canaanites, the Hittites, the Amorites, the Perizzites, the Hivites and the Jebusites' (Jud 3, 3; Jos 13, 2-6). They had to defend the territory they occupied against others who wished to follow in their footsteps, and they slowly extended their occupation at the expense of their Canaanite neighbours. We know very little about the history of this period between the first settlements and the great expansion under David at least two hundred years later. Epic stories of the struggles that went on during this time were proudly handed on from generation to generation,[19] but since their purpose was not that of merely historical record, we learn little of the historical detail of this long and hard fought struggle. We are not however entirely bereft of information. We know for instance that the southern tribes had to repulse the invasion of the Edomites (Jud 3, 10 emending Aram to Edom).[20] The Moabites, Amorites and Amalekites following the same path as the Israelites, crossed the Jordan near Jericho and tried to enter the central hill region, but were successfully repulsed (Jud 3, 11-30). The northern tribes took the offensive against the Canaanites, and a great victory over them was immortalised in the Song of Deborah

---

[19]Many of these are preserved, particularly in the book of Judges.
[20]cf Bible de Jérusalem ad vers.

(Jud 5). The Midianites, another nomadic tribe attempting to emulate the Israelites, gave considerable trouble. Though they were closely akin to the Israelites (cf Gen 25, 1-6) they could not be tolerated, since they robbed the sedentary people of their food. But it seems clear that the Israelites suffered greatly from annual invasion by these nomads (Jud 6, 1-6).

In the latter half of this period of consolidation the principal enemy was the Philistines, a non-semitic race who were far better equipped for war than the other inhabitants of Canaan. Having gained a foothold on the southern part of the coastal plain their aim was to penetrate the whole of Canaan, moving eastwards by way of the valleys, into the hill region. It is certain that they had a considerable success, and they constituted the most serious threat that the Israelites had had to face. This had a most important consequence for Israel, since the Philistines weakened their Canaanite opponents and at the same time forced the Israelitic tribes to unite with one another far more closely than they had ever done before. By the time the Philistines had penetrated to the eastern end of the valley of Jizreel the Israelites felt the need of a king to bind them together and lead them in one united effort. Thus Saul began the struggle which was so successfully concluded by David.

Under David the tribes were welded together into one nation of considerable political significance, with its capital at Jerusalem, a city newly captured from the Jebusites, and one therefore which had never been previously associated with any of the old tribes. Its geographical position was well suited for the cause of unity, since it stood between the southern and the northern tribes. This was an event of prime importance in the history of Israel, which particularly under Solomon increased in power and wealth, and came near to an effective rule of the whole of Canaan and its neighbouring territories. The independence of such Canaanite cities as Megiddo, Taanack and Bethshan was destroyed (2 Sam 8). In the north a number of Aramean states were subjugated; the Ammonites, Moabites and Edomites to the east and south were kept under control. The Philistines were confined to their original territory on the south-west coast. It is not surprising then that the reign of Solomon was always looked back on as the period of Israel's greatest glory. But it was ephemeral. The union of the southern and northern tribes did not survive Solomon's death, and there followed the period of the divided kingdom, with one king in Jerusalem and another in Samaria. There was a general decline in strength, which put the Israelites at the mercy of the expanding Assyrian power. Samaria fell to them in 721 B.C. and many Israelites were exiled. In 586 it was Jerusalem's turn, and the holy city was destroyed by the Babylonians who took many of the Judans into exile. David's great kingdom of united Israel had at last been finally destroyed, and the possession of Canaan had proved no more than a dream.

The Religious History

This brief outline of the history of Israel from the settlement in Canaan until the destruction of Jerusalem in 586 must be supplemented by a brief consideration of the history of religious practice during this same period, for it is here above all that the key to the understanding of the earlier prophets is to be found. As we saw, there was at first little to unite the Israelitic tribes who were slowly and laboriously making a home for themselves in Canaan. They were of the same race, and there were loose ties of kinship; but they largely went their own ways. Yet there was one bond of union between them which alone explains why they survived and why in spite of their isolation they regarded themselves as constituting Israel the chosen people. This was their common belief that Yahweh was their God; their common acceptance of the covenant; their common purpose to observe the law given to Moses on Sinai. This common belief and common purpose were kept alive and strengthened by solemn convocations of the tribes, the memory of which provides the framework for Jos 24, where we read of the meeting at Sichem. Josue calls upon the tribes to choose between Yahweh on the one hand or on the other the gods worshipped by their ancestors in Mesopotamia and the gods worshipped by the Canaanites among whom they are now living (Jos 24, 14-15). When the tribes shout : 'We will serve Yahweh' (Jos 24, 21) and 'Yahweh our God we will serve, and His voice we will obey' (v. 24) Josue replies : 'Then put away the foreign gods which are among you, and incline your heart to Yahweh, the God of Israel' (Jos 24, 23; cf Gen 35, 2-4).

It is difficult to know on how big a scale or how frequently these solemn convocations of the tribes took place. There is no reason to call in question that they were liturgical celebrations in which the ark was the central object of the cult, and that the central place of pilgrimage was first Sichem (cf Jos 24, 1) and later Siloh[21] (cf Jos 18, 1; 1 Sam 1, 3). It was perhaps an annual festival. But though there is very little information about the preservation of belief in Yahweh and the practical consequences of this belief during the period between 1250 and 1050 B.C., the fact that it did survive is astonishing evidence of God's determination, when we consider the obstacles this faith had to overcome.

It may seem strange at first sight that we have far more information concerning these obstacles than we have concerning the preservation of orthodoxy. Yet such is the purpose of the sacred books that we can, on their evidence alone, reconstruct the sombre side of Israel's religious history in considerable detail, and this reconstruction is further helped by the contributions of archaeology. The simple truth is that the Israelitic tribes were influenced by the Canaanite beliefs and practices to a degree which is perhaps surprising to anyone who has not really thought of its possibility before.

But is it really so surprising? The Israelitic tribes settled in Canaan, where there was already a well established popula-

[21]The last permanent resting-place of the Ark before it was brought to Jerusalem by David.

tion, with a highly organised way of life suited to the land in which they were living. This population lived by raising crops and tending cattle and sheep. Their cities enjoyed a fairly high level of civilisation. By comparison the semi-nomadic tribes, newly arrived in Canaan were inferior and needed instruction in the art of living the sedentary life which had been the goal of their ambition. The Israelites had much to learn from the Canaanites, much that was necessary for their prosperity and much which in any case seemed highly desirable. It is not then surprising that the immigrants were greatly influenced by their Canaanite neighbours, with whom they clearly came to an understanding in order that they might enjoy the relative prosperity of this country.

But in learning how to live in Canaan the Israelites were bound to learn the religious practices of the Canaanites, for the modern separation between religion and economics did not exist at that time (cf Os 2, 7-10). To be a prosperous farmer the Canaanite must be devoutly religious. Canaanite religion[22] was basically a declaration of faith in the deified forces of nature which provided the necessities of life.[23] The rain and the sun, the soil and the seed, were so many forces which must fulfil their task in an ordered cycle of events if human life was to continue. These forces were beyond human control, and yet they were indispensable to man. When on occasion the rain failed, famine must inevitably follow. When on occasion the ewes were barren, their owners were impoverished. If the sun shone too soon and too strongly then the harvest was inadequate

[22]Our knowledge of the Canaanites depends largely on discoveries made at *Ras Shamra,* the ancient Ugarit. The most important result of excavations carried out there, is that we now possess a considerable amount of Canaanite literature cf G. Ernest Wright, *Biblical Archaeology* 1957, pp. 105-115; G. R. Driver, *Canaanite Myths and Legends* 1956; John Gray, *The Legacy of Canaan,* 1957.

[23]For the following interpretation of the Ugaritic texts, cf my article, 'The Literary Influence of the Ugaritic Fertility Myth on the Old Testament' in *Vetus Testamentum,* 1953, pp. 273-297.

for man's needs. In a land which was not over fertile there were many ways in which things could go wrong, and the margin between prosperity and poverty was small. It was therefore of supreme importance in the life of the Canaanite that he should do all that was possible to influence the forces controlling this cycle of productivity.

In Canaan the most important element was the rain. Without it the land was an arid desert, and it had been to escape the desert that the Canaanites had settled here. Nothing was more important than the coming of the rains at the due season and in the right quantity. Nothing could equal the joy of hearing the rumble of the thunder and seeing the lightning flash among the rain-laden clouds, for it heralded the beginning of another year's life. Baal the god of the rain was riding the clouds, brandishing his thunder bolts and his lightning : the warrior who will conquer sterility is once more asserting his position as prince and lord of the earth, with a strength and a vigour like that of the young bull among the heifers.

But just as the heifer is necessary to the bull, the ewe to the ram, the soil to the rain, so there must be a goddess for the god. Asherah the goddess who gives fertility has an equally important part to play, or is it perhaps a more important part? The slow process of germination must continue after the rains have gone; many dangers threaten the unborn lamb or calf, or the seed hidden in the ground. Barrenness is all too common an enemy and therefore Asherah must be cajoled and placated with perseverance and generosity. Shamash the Sun must also do his part, moving across the sky with precise regularity and giving his light and warmth. But at last the soil on which the rain had fallen bears its fruit, and the grain ripens : this is the god Mot making his appearance, Mot the son of Asherah and the beloved son of Il. The grain must be harvested and ground and already the good farmer must begin to entreat Baal to return. The cycle of nature must begin again; the gods must take up their allotted tasks once more; Il, supreme god and the master of the heavenly household must see to it that his family of gods carry out their tasks in due order.

But man must do his part. The gods must be worshipped, for their anger brings famine, their favour brings prosperity. Hence the inhabitants of every Canaanite town had their sanctuary where sacrifices and prayers could be offered to ensure the favour of the gods. These sanctuaries were in the open air, outside the town and if possible on the top of a hill, a feature which seems to have determined their name *bamah*, conventionally translated 'high-place'. Here were set up the altar, the stone pillars called *massaboth* along with the *'asherim* which were either trees or wooden stakes as a conventional representation of trees. Doubtless there was also a small building to provide shelter for priests and devotees who might wish to spend the night at the shrine.[24]

Here at the high-place the Canaanites worshipped their gods by offering sacrifices of certain animals, by pouring out libations and by carrying out the ritual which by its re-enacting of the myth was designed to ensure the continuing cycle of nature. An important part of this ritual was the liturgical lament for Baal, since the passing of the rains marked his death. He had gone down into the earth and been swallowed up by Mot. This lamentation was an elaborate expression of grief, involving loud wailing, lacerations, sack-cloth and ashes. Another part of the Canaanite ritual was the re-enactment of the fertilising of Asherah by the use of the prostitutes who were to be found at the high-places. Harvest time brought great rejoicing both because nature's cycle had come to its appointed end, and also because this heralded the beginning of the next cycle, with the return of Baal from the dead.

Canaanite religion was a fertility cult, closely linked with the agricultural seasons of the year. Essentially it was the acknow-

[24]cf L. H. Vincent, 'La notion biblique du Haut-Lieu' in *Revue biblique* 1948, pp. 245-278; 438-445.

ledgment that the source of life lay beyond man's power. The carrying out of its ritual was thought to be necessary for the preservation of life; and at the same time it satisfied the demands of their natural appetite. The quantity of small clay plaques bearing the image of Asherah as a nude woman with pronounced sexual features, which archaeologists have found throughout Palestine, is a good indication of the devotion shown to the goddess of fertility.[25]

These then were the Canaanite religious practices which had a great influence upon the immigrant tribes. The distinction between Canaanite religion and Canaanite agricultural methods was not so obvious to them as it is to us. The beliefs of a people more prosperous and more civilised were bound to impress the newcomers. Living side by side, and inter-marrying with the Canaanites had disastrous consequences : 'They took their daughters to themselves for wives, and their own daughters they gave to their sons; and they served their gods. The people of Israel did what was evil in the sight of Yahweh, forgetting Yahweh their God, and serving the Baals and the Asheroth.' (Jud 3, 6-7). There is overwhelming evidence in the Old Testament that Canaanite influence was strongly felt by the Israelites. In the first place it undoubtedly made considerable contributions to the evolution of orthodox Israelite liturgy and religious language. The tradition of Israelite worship had been associated with the tabernacle and the ark, and had been suited to the life and customs of semi-nomadic tribes. Clearly the change in manner of life was bound to modify this tradition. As we have already mentioned the tradition of a solemn convocation of the tribes was continued. But this could only take place on rare occasions, perhaps once a year. For the rest the Israelitic tribes needed local meeting places and a liturgy which would preserve their faith and give them guid-

[25]cf illustrations in James B. Pritchard, *The Ancient Near East in Pictures* 1954, pp. 161-2; L. H. Grollenberg, *Atlas of the Bible* 1956, p. 56.

ance in their daily lives. There were many places in Canaan which were associated with the patriarchs and these provided the obvious centres for the tribal worship of Yahweh. For instance Mambre with its famous oak tree was a place near Hebron which was associated with Abraham, for he had pitched his tent there (Gen 13, 18), and had entertained three mysterious visitors through whom he also received a revelation from Yahweh that Sarah would bear him a son (Gen 18 1-15). Though the name is never mentioned apart from the patriarchs it is reasonable enough to suppose that Mambre provided a place of worship for the tribe of Judah which was settled around Hebron.

Bethel in the southern region of the hill country was far more famous. Abraham had built an altar near Bethel (Gen 12, 8; 13, 4), and it was here that Jacob had seen in his dream the ladder reaching up to heaven. On waking he had exclaimed: 'Truly Yahweh is here, but I did not know it' (Gen 28, 16; cf 31, 13; 35, 7). Here therefore there was doubtless a place of worship of the tribe of Ephraim (Jos 16, 1; but cf Jos 18, 22; Jud 1, 22; 20, 18. 26; 21, 2). In Transjordan where the tribe of Gad had settled there was Penuel where Jacob had wrestled with God (Gen 32, 20. 31); cf Jud 8, 8). Sichem also was associated with the patriarchs: Abraham had built an altar there (Gen 12, 7); Jacob did likewise (Gen 33, 20); it had been given by Jacob to Joseph (Gen 48, 22) and it lay within the territory occupied by Manasseh (Jos 17, 2. 7). In the extreme south where the tribes of Judah (Jos 15, 28) and Simeon (Jos 19, 2) were situated, there was Beersheba, associated with Abraham (Gen 21, 33; 22, 19), and the place where Israel had a vision and built an altar (Gen 26, 25; 46, 1).

There were other sanctuaries which had no link with the patriarchs, but were used by the tribes and which played an important part in the preservation of ancient traditions: Gilgal near Jericho originally associated with the tribe of Benjamin (cf Jos 18, 12), and Siloh in the territory of Ephraim. We know very little about the tribes north of the great plain, but in Deut 33, 19 there is mention, in connection with Zabulon and Issachar of 'the mountain where the peoples come to pray and offer sacrifices of good augury': this is probably Mount Tabor (Os 5, 1).

In these places therefore, and doubtless elsewhere the Israelites had their legitimate sanctuaries:[26] their high-places or *bamoth*. From the evidence which the Old Testament itself provides, as it were in spite of its set purpose,[27] it is clear that the local cultus of Yahweh at these high-places was for a long time a legitimate feature of the true religion. At the high-place of Rama for example the prophet Samuel officiated on those days when there was a sacrifice for the people (1 Sam 9, 12-13). Gabaon had the most important high-place, and Solomon offered a thousand sacrifices on its altar (1 Kgs 3, 4). It was here also that Yahweh appeared to him and gave him wisdom, although the Ark had by this time been brought to Jerusalem (cf 1 Kgs 3, 15; 2 Sam 6, 1-19).

The practical advantages of local sanctuaries are clear enough, but the dangers are no less obvious. Close contact with the Canaanites and a close imitation of their liturgy threatened the purity of the Israelite faith. It was in fact more than a threat, for Israelite religious practices were constantly contaminated by Canaanite errors, as can be seen from the activities and pronouncements of the prophets. It is not always possible to decide whether the prophets are condemning complete apostasy or simply a contaminated form of the worship of Yahweh, for there was not the same clear-cut distinction

[26]cf R. de Vaux, *Les institutions de l'ancient testament II*, 1960, pp. 112-3.

[27]By the time the Old Testament was given its definitive form, worship at local shrines was unlawful cf Deut 12, 2-14. The later legislation against Canaanite practices is itself proof that these had previously been widespread in Israel cf Ex 23, 24; 34, 13; Lev 26, 1; Deut 7, 5; 16, 22; Mich 5, 12. Deut 16, 22 forbids a practice which the patriarchs had followed without blame, and cf Os 3, 4.

as exists in our minds between the worship of false gods and a debased worship of the true God. One may indeed wonder whether our distinction is even today more scholastic than practical, for people in general do not distinguish as clearly as the theologian may imagine. Be this as it may the prophets were concerned not with theological formulations of religious doctrine, but with the practical worship of Yahweh and its consequences. There is every reason to think[28] that when Jeroboam organised the sanctuaries of Bethel and Dan and put there the golden calves, he was not initiating idolatry but providing two sanctuaries where Yahweh could be worshipped without the political inconvenience of his people continuing to go up to Jerusalem in order to fulfil their religious obligations. Yet the practical consequences were disastrous, because the use of the golden calf as a substitute for the Ark made the cultus of Yahweh all the more Canaanite in appearance, since Baal was represented as standing on the back of a young bull.[29] The prophet Osee voices God's complaint that the people have made offerings to the Baals and forgotten Him (2, 15). He condemns them because they are aping the ways of the Canaanites : 'My people inquire of a thing of wood, and their staff gives them oracles. For a spirit of harlotry has led them astray, and they have left their God to play the harlot. They sacrifice on the tops of the mountains, and make offerings upon the hills, under oak, poplar, and terebinth, because their shade is good. Therefore your daughters play the harlot, and your brides commit adultery. I will not punish your daughters when they play the harlot, nor your brides when they commit adultery; for the men themselves go aside with harlots, and sacrifice with cult prostitutes, and a people without understanding shall come to ruin' (4, 12-14; cf 8, 11; 9, 1; 10, 5. 8; 11, 2; 12, 11; 13, 1-2). The people of the northern kingdom have become rich and prosperous : 'Ephraim has said : Ah, but I

[28]cf the note in *Bible de Jérusalem* at 1 Kgs 12, 28.
[29]cf Pritchard, *op. cit.,* p. 170.

167

am rich, I have gained wealth for myself' (12, 8). They have learned well the lessons which the Canaanites have taught them. But 'threshing floor and wine vat shall not feed them, and the new wine shall fail them' (9, 2). Prosperity has led to abandoning Yahweh in favour of the gods of fertility and wealth : 'Israel is a luxuriant vine that yields its fruit. The more his fruit increased the more altars he built; as his country improved he improved his pillars. Their heart is false; now they must bear their guilt. Yahweh will break down their altars and destroy their pillars' (10, 1-2). The disaster can be explained in one prosaic phrase : 'Ephraim mixes himself with the peoples' (7, 8).

This 'mixing' with the Canaanites and the resulting contamination of their faith continued throughout the whole period of Israel's occupation of Canaan until the exile in 586. And though Canaanite beliefs and practices were the major ingredient of this pernicious syncretism there were others contributed by the surrounding nations. When Israel attained political prominence as a strong and wealthy nation she became interested in her more distant neighbours and sought various alliances (cf, e.g., 1 Kgs 15, 18-20). For this purpose Solomon married foreign women and the latter prevailed upon him to erect shrines in honour of their gods (1 Kgs 11, 1-8). Without doubt the cult of these gods attracted the interest of the Israelites. It would seem that they did not always stop short even of the sacrifice of children to Molok (cf 2 Kgs 23, 10; cf 16, 3; Jer 32, 35) in imitation of the Ammonites and Moabites (1 Kgs 11, 7; 2 Kgs 3, 27). During the reign of Achab who had married the Sidonian princess Jezabel (1 Kgs 16, 31) the prophets of Baal were in such a powerful position that the worship of Yahweh was threatened with extinction. Achaz had an altar of the temple at Damascus copied and erected in the Temple at Jerusalem, presumably to be used for rites in which he himself had taken part at Damascus (2 Kgs 16, 10-16). The situation reached its climax during the reign of Manasses of Judah (687-642): 'He rebuilt the high places ... and he erected altars for Baal and made an Asherah ... and worshipped all the host of heaven and served them. And he built altars in the house of Yahweh.... And he built altars for all the host of heaven in the two courts of the house of Yahweh. and he burned his son as an offering, and practised soothsaying and augury, and dealt with mediums and with wizards. ... And the graven image of Asherah that he had made he set in the house of which Yahweh said ...' (2 Kgs 21, 3-7).[30]

The *actual history* of Israel's occupation of Canaan therefore is one of constant struggle against pagan influences, and a struggle which was far from being wholly successful. It is necessary to insist that these facts of Israel's history during the period covering 1250-586 have been taken from the Old Testament itself, and they show without any doubt whatsoever that the Israelitic tribes never gained complete possession of Canaan, nor were ever free from contamination by false religions In other words they never conquered all the land, still less did they destroy all its inhabitants. They borrowed much from the Canaanites and for a long time worshipped Yahweh quite legitimately at local shrines. They constantly yielded to the attractions of the Canaanite cult, and were therefore constantly unfaithful to Yahweh. To use the biblical expression which in view of Canaanite rites is a particularly apt one, they constantly committed adultery against Yahweh, prostituting themselves to many strange gods. It is essential to bear in mind this sad *history* of what in actual fact took place when Israel came to Canaan, in order that the *theology* of Israel's inheritance of the Promised Land may be properly understood.

The Theology of the Promised Land

The history of Israel in Canaan, such as we have just des-

[30]For further examples cf Jud 3, 7; 6, 25; 1 Kgs 14, 15. 23; 15, 13; 16, 33; 18, 19; 2 Kgs 13, 6; 17, 10. 16; 18, 4; 21, 3. 7; 23, 4. 6. 7. 14. 15; Is 17, 8, 27, 9; Jer 17, 2.

cribed it, evokes no act of faith, for it follows a pattern which can be paralleled time and again in the histories of other peoples. It presents a surprisingly ordinary and down-to-earth picture of the struggles and the limited success of certain migrant tribes. No more than a passing reference has been made to the common faith of these tribes in Yahweh their God, and to the covenant between them with its common code of law. Yet this common faith is in the end the only historically valid explanation of the remarkable survival of Israel, alone of all the nations which existed at that time. And much more important, it is this faith which is our Christian heritage. Israel's history is of importance to us only because it is the instrument of God's revelation, and supplies the terms in which this divine revelation is offered for the assent of our faith.

This divine revelation, the object of Israel's faith, permeates the whole of the Old Testament, and it may be summed up as the belief that Yahweh had chosen one people, Israel, to make Himself known to the world, through their living in perfect accordance with His law in the land of Canaan, where the complete happiness of that life will testify that Yahweh is the one God, Who alone is the end of man's desires. Any contrast there may be between this belief and historical experience is for the most part, according to Israel's faith, the result of failing to live in perfect accordance with God's law.

This declaration of faith is set forth most categorically, and as it were *ex professo,* in the books of Deuteronomy and Josue. The need for such a reiteration and insistence is clear in the light of Israel's historical experience.[31] If indeed this was as we have tried to describe it then it must have come near to extinguishing Israel's faith. The reaction of the Israelites in face of their historical experiences must have been somewhat the

[31]The book of Deuteronomy—as distinct from most of the material used in its making, belongs to the 7th century, cf p. 17, ftn. 13. The influence of the Deuteronomists on the books of Josue and Judges can be clearly seen, cf the authors cited on p. 152, ftn. 16.

same as our first reaction on reading about them, namely that there is no trace of God's hand in them, and nothing to distinguish them from the experiences of other nations who did not know Yahweh.

Was it then indeed true that Yahweh had chosen Israel to be His people? Was it true that the contrast between faith and experience was due to their infidelity? There must have been many who, finding God's law so difficult to observe, answered these questions in the negative. The faith even of the good, who tried to live according to the divine law, must have been greatly tried in face of the contrast that experience forced upon their attention. It was therefore imperative that their faith should be strengthened, and that the wicked should be brought to the reacceptance of that faith. This task, which was carried out pre-eminently by the prophets,[32] was essentially the reaffirming of this faith in the light of historical experience : in other words they must both strengthen belief in God's choice of Israel, and at the same time counteract the damaging effect of experience by showing clearly and compellingly that the historical facts which called their faith in question were the consequences of infidelity.

We have already seen the declaration and reaffirmation of the divine election of Israel in the story of the deliverance from Egypt and the journey through the wilderness. We must now see how the settlement in Canaan is made to serve the same purpose.

Canaan God's Gift to Israel

'Behold, I have set the land before you; go in and take possession of the land which Yahweh swore to your fathers, to Abraham, to Isaac and to Jacob, to give to them and to their descendants after them' (Deut 1, 8). This land is defined as the southern hill country of the Amorites, the Arabah, the

[32]The same spirit pervades Deuteronomy and the prophetical writings cf H. Cazelles *op. cit.*, pp. 16-17.

central hill region, the lowland or Shephelah, the Negeb, the seacoast, Lebanon and as far as the great river, the river Euphrates. (cf Deut 1, 7. 20; 11, 24; Jos 1, 4; Gen 15, 18; Ex 23, 31; Is 27, 12). The limits therefore from south to north are the wilderness, or the torrent of Egypt, or even the Red Sea, to Lebanon, and from east to west the river Euphrates to the sea, (Deut 11, 24) limits far greater than those which define Canaan as we usually understand the term. It is the good land, as Deuteronomy insists so frequently,[33] offering everything the Israelites could long for: 'A land of brooks of water, of fountains and springs, flowing forth in valleys and hills, a land of wheat and barley, of vines and fig trees and pomegranates, a land of olive trees and honey, a land in which you will eat bread without scarcity, in which you will lack nothing, a land whose stones are iron, and out of whose hills you can dig copper. And you shall eat and be full, and you shall bless Yahweh your God for the good land He has given you' (Deut 8, 7-10). This land will bring all the happiness and prosperity a man can imagine: here in the Promised Land Yahweh 'will love you, bless you and multiply you; He will also bless the fruit of your body and the fruit of your ground, your grain and your wine and your oil, the increase of your cattle and the young of your flock, in the land which He swore to your fathers to give you. You shall be blessed above all peoples; there shall not be male or female barren among you, or among your cattle. And Yahweh will take away from you all sickness; and none of the evil diseases of Egypt, which you knew, will He inflict upon you' (Deut 7, 13-15; cf Ex 3, 8). In a word, Canaan is a land which offers the luxuries of life in abundance, the land which veritably flows with milk and honey,[34] sur-

[33] 1, 25. 35; 3, 25; 4, 21. 22; 6, 18; 8, 10; 9, 6; 11, 17; cf Jos 23, 16.
[34] Ex 3, 8. 17; 13, 5; 33, 3; Lev 20, 24; Num 13, 27; 14, 8; 16, 13-14; Deut 6, 3; 11, 9; 26, 9. 15; 27, 3; 31, 20; Jos 5, 6; Jer 11, 5; 32, 22; Ez 20, 6. 15. Milk and honey were delights highly prized cf Cant 4, 11; 5, 1. 12, and to have them in such abundance was delight beyond imagining cf Joel 3, 18.

passing even the luxury of Egypt, the El Dorado of all nomadic tribes in this part of the world: 'For the land which you are entering to take possession of it, is not like the land of Egypt, from which you have come, where you sowed your seed and watered it with your feet,[35] like a garden of vegetables; but the land which you are going over to possess is a land of hills and valleys, which drinks water by the rain from heaven, a land which Yahweh your God cares for; the eyes of Yahweh your God are always upon it, from the beginning of the year to the end of the year' (Deut 11, 10-12).

This is the fabulous land which Yahweh has promised to Israel. This land of Canaan is Israel's inheritance, not by any natural law but by divine gift (Deut 4, 21). Just as the descendants of Esau had dispossessed the Horites and taken the land of Seir, so Israel would do for 'the land of their possession' (Deut 2, 12). By natural right Canaan belonged to nations greater and mightier than Israel (Deut 4, 38). They could not possibly take possession of this enviable land by their own strength. But Yahweh had given it to them, and would drive out the nations whose right of possession He had cancelled in their favour (Deut 19, 1). Because of His steadfast love for them they had inherited this land, 'with great and goodly cities which you did not build, and houses full of all good things, which you did not fill, and cisterns hewn out, which you did not hew, and vineyards and olive trees, which you did not plant' (Deut 6, 10-11).

Clearly such a land could never have come into the possession of Israel except by gift from Yahweh. Moreover how can anyone imagine this happening without including the conquest of its inhabitants? Yahweh must dispossess those nations, greater and mightier than Israel, by force of arms, just as the

[35]A reference to the work of irrigating the soil, though it is not clear in what particular method the feet were used: possibly in the making and damming of the rills which carried the water over the cultivated area cf A. Clamer, *La Sainte Bible* II, 1940, p. 584.

Pharaoh of Egypt or the king of Assyria gained possession of territory not originally his own. In all truth Yahweh is a warrior[36] more powerful than any other, and it was His strength and military skill which would enable so weak and insignificant a people as Israel to gain possession of the most desirable land that man might imagine. It would have been sheer folly for the Israelites even to think of setting foot in Canaan if they had not believed that Yahweh was at their head, directing them as the wisest of strategists, fighting for them as the strongest and bravest of warriors, and overcoming the most formidable of enemies. Their hearts had melted with fear when their spies had reported: 'The people are greater and taller than we; the cities are great and fortified up to heaven; and moreover we have seen the sons of the Anakim there.' But Moses could reassure them: 'Do not be in dread or afraid of them. Yahweh your God Who goes before you will Himself fight for you, just as He did for you in Egypt before your eyes' (Deut 1, 28-30; cf 3, 22; Num 13, 23, 28-33). 'Thou shalt not be in dread of them; for Yahweh thy God is in the midst of thee, a great and terrible God' (Deut 7, 21).

The Divine Conquest

These were no empty promises. The inheriting of Canaan, the very paradise of delights, was something more than wish-

[36]The prophetical view of God's saving action on behalf of Israel was conceived as the triumphant advance of a victorious army, that is of Israel with Yahweh leading them, from Egypt to Canaan. Moreover the origin of the title *Yahweh Sebaoth,* conventionally translated as Lord of Hosts or Armies, seems to have originated in the concept of Yahweh as the warrior Who led the armies of Israel in their wars against the Philistines (cf 2 Sam 17, 45; Ps 24, 8. 10). Strangely enough, however, this title is never found in Genesis-Judges, and in its use by the prophets there seems to have been included the idea of Yahweh as commander of the 'heavenly army' of cosmic forces. Problems connected with this name remain, cf R. de Vaux, *Revue biblique* 1948, pp. 587-590; Walther Eichrodt, *Theologie des Alten Testaments* I, 1957, pp. 120-1; Gerhard von Rad, *Theologie des Alten Testaments* I, 1961, pp. 27-8.

ful thinking; it was something more than a gift of God to be handed over in the dim and distant future. Yahweh is not one to promise only: He fulfills His promises, lest His people should weary of trusting in His word. Yahweh not only promises salvation: Yahweh *is* salvation: *Yehoshua'*. To carry out His promises He chose as successor to Moses, Osee son of Nun, of the tribe of Ephraim, and in order to proclaim the fulfilment of God's promises through his servant, Osee's name was changed to *Yehoshua'*, Joshua[37] (Num 13, 8. 16). Under his leadership *all* Israel including those tribes which were settled in Transjordan (Jos 1, 12-18) entered the land which Yahweh had given to them.

After three days of solemn preparation the whole nation of Israel (Jos 3, 17; 4, 1) crossed the Jordan, with the ark of the covenant at its head. It was the liturgical procession of God's people crossing the river in the presence of Yahweh. 'On that day Yahweh exalted Joshua in the sight of all Israel' (Jos 4, 14). Neither the Jordan nor the great city of Jericho, so formidable an obstacle in the way of any ordinary people attempting to enter Canaan, was a barrier in the path of God's people entering into their inheritance. In solemn procession they circled its walls for seven days, in the manner of celebrating a great feast, the ark borne aloft and the seven priests with trumpets. The great ramparts crumbled away, and Jericho was destroyed. Yahweh's word to Joshua was being fulfilled: 'Every place that the sole of thy feet will tread upon I have given to thee, as I promised to Moses. From the wilderness and this Lebanon, as far as the great river, the river Euphrates, all the land of the Hittites to the Great Sea toward the going down of the sun shall be your territory. No man shall be able to stand before thee all the days of thy life; as I was with Moses, so I will be with thee; I will not fail thee or forsake thee. Be strong and of good courage; for thou shalt cause this people to inherit the land which I swore to their fathers to give them' (Jos 1, 3-6).

[37]The Greek form of this name is Jesus.

The conquest of Jericho was followed by the destruction of Ai, and thus the whole of the central portion of the promised land came into the possession of Israel. The southern region was then conquered by Joshua's glorious victory over its five kings, or rather it was Yahweh Who 'threw them into a panic before Israel, who slew them with a great slaughter at Gibeon. . . . And they fled before Israel, while they were going down the ascent of Bethhoron, Yahweh threw down great stones from heaven upon them as far as Azekah, and they died; there were more who died because of the hailstones than the men of Israel killed with the sword. . . . The sun stayed in the midst of heaven, and did not hasten to go down for about a whole day. There has been no day like it before or since, when Yahweh hearkened to the voice of a man; for Yahweh fought for Israel' (Jos 10, 10-14). It could hardly be stated more clearly, that this is truly a divine conquest, a supernatural victory.

There only remained the northern part of Israel's inheritance. The kings of this region joined together in an attempt to withstand the advance of Joshua: 'They came out, with all their troops, a great host, in number like the sand that is upon the seashore, with very many horses and chariots. And all these kings joined their forces, and came and encamped together at the waters of Merom, to fight with Israel' (Jos 11, 4-5). It was all in vain, for they were seeking to withstand the inevitable execution of Yahweh's purpose. Joshua had no need to fear this multitude with all its horses and chariots, for Yahweh said to him: 'Do not be afraid of them, for tomorrow at this time I will give over all of them, slain to Israel.' (Jos 11, 6). With their defeat, the conquest of Canaan was completed, and Israel entered into her inheritance: 'So Joshua took the whole land, according to all that Yahweh had spoken to Moses; and Joshua gave it for an inheritance to Israel according to their tribal allotments. And the land had rest from war.' (Jos 11, 23).

The Herem

Canaan was now Israel's exclusive possession. It was the gift of God to His people, and had passed into their possession by right of divine conquest. It belonged to all Israel and only to Israel, for it was the land in which God's people were to live in perfect happiness. Here they were to observe His law and thus proclaim His name. There was no place here for those who did not know Yahweh. Canaan is henceforth the home of 'a people holy to Yahweh ... a kingdom of priests and a holy nation' (Deut 7, 6; Ex 19, 6). It is Yahweh's home also, since He lives in the midst of Israel (Deut 6, 15). But it must be remembered that He cannot tolerate those who hate Him (Deut 7, 10), nor those who hate His son Israel (Deut 1, 31): upon them He will lay the evil diseases of Egypt from which He had rescued Israel. (Deut 7, 15). Moreover the presence in Canaan of those who do not know Yahweh is not only something repugnant in itself, it is a threat to God's people who may be led astray by them. Unless therefore all the nations who were to be found in Canaan were destroyed, the promised land could not be the paradise it was intended to be, the place of peace and tranquility, where Israel would keep the law of God to perfection.

This is why the taking possession of Canaan must include the destruction of the nations living there. And just as the military operation was led by Yahweh Himself, and the conquest was a divine and sacred action, so too this destruction of Israel's and God's enemies was a sacred act, commanded by God Himself. The nations were to be set apart, they were to be made a *herem,* something belonging exclusively to Yahweh and therefore not to be used or even approached by men. Just as any gift declared *herem,* that is the exclusive possession of God, could neither be sold nor bought back, but must be destroyed as the sign of God's exclusive right to it (Lev 27, 21. 28-29; but cf Num 18, 4), the naming of the nations as a *herem* involved their destruction.

On entering Canaan therefore, Israel must obey God's command, in regard to the seven nations greater and mightier than themselves: 'When Yahweh your God gives them over to you and you defeat them, then you must utterly destroy them; you shall make no covenant with them, and show no mercy to them. You shall not make marriages with them, giving your daughters to their sons or taking their daughters for your sons. For they would turn away your sons from following me, to serve other gods; then the anger of Yahweh would be kindled against you, and He would destroy you quickly. But thus shall you deal with them: you shall break down their altars, and dash in pieces their pillars, and hew down their Asherim, and burn their graven images with fire. For you are a people holy to Yahweh your God' (Deut 7, 2-6). 'You shall destroy all the peoples that Yahweh your God will give over to you, your eye shall not pity them; neither shall you serve their gods, for that would be a snare to you' (Deut 7, 16).

This command Joshua fulfilled when, as Yahweh's servant, he led all Israel into the Promised Land. Jericho was made a *herem*: 'They utterly destroyed[38] all in the city, both men and women, young and old, oxen, sheep and asses, with the edge of the sword' (Jos 6, 21). After destroying the city of Ai the Israelites slew its inhabitants, 'until there was left none that survived or escaped.... And all who fell that day, both men and women, were twelve thousand, all the people of Ai. For Joshua did not draw back his hand with which he stretched out the javelin, until he had utterly destroyed all the inhabitants of Ai' (Jos 8, 22. 25-6). It was the same with regard to Joshua's conquest of the south. After the mention of each city's destruction there recurs the refrain: 'He utterly destroyed every person in it, he left none remaining' (Jos 10, 28. 30. 32. 33. 35. 37. 39), and the recital of this conquest ends: 'So Joshua defeated the whole land, ... and all their kings; he left none remaining, but utterly destroyed all that breathed, as Yahweh

[38]*wayyaharîmû*: 'they made a *herem*'

178

God of Israel commanded' (Jos 10, 40). Finally when he conquered the northern part of Canaan at the battle of Merom, 'They smote them, until they left none remaining' (Jos 11, 9). As Israel went from city to city in this region, 'they put to the sword all who were in it, utterly destroying them; there was none left that breathed' (Jos 11, 11. 14).

The law of *herem,* God's command that the nations should be destroyed in order that Israel alone might dwell in Canaan and be perfectly faithful to Him, had been carried out: 'As Yahweh had commanded Moses his servant, so Moses commanded Joshua, and so Joshua did; he left nothing undone of all that Yahweh had commanded Moses' (Jos 11, 15). In Yahweh's strength Joshua had conquered, and Israel had been saved, to live in Canaan the land He had sworn to give them. Only one thing remained: 'And now, Israel, what does Yahweh your God require of you, but to fear Yahweh your God, to walk in all His ways, to love Him, to serve Yahweh your God with all your heart and with all your soul, and to keep the commandments and statutes of Yahweh, which I command you this day for your good. . . . You shall fear Yahweh your God; you shall serve Him and cleave to Him, and by His name you shall swear. He is your praise; He is your God' (Deut 10, 12-13. 20-1).

The Contrast Between the History and the Theology of Israel in Canaan

This theological presentation of Israel's inheritance of the Promised Land stands out in sharp contrast to the history of the settlement in Canaan. The boundaries of the Promised Land are larger than the land which Israel at any time occupied. Its fertility surpasses anything they ever experienced. The rapidity and completeness of its conquest, the union of all Israel under Joshua, and the extermination of Israel's enemies are all details which do not correspond to the historical picture we have drawn from Old Testament sources. Yet not a detail is utterly fantastic and devoid of historical foundation. In the

179

reign of David for instance, his empire spread beyond the more usual limits of Dan and Beersheba, and for one very short period there had been an Israelitic empire which came near to embracing the Canaan of Deuteronomist theology (cf 2 Sam 8, 1-14; 10, 19; 1 Kgs 2, 39). Moreover the fertility of Canaan was indeed considerable, especially by comparison with the arid wilderness surrounding it. Lastly the Israelites did succeed in conquering Canaan even though that conquest was gradual and incomplete. And there can be no doubt that in the process they slew many of their enemies. The language of God's promise to Israel and of its fulfilment through Joshua was the language of history. But history always fell short of the truths that language enunciated.[39]

This is a paradox of fundamental importance and to attempt to gloss over the contrast is fatal to the divine revelation. The Israelites themselves made no such attempt.[40] It is nothing short of arrogance to suppose that the contradictions were too

[39]It is perhaps necessary to point out that apologetical questions are distinct from questions of theology, since many Christian readers allow themselves to be so pre-occupied with apologetical difficulties that they cannot profit by a theological consideration of the Scriptures in whose truth they *believe*. In this instance, the emphasis placed upon the contrast immediately raises in some minds the question: 'How then are we going "to prove" that the scriptures are true?' But it is a mistake to allow such a question to intrude here. Its proper place is in a consideration of Christian apologetics. In actual fact anxieties on this score are greatly exaggerated: 'It is important indeed that the biblical history should be shewn to be a real history of real men and women, and not a fictitious romance about mythical heroes and events; but there is no likelihood of its ever being thought to be unhistorical in the latter sense. The Bible will remain a book of real history, and as such it will continue to be a "source" of supreme interest and value to the historian of the ancient world. But it is not as a source-text of ancient history that it is valued by Christians; we no longer suppose that the corroboration of its archaeological and historical information by modern research guarantees its supernatural origin as an oracle of divine and infallible truth.' Alan Richardson, *The Bible in the Age of Science*, 1961, p. 166.

[40]Or only on a very small scale, in order to preserve an appearance of historical continuity, cf e.g., Jos 13, 1-6; Jud 2, 7-10; 2, 21.

subtle for the simple Israelites, and needed the critical eye of the modern, scientific scholar to unmask them. The same readers who treasured and preserved the book of Judges for us did the same with Deuteronomy and Josue, and we have no right to suppose they were too simple minded to see that the former seemingly cancelled out the latter. There is ample evidence that they were well aware of the contrasts, and in fact we have oversimplified the evidence by giving the impression that the contrasts only exist between different *books*. We have suggested that the books of Deuteronomy and Josue are all theology whilst the book of Judges is all history. But whilst this is accurate enough as a general definition of their distinctive purposes, we see when we examine the books more closely that it is a vast over-simplification. There are many 'contradictions' within the same book. For example Deut 9, 3 is a clear statement that the conquest of Canaan will be rapid and complete, whereas the same book states equally clearly: 'Yahweh your God will clear away these nations before you little by little' (7, 22 cf Ex 23, 29). Are we to 'reconcile' these two verses in the same book, by saying that '*Quickly* (7, 22) is of course a relative term, and must be understood here of a shorter period than in 9, 3 : it corresponds to "in one year" in Ex 23, 29'?[41] Have we thereby 'saved' Deut 9, 3 from a charge of inaccuracy? even the same author, faced with another so-called contradiction, the enormous size of Israel (Deut 1, 10; 4, 6; 10, 22; 26, 5), which on the other hand is termed 'the fewest of all peoples' (Deut 7, 7; cf 4, 38; 9, 1; 11, 23) comments that 'the representation of Israel's numbers and power appears to vary, in different passages, according to the thought which the writer at the time desires to impress'.[42] Fortunately he refrains from 'reconciling' them by suggesting that Israel had grown in

[41]S. R. Driver, *Deuteronomy* (*International Critical Commentary*) 1902, p. 104.

[42]*ibid*., p. 100.

numbers during their forty years in the wilderness. Are we to reconcile' the rapid and complete conquest of Joshua with the slow and painful struggles of the judges by saying that Joshua's campaign though extensive and successful was nevertheless short-lived? There is no evidence that the book of Judges tells the story of attempts to recover what Joshua had won, only to be lost again over some undefined period. This explanation would in any case seem very inadequate if we recall that Joshua had exterminated everyone that breathed. This all seems absurd, and yet it is unfortunately true that the Scriptures have often been subjected to this sort of indignity, because it was assumed that they had at all costs to be reconciled.

They do not have to be reconciled in this way. They must not be reconciled, because this involves a fatal misunderstanding of the divine message. The very fact that the Israelites themselves felt little need for reconciling of this kind should be a warning that they understood in a different way what appear as contradictions to us. If they felt no need to remove the violent contrasts then neither ought we. In other words, the existence of these contrasts and so-called contradictions must lead us to a reappraisal of the books concerned. This we have in fact already done by considering them under the two aspects of history and theology.

But such a distinction, though it is completely justified by the so-called contradictions of these books, raises the further question : why was there this violent contrast between the banality of Israel's historical experience and the magnificence of God's promise and its fulfilment?[43] The answer to this question is given over and over again in the Scriptures. Far from wishing to gloss over the contrasts the sacred authors considered it important to emphasise them to the full, for only in so doing could another great truth of revelation be proclaimed in a

[43]God's promise had been fulfilled, in the sense that God, unlike man, not only promises but acts accordingly. But the fulfilment had not 'reached' Israel.

compelling and insistent way. God not only promised but actually gave to all Israel the complete possession of Canaan, the land of perfect happiness. But there was one condition which Israel constantly failed to observe. Canaan was their home in order that they might fear and love and serve God, and it was their home only in so far as they did this. Here we have the *theological* explanation of why so great a contrast existed between the theology and the history of Israel in Canaan. Or to put it another way, the contrast which constantly made itself felt provided the recurring opportunity of reiterating another truth of faith : 'Yahweh your God is God, the faithful God Who keeps covenant and steadfast love with those who love Him and keep His commandments, to a thousand generations, and requites to their face those who hate Him, by destroying them; He will not be slack with him who hates Him, He will requite him to his face. You shall therefore be careful to do the commandment, and the statutes, and the ordinances, which I command you this day' (Deut 7, 9-11).

The book of Judges is the principal source for this truth. Throughout the book we have it constantly repeated that Israel was unfaithful and *therefore* Canaan was not the place of happiness God had intended. Yet every time that Israel turned back from its evil ways, God rescued them from their misery and through the judges,[44] each as it were another Joshua, began once more to make Canaan the fitting home of His chosen people. The whole book is summed up and interpreted in this way by its introduction[45] : 'Because this people have transgressed My covenant which I commanded their fathers, and have not obeyed My voice, I will not henceforth drive out before them any of the nations that Joshua left when he died,

[44]The term in this context, approximates to 'saviour', cf A. Vincent, *Le livre des Juges, le livre de Ruth (Bible de Jérusalem)* 1958, pp. 9-10.

[45]Jud 2, 6-3, 6 constituted the original introduction; 1, 1-2, 5 is a later addition cf George F. Moore, *op. cit.,* p. xv.

that by them I may test Israel, whether they will take care to walk in the way of Yahweh as their fathers did, or not. So Yahweh left those nations, not driving them out at once, and He did not give them into the power of Joshua' (2, 20-3). It is precisely because the book of Judges is concerned mainly with this theological truth that it was our chief source for the reconstruction of the actual history of Israel's entry into Canaan. But it should now be clear that Judges is no more intended as a history book than are Deuteronomy and Josue. There is not a single book in the Bible so intended. However, precisely because it is concerned with the theological explanation of the misfortunes of Israel's history, it gives us more evidence of the actual historical facts than do the other two books.

Yet these latter are not blind to the contrasts. Though they concentrate much more strongly on the divine action on behalf of Israel, the experience of the consequences of Israel's failure to act in accordance with the divine will cannot be wholly ignored. The same book which defines Canaan's ideal boundaries (Deut 1, 7) also points out that the establishing of these boundaries depends upon one condition : 'Provided you are careful to keep all this commandment, which I command you this day, by loving Yahweh your God, and by walking ever in His ways' (19, 9; cf 11, 22). Deuteronomy insists that God has truly given Canaan to be Israel's inheritance; but this does not exclude the possibility of Israel's losing it, and therefore there is need of the warning : 'Beware lest you say in your heart : My power and the might of my hand have gotten me this wealth. . . . And if you forget Yahweh your God and go after other gods and serve them and worship them, I solemnly warn you this day that you shall surely perish' (Deut 8, 17. 19; cf 4, 23-8). The very fertility of Canaan depends upon Israel's observance of God's law : 'And if you will obey my commandments which I command you this day, to love Yahweh your

God, and to serve Him with all your heart and with all your soul, He will give the rain for your land in its season, the early rain and the later rain, that you may gather in your grain and your wine and your oil. And He will give grass in your fields for your cattle, and you shall eat and be full' (Deut 11, 13-15; cf 11, 8-9; 7, 12; Ex 23, 25)[46]. Similarly the book of Josue introduces the proclamation of the divine conquest of Canaan on behalf of Israel, with the warning that all depends upon fidelity to the law : 'Only be strong and very courageous, being careful to do according to all the law which Moses My servant commanded you; turn not from it to the right hand or to the left, that you may have good success wherever you go. This book of the law shall not depart out of your mouth, but you shall meditate on it day and night, that you may be careful to do according to all that is written in it; for then you shall make your way prosperous, and then you shall have good success' (1, 7-8). Moreover the only set-back in Joshua's victorious progress came through the disobedience of Achan when he broke the law of *herem* (Jos 7).

The contrast, lastly, between this law of *herem* and the continued existence of the nations in Canaan is clearly realised, as can be seen from the variations in its formulation. According to Deut 20, 16-18 not one is to be left alive. Yet in Deut 7, 2-5 after commanding the Israelites to smite the nations and make them a *herem,* the law goes on to forbid alliances and intermarriage with them. It sometimes demands the destruction of all the people and all their possessions (1 Sam 15, 3), at other times, of all the people but not their possessions (Deut 2, 34-35; 3, 6-7; 8, 26-7), except the gold and silver covering their idols (Deut 7, 25-6). Even in the book of Josue, where the fulfilling of this law recurs like a refrain, it is not ignored that the family of Rahab and the Gabaonites were spared (6, 22-23; 9), whilst

---

[46]Neither does Deuteronomy ignore the continued existence in historical fact of other nations within the ideal boundaries cf Deut 2, 5. 9. 19.

in Judges the heroes of Israel are never credited with its execution.[47]

These three books therefore, all concerned with Israel's settlement in Canaan, proclaim the revealed truths that on the one hand God has not only promised salvation for Israel but fulfilled His promises and on the other, that this fulfilment will be enjoyed if Israel loves and serves God according to His law. Both these truths are essential, for the first without the second leaves unsolved the enigma of Israel's existence with all its suffering and frustration; the second without the first makes intolerable demands upon their trust in God's word. The constant alternation of these two truths may make the books mystifying and complicated for the reader who does not share the faith of Israel, and he may well feel that more explicit indications of which of the two truths is being proclaimed would greatly facilitate his understanding. But the Christian reader should find no such difficulty. He shares the faith of Israel and experiences the same alternation in the New Testament for the divine revelation is homogeneous from beginning to end.

The New Testament shows the same paradox and the same contrast between the saving acts of God and the historical experience of the Church which is the New Israel. It explains the contrast in the same way, namely as the revelation of the need for the Church to keep God's law if she is to enjoy to the full the divine salvation. The gospel proclaims the coming of the kingdom, the redemption of the world, the conquest of sin and death, and the rebirth to eternal life. All this is not simply announced as God's promise but as actually realised in Jesus Christ. Yet this same gospel demands the obedience and co-operation of every Christian if he is to share in this salvation through Christ, and the failure to respond to this demand is

[47]The word only occurs twice, in Jud 1, 17; 21, 11. For the practical rules of warfare cf Deut 20, 10-15. 19-20; 21, 10-14; Num 31, 8. 22.

the gospel's explanation[48] of why there is so great a contrast between both the Church as the body of the risen and exalted Christ and her historical vicissitudes, and every Christian's new life in Christ and his present wretchedness. Are we already saved? Is the kingdom of God already come? Have sin and death already been conquered? The answers to these questions are not truly Christian unless they are paradoxical. The answer in every case must be both Yes and No.[49]

Why is it then that there are unfortunately many Christians whose reading of the New Testament with all its paradoxical message, supports and revivifies their faith, but who cannot read the Old Testament to the same end, because they find this paradox an obstacle? Probably the reason is that the Old Testament, and particularly in its earlier books, is much more closely tied to the language of history than is the New. The New Testament is in one sense just as intimately linked with history, in so far as God's revelation is made through the historical events of Christ's life, death and resurrection. But in the progress of revelation the language which interprets God's saving actions has become less dependent upon history. The salvation of the New Israel stands revealed in the resurrection and exaltation of Christ to the right hand of God. It is not accomplished until Christ leaves this historical sphere and enters the world which is beyond the reach of history. Similarly the proclamation of our salvation through Christ no longer depends exclusively on the language of history. We are saved because we have died and risen with him to a new life; our old selves have been crucified with him; 'Even when we were dead through our trespasses, (God) made us alive together with Christ (by grace you have been saved), and raised us up

[48]Not of course exclusively so, for the mystery of iniquity receives a Christian explanation in the value of suffering.

[49]The distinction of the Christian theologian between the *objective* and *subjective* redemption is another way of answering these questions.

with him and made us sit with him in the heavenly places in Christ Jesus' (Eph 2, 5-6). The kingdom of God has become the kingdom in heaven, and the proclamation of our salvation is no longer wholly restricted to the language of history. Hence there is no need for instance to describe in an apparently historical narrative the crucifixion of an innumerable multitude and their resurrection on the third day. The proclamation of our salvation in Christ uses the language of history in so far as it proclaims the historical resurrection of Christ, but discards it in proclaiming that we have been raised along with him. This is only possible because the supra-historical character of divine salvation has now been revealed to us.

It was not possible when the proclamation of God's salvation was first made. God's action showed forth in the historical events leading to the settlement of the Israelitic tribes in Canaan. But His action was in His intention the settlement of all Israel in perfect peace and uninterrupted life with Him. Tied to the language of history this could only be proclaimed in terms of the divine conquest of Canaan through Joshua. In other words the historical events which gave glimpses of the divinely implanted faith of Israel had at the same time to provide the language in which that faith was fully proclaimed.[50] In the Christian gospel on the other hand the historical event, stated in the language of history, is that Christ rose from the dead. But the profession of faith: God has raised us up together with Christ, goes beyond not only the historical event, but also the historical language in which the latter was couched, since it implies statements such as 'Being united with him in a death like his' (Rom 6, 5) or 'Having died to the law through the body of Christ' (Rom 7, 4), statements not made

[50]By way of analogy, one might try to imagine composing a proclamation of the Christian faith, using nothing except material provided by chroniclers and hagiographers of the first four centuries of the Church. One would of course find that this material itself was already, in varying degrees, a proclamation of faith.

188

in the language of history. Because the book of Josue, and the Old Testament in general, does not break free from the language of history, the profession of faith is for us obscured. And since we are unfortunately all too inclined to think that every unhistorical statement is untrue, we not only fail to perceive the profession of faith, but regard the book of Josue as nothing more than exaggerated, tendencious and, quite bluntly, false history.

To give another example of the contrast *in language* between the confession of faith made by the Israelite and the Christian, we proclaim that Christ is the conqueror of evil and lord of the world: he himself said 'I have overcome the world' (John 16, 33). If an unbelieving historian were to retort: 'There is no evidence to show that this is true, and in fact there is abundant evidence to the contrary,' we would call his attention to Christ's miracles, his calming of the storm, his walking on the water, his curing of diseases and his raising of the dead. And we would also point to the endurance and progress of Christianity. But his reply might well be that all this evidence falls far short of the categorical and all-embracing statement that Christ is lord of the world. Now let us suppose that instead of making this short statement, we professed our faith in the form of a narrative, perhaps for the sake of children. We recount how Our Lord expelled the demons and cured the sick in Palestine, and how he was greeted with 'Hosanna to the Son of David.' Then he went to China, and was there acclaimed as king. From there he went to Australia and having overcome the wicked rulers there, established his own kingdom of peace and happiness, and so on throughout the world: Christ is lord of the world. At first sight such a narrative creates far more difficulty than the simple statement, since it is so much the more obviously unhistorical. Yet, if we penetrate beyond the superficiality of the language used, the difficulty is no greater than that which arises from the statement: 'Christ is lord of the world', for whether the profession be made in this way, or through a discursive narrative historical in appearance, the same contrast remains between the profession of faith and the historical evidence.

The book of Josue seems all the more unhistorical because the profession of faith is couched in a discursive narrative which on the surface appears as nothing more than a recital of history. The incidents from which this narrative is composed have a real basis in history;[51] but the characteristics which give the narrative its finished form and which make it suited to its proper purpose are unhistorical. Yet this must not lead us to question the truth of the narrative, considered as it is intended, namely as a profession of faith in the divine salvation of Israel. If only we can overcome the obstacle created by its superficial appearance of being simply a history of Israel's entry into Canaan, we will be able to read it in the one way it is intended to be read, namely as a profession of *our* faith in God our saviour, and with a strengthening of *our* confidence in God Who from the very first moment of His choosing Israel to be His people, has striven and continues to strive for their entry into a place of peace and happiness where He may dwell in their midst. It is a most wonderful, a most astonishing sign of God's presence in Israel that our forefathers could preserve their faith when its proclamation was wholly in the language of history, and therefore completely at the mercy of a comparison with historical experience. Are we, to whom God's revelation has come in the person of Jesus Christ and ascended with him into the world which is beyond history, to be found of less faith than they for whom faith was so much more difficult? The unbeliever may scoff and ask : How can you believe all that is written in the book of Josue? But remember that he might as easily ask : How can you believe you are saved through Christ? In both cases he might legitimately word his question : How can you believe in a salvation which cannot be wholly verified by history? The plain answer is : By the power of the Spirit

[51]cf F. M. Abel, *op. cit.*, p. 9.

of God. What would be impossible to unaided reason, is possible through the supernatural gift of faith. As we look back over the history of God's Israel to the day He brought us out of Egypt, we may indeed point to many signs that what we believe is true, but there is far more there to show that we believe *in spite of* the contradictions of history. Then it is that the faith of Israel through the centuries shows forth in all its glory.

The Church's Prayer

The Christian therefore can and ought to read of God's gift to Israel of the Promised Land with devotion, and with the clear realisation that he is thereby professing his faith in the divinely revealed truths there expressed. Far from having to adopt the pose of a simple and gullible illiterate he can be assured that in reading the word of God as a profession of his faith he is making use of the sacred scriptures in precisely the way which modern historical and scientific criticism shows they were intended to be used. He is making use of the ancient historical traditions of the Israelitic tribes in precisely the same way as the prophets did, when they gathered together these traditions to form the books of Deuteronomy, Josue and Judges, namely for the purpose of proclaiming the divine goal in history, and the divine plan for mankind, known only to those who believe in God's word. Here he finds the answer, as the prophets intended he should, to the disturbing questions raised by the contrast between his faith in God his Saviour, and the trials of this present life. Here too he discovers for what he must pray in order that God's will may be fully accomplished in the sight of all mankind.

He must earnestly pray that the Church, God's Israel, may enter into full possession of the Promised Land. He must lament the attacks of her enemies which impede this, and beg for their speedy overthrow. The law of *herem,* far from being the stumbling-block so many Christians find it, has still its meaning and its full validity. From the very first moment it was formulated by the prophets, it was a statement, not of historical fact but of theological truth. It was the prophetic interpretation of God's will, in human language, and within that human framework of the holy war and its conquests, in which they presented the execution of God's will. And the will of God they were in this way revealing to us, is that all wickedness should be destroyed, and that He should triumph over all who will not acknowledge Him.

This, we must insist, is as essential a part of divine revelation as is Our Lord's injunction to love our enemies and do good to those who persecute us. To contrast the law of *herem* with the Sermon of the Mount in order to show *the difference* between the Old Testament and the New is to do a grave injustice to the divine revelation. The comparison should be between the law of *herem* and the judgment of the king: 'Depart from me, you cursed, into the eternal fire prepared for the devil and his angels.' (Mt 25, 41). This comparison would show not the contrast but the agreement between Old Testament and New, for throughout the whole of Divine revelation it has been made clear that those who refuse to acknowledge God 'will go away into eternal punishment, but the righteous into eternal life' (Mt 25, 46).

The nations whose destruction is commanded in the law of *herem* are those who do not know Yahweh, and who therefore refuse to obey His commandments; and it is precisely for this reason that they must be destroyed along with their abominable practices (Deut 18, 9-14). It is not because they are Amorites, or Canaanites or Perizzites or the rest, but because they worship false gods and lead Israel astray (Deut 20, 18). Israel herself is constantly warned that she also may become one of the nations who know not Yahweh, and she is constantly threatened with the same destruction. It is too easily forgotten that the law of *herem* applies to Israelites as well as non-Israelites. If an *Israelite* city should fall into idolatry then the law of *herem* must be executed against it in its fullest rigour:

'You shall surely put the inhabitants of that city to the sword, destroying it utterly,[52] all who are in it and its cattle, with the edge of the sword. You shall gather all its spoil into the midst of its open square, and burn the city and all its spoil with fire, as a whole burnt offering to Yahweh your God; it shall be a heap for ever, it shall not be built again. None of the devoted things shall cleave to your hand; that Yahweh may turn from the fierceness of His anger, and show you mercy, and have compassion on you, and multiply you, as He swore to your fathers' (Deut 13, 15-17). Moreover, Israelites who aped the abominable practices of the nations must be destroyed, whether it was for worshipping false gods (Deut 17, 2-7), for refusing to obey the priest or judge (Deut 17, 12), for indulging in magical practices (Deut 18, 9-12), for murder (Deut 19, 12), for dishonouring parents (Deut 21, 21), for fornication (21, 21) or for adultery (Deut 22, 22-4). These are 'mortal' sins, and their perpetrators are to be put to death, for they are an evil in the midst of Israel which must be purged away. Moreover, abominable practices whether of whole nations or of individuals, whether Canaanite or Israelite, are judged in relation to Israel: every sinner must be considered in relation to the whole of God's people and judged unfit to dwell with them in the promised land, for nothing defiled is to exist there.[53]

Christians therefore who find the law of *herem* primitive and unchristian must face St Paul's question: 'Do you not know that the unrighteous will not inherit the kingdom of God?' (1 Cor 6, 9; cf Gal 5, 21; Ephes 5, 5; Rom 1, 32; 1 Pet 4, 18). Or is it that they are so badly deceived by the differences of language and human imagery as to find the law of *herem* a more cruel and more terrible fate than the eternal punishment of hell which is the penalty of mortal sin? The wrath of God against the wicked and their eternal destruction is an authentic part of the Christian revelation, and the terms in

[52]lit. 'making it a *herem*'.
[53]cf Deut 17, 4. 7. 12; 19, 13. 19; 21, 21. 22. 24.

which the New Testament proclaims this truth are no less terrible than those of the Old.

That the law of *herem* is an ideal law concerned not with non-Israelites in the racial or 'national' sense, but with those, whether Israelite or non-Israelite, who indulge in 'abominable practices' is confirmed by the solicitude of the same law code[54] for the *ger*, namely the stranger[55] settled in the midst of Israel. Not only must the rights he enjoyed under Israelite law be carefully preserved (Deut 1, 16; 24, 17; 27, 19), but the Israelites are commanded: 'Love the stranger therefore, for you were strangers in the land of Egypt' (Deut 10, 19), and he is loved by Yahweh Himself (Deut 10, 18). The stranger in fact became more and more closely bound with Israel: 'When a stranger sojourns with you in your land, you shall not do him wrong. The stranger who sojourns with you shall be to you as the native among you, and you shall love him as yourself; for you were strangers in the land of Egypt' (Lev 19, 33-34). They had the obligation and the privilege of observing the Sabbath (Deut 5, 14) and the day of atonement (Lev 16, 29). They could offer sacrifices (Lev 17, 8; Num 15, 14-15), and take part in the feasts (Deut 16, 11. 14). They could even accept circumcision and eat of the Pasch (Ex 12, 48-9; Num 9, 14). Finally, in Ezechiel's vision of the restored Israel they are seen as co-citizens with equal rights: 'So you shall divide this land among you according to the tribes of Israel.

---

[54] A. Clamer, *op. cit.*, p. 581, feels the incongruity of the law of *herem* being found side by side with the legislation for the protection of the *ger* in the same book, but his attempt at a reconciling explanation is misplaced.

[55] cf Kuhn in *Theologisches Wörterbuch zum neuen Testament* VI, 728-730. R. de Vaux, *Les institutions de l'ancien testament* I, pp. 116-118. The latter, whilst pointing out that the term *ger* was sometimes used of an Israelite who resided with another tribe, states that 'They were the ancient inhabitants (of Canaan) not assimilated by marriage nor reduced to slavery... and to them were added immigrants.' (p. 116).

You shall allot it as an inheritance for yourselves and for the strangers who reside among you and have begotten children among you. They shall be to you as native-born sons of Israel; with you they shall be allotted an inheritance among the tribes of Israel' (Ezech 47, 21-2; cf Ephes 2, 19).

When therefore in the communal laments of the Psalter Israel bemoans the presence of her enemies in the land that is her inheritance, and pleads for their speedy overthrow, she is expressing her longing for the final and perfect fulfilment of God's own will. It is God's salvific will that Israel should enjoy the complete and uninterrupted life with Himself, and it is His will that all those who hate Israel and afflict her should be destroyed. These psalms are the true expression of Israel's prayer, whether we consider Israel living in the days of the Babylonian exile or of the nineteen sixties. Without doubt the language of revelation has changed along with its progress, and the Christian does at first find the language of these psalms disconcerting. But the remedy lies, not in a rejection or an allegorising of this language, but in a deeper understanding of its meaning. It should now be clear that the meaning these ancient poems had when they were first written remains valid and necessary for the Christian Church today. If we are truly conscious of our solidarity and if the sufferings of our brethren persecuted in so many parts of the world today are truly our sufferings, then we can with great sincerity lament: 'Hast thou not rejected us, O God? Thou dost not go forth, O God, with our armies. O grant us help against the foe, for vain is the help of man' (Ps 60, 10-11). Conscious of the many damaging blows aimed against the Church, the devouring of Jacob and the laying waste of his habitation (cf Ps 79, 7), we ought insistently to remind God that 'We have become a taunt to our neighbours, mocked and derided by those round about us. How long, Yahweh? Wilt thou be angry for ever?' (Ps 79, 4-5). With confidence we should remind God that in seeking to destroy His Church the wicked are seeking to destroy the knowledge of His name from the face of the earth: 'Lo, Thy enemies are in tumult; those who hate Thee have raised their heads. They lay crafty plans against Thy people; they consult together against Thy protected one, They say: Come, let us wipe them out as a nation; let the name of Israel be remembered no more. Yea, they conspire with one accord; against Thee they make a covenant' (Ps 83, 2-5).

As God's Church, surrounded by dangers, suffering loss and humiliation, we have the solemn obligation to beg that for the glory of God's name our enemies may soon be destroyed: *Ut inimicos sanctae ecclesiae humiliare digneris.* In her liturgy the Church prays: 'Almighty and everlasting God, under whose control are the powers of all men and the rights of all kingdoms, look to the help of Christians, in order that heathen nations, who rely on their own ferocity may be crushed by Thy powerful right arm.[56] Similarly in these psalms she prays without hesitation and without qualm: 'Pour out Thy anger on the nations that do not know Thee, and on the kingdoms that do not call on Thy name. . . . Let the avenging of the outpoured blood of Thy servants be known among the nations before our eyes. Let the groans of the prisoners come before Thee; according to Thy great power preserve those doomed to die. Return sevenfold into the bosom of our neighbours, the taunts with which they have taunted Thee Yahweh' (Ps 79, 6. 10-12).

What we are concerned with at this particular moment of prayer, is uniquely the triumph of God and His Church over their enemies. That God may in His mercy turn enemies into friends is also oftentimes our prayer, but not at this moment, and the fervour of our desire for God's final triumph ought not to be lessened by any mistaken feeling that the one truth must give way, here and now, to the other. We must indeed be careful not to lose sight of the fact that we are praying for the destruction of the enemies *of the Church,* and not the enemies

[56]Collect from the votive Mass *pro Ecclesiae defensione,* until recently known as *contra paganos.*

196

of our nation or of our particular way of life.[57] The war which we here urge God to wage is no war of this world, with nuclear weapons and supersonic aircraft. God wages war on behalf of His people insofar as they constitute Israel, the means whereby He has chosen to make Himself known to the world. He wages war against the nations insofar as they refuse to acknowledge Him as their God. This was made clear long ago by the prophets themselves, who so strongly condemned the worldly power[58] and ambition even of Israel's kings. 'Woe to those who go down to Egypt for help and rely on horses, who trust in chariots because they are many and in horsemen because they are very strong, but do not look to the Holy One of Israel or consult Yahweh' (Is 31, 1; cf 22, 8-11). Just as in the beginning : 'Not by their own sword did they win the land, nor did their own arm give them victory; but Thy right hand, and Thy arm, and the light of Thy countenance; for Thou didst delight in them' (Ps 44, 3), so it will be on the Day of Yahweh, when 'I will have pity on the house of Judah, and I will deliver them by Yahweh their God; I will not deliver them by bow, nor by sword, nor by war, nor by horses, nor by horsemen' (Os 1, 7; cf Mich 5, 10, 15; Ps 33, 16-22; 147, 10-11).[59]

We must pray earnestly for the hastening of that day, the day of the final battle, the day of God's triumph and the

[57]The Christian's attitude towards the wars between nations is altogether another question. It is an undeniable fact that much use has been made of the Old Testament in support of wars of this kind, whether between Christians and infidels, or Christians and Christians, and attempts have been made to elaborate a *theology* of war in this sense cf M. D. Chenu, 'L'évolution de la théologie de la guerre' in *Lumière et Vie* No. 38, 1958, pp. 76-97. How far such attempts have succeeded is open to question.

[58]David's carrying out a census (2 Sam 24, 1-17) is condemned because it was designed to provide him with conscripts for 'profane' war.

[59]The eschatological intervention of God finally to destroy the nations was part of the prophetic vision: Is 10, 24-27; 14, 24-27; 30, 27-33; 31, 4-9; Ez 38, 19-22; Mich 4, 11-13; Agg 2, 21ff; Zach 14.

vindication of Israel, God's Church : 'Since indeed God deems it just to repay with affliction those who afflict you, and to grant rest with us to you who are afflicted, when the Lord Jesus is revealed from heaven with his mighty angels in flaming fire, inflicting vengeance upon those who do not know God and upon those who do not obey the gospel of our Lord Jesus. They shall suffer the punishment of eternal destruction and exclusion from the presence of the Lord and from the glory of His might, when he comes on that day to be glorified in his saints, and to be marvelled at in all who have believed, because our testimony to you was believed.' (2 Thess 1, 6-10; cf Apoc 19, 11-21; 21, 7-10).

On that day, and our prayer is that it should come soon, we will see a new heaven and a new earth, and the new Jerusalem descending into the Promised Land, and we shall hear a great voice from the throne saying : 'Behold the dwelling of God is with men. He will dwell with them, and they shall be His people, and God Himself will be with them; He will wipe away every tear from their eyes, and death shall be no more, neither shall there be mourning nor crying nor pain any more, for the former things have passed away.' (Apoc 21, 3-4).

READINGS FROM THE PSALMS

READINGS FROM THE PSALMS

THE REDEMPTION OF ISRAEL

Psalm 105

Proclaim Yahweh : call out His name !
Make His deeds known among the peoples !
Sing of Him : sing His praises !
Tell of all His wonderful works !
Glory in His holy name !
Let the hearts of those who seek Yahweh rejoice !
—Seek Yahweh and His strength,
    seek His presence always—
Remember the wonderful works He has done,
    His miracles and the judgements He has uttered,
O offspring of Abraham His servant,
O sons of Jacob His chosen ones !

He is Yahweh, our God,
His judgements are in all the earth.
He is mindful of His covenant for ever,
    of the word that He commanded, for a thousand
                                 generations,
    the covenant which He made with Abraham,
    His sworn promise to Isaac
    which He confirmed to Jacob as a statute,
    to Israel as an everlasting covenant,
    saying : 'To you I will give the land of Canaan
    as your portion for an inheritance.'

When they were few in number,
    of little account, and sojourners there,
    wandering from nation to nation,
    from one kingdom to another people,

He allowed no one to oppress them;
    He rebuked kings on their account,
        saying : 'Touch not my anointed ones,
    do My prophets no harm'
When He summoned a famine on the land,
    and broke every staff of bread,
He sent a man ahead of them,
    Joseph who was sold as a slave.
His feet were hurt with fetters,
    his neck was put in a collar of iron.
Until what he had said came to pass
    the word of Yahweh tested him.
The king sent and released him,
    the ruler of the peoples set him free.
He made him lord of his house,
        and ruler of all his possessions,
        to instruct his princes at his pleasure,
    and to teach his elders wisdom.

Then Israel came to Egypt;
Jacob sojourned in the land of Ham.
And Yahweh made His people very fruitful,
    and made them stronger than their foes.
He turned their hearts to hate His people,
    to deal craftily with His servants.
He sent Moses His servant,
    and Aaron whom He had chosen.
They wrought His signs among them,
    and miracles in the land of Ham.
He sent darkness and made the land dark;
    they rebelled against His words.
He turned their waters into blood,
    and caused their fish to die.
Their land swarmed with frogs,
    even in the chambers of their kings.
He spoke, and there came swarms of flies,
    and gnats throughout their country.
He gave them hail for rain,
    and lightning that flashed through their land.
He smote their vines and fig trees,
    and shattered the trees of their country.

He spoke, and the locusts came,
    and young locusts without number,
    which devoured all the vegetation in their land,
    and ate up the fruit of their ground.
He smote all the first-born in their land,
    the first issue of all their strength.

Then He led forth Israel with silver and gold,
    and there was none among His tribes who stumbled.
Egypt was glad when they departed,
    for dread of them had fallen upon it.
He spread a cloud for a covering,
    and fire to give light by night.
They asked and He brought quails,
    and gave them bread from heaven in abundance.
He opened the rock and water gushed forth;
    it flowed through the desert like a river.
For He remembered His holy promise,
    and Abraham His servant.
So He led forth His people with joy,
    His chosen ones with singing.
And He gave them the lands of the nations;
And they took possession of the fruit of the peoples' toil,
    to the end that they should keep His statutes,
    and observe His laws.
        Halleluyah

Psalm 106

Halleluyah
Proclaim Yahweh : Truly He is good !
Truly His steadfast love endures for ever !
Who can utter the mighty doings of Yahweh,
    or announce all His praise ?
Blessed are they who observe justice,
    who do righteousness at all times !
Remember me, Yahweh, when Thou showest favour
                                to Thy people.

Help me when Thou deliverest them;
    that I may see the prosperity of Thy chosen ones,
    that I may rejoice in the gladness of Thy nation,
    that I may glory with Thy heritage.
Both we and our fathers have sinned.
We have committed iniquity,
    we have done wickedly.
Our fathers, when they were in Egypt,
    did not consider thy wonderful works.
They did not remember the abundance of Thy
                                    steadfast love,
    but rebelled against the Most High at the Red Sea.
Yet He saved them for His name's sake,
    that He might make known His mighty power.
He rebuked the Red Sea, and it became dry;
    and He led them through the deep as through
                                    a desert.
So he saved them from the hand of the foe,
    and delivered them from the power of the enemy.
And the waters covered their adversaries;
    not one of them was left.
Then they believed His words;
    they sang His praise.

But they soon forgot His works;
    they did not wait for His counsel.
But they had a wanton craving in the wilderness,
    and put God to the test in the desert.
He gave them what they asked,
    but sent a wasting disease among them.
When men in the camp were jealous of Moses,
    and Aaron, Yahweh's holy one,
    the earth opened and swallowed up Dathan,
    and covered the company of Abiram.
Fire also broke out in their company;
    the flame burned up the wicked.

They made a calf in Horeb,
    and worshipped a molten image.
They exchanged the glory of God
    for the image of an ox that eats grass.

They forgot God their Saviour,
    Who had done great things in Egypt,
    wondrous works in the land of Ham,
    and terrible things by the Red Sea.
Therefore He said He would destroy them—
      had not Moses, His chosen one
    stood in the breach before Him,
    to turn away His wrath from destroying them.
Then they despised the pleasant land,
    having no faith in His promise.
They murmured in their tents,
    and did not obey the voice of Yahweh.
Therefore He raised His hand and swore to them
    that He would make them fall in the wilderness,
    and would disperse their descendants among the
                            nations,
    scattering them over the lands.

Then they attached themselves to the Baal of Peor,
      and ate sacrifices of the dead.
They provoked Yahweh to anger with their doings,
    and a plague broke out among them.
Then Phinehas stood up and gave judgement,
    and the plague was stayed.
And that has been reckoned to him as righteousness
    from generation to generation for ever.
They angered Him at the waters of Meribah,
    and it went ill with Moses on their account.
For they made his spirit bitter,
    and he spoke words that were rash.

They did not destroy the peoples,
    as Yahweh commanded them.
But they mingled with the nations,
    and learned to do as they did.
They served their idols, which became a snare to them
They sacrificed their sons and their daughters to the
                            demons.
They poured out innocent blood,
    the blood of their sons and daughters,
    whom they sacrificed to the idols of Canaan.

And the land was polluted with blood.
Thus they became unclean by their acts,
   and played the harlot in their doings.

Then the anger of Yahweh was kindled against His
                                            people,
   and He abhorred His heritage.
He gave them into the hand of the nations,
   so that those who hated them ruled over them.
Their enemies oppressed them,
   and they were brought into subjection
   under their power.
Many times He delivered them,
   but they were rebellious in their purposes,
   and were brought low through their iniquity.
Nevertheless He looked on their distress
   when He heard their cry.
He remembered for their sake His covenant,
   and relented according to the abundance of His
                                 steadfast love.
He caused them to be pitied
   by all those who held them captive.

Save us, Yahweh our God,
   and gather us from among the nations,
   that we may proclaim Thy holy name,
   and glory in Thy praise.

Psalm 135

Halleluyah

Praise the name of Yahweh, praise,
   O servants of Yahweh,
   you that stand in the house of Yahweh,
   in the courts of the house of our God !
Praise Yahweh : truly Yahweh is good.
Sing His name's praise : truly He is gracious !
Truly Yahweh has chosen Jacob for Himself,
   Israel as His Own possession.

206

Truly I know that Yahweh is great,
and that our Lord is above all gods.
Whatever Yahweh pleases He does,
in heaven and on earth,
in the seas and all deeps.
He it is Who makes the clouds rise at the end of the
earth.
Who makes lightnings for the rain,
and brings forth the wind from His storehouses.

He it was Who smote the first-born of Egypt,
both of man and of beast.
Who in thy midst, O Egypt, sent signs and wonders
against Pharaoh and all his servants.
Who smote many nations,
and slew mighty kings :
Sihon, king of the Amorites,
and Og, king of Bashan,
and all the kingdoms of Canaan,
and gave their land as a heritage,
a heritage to His people Israel.

Thy name, Yahweh, endures for ever ;
Thy renown, Yahweh, throughout all ages.
For Yahweh will vindicate His people,
and have compassion on His servants.
The idols of the nations are silver and gold,
the work of men's hands.
They have mouths, but they do not speak,
they have eyes, but they do not see,
nor is there any breath in their mouths.
Like them be those who make them !
Yea, every one who trusts in them !

O house of Israel, bless Yahweh !
O house of Aaron, bless Yahweh !
O house of Levi, bless Yahweh !
You that fear Yahweh, bless Yahweh !
Blessed be Yahweh from Sion,
He who dwells in Jerusalem !
Halleluyah

YAHWEH THE CONQUEROR OF ISRAEL'S ENEMIES

Psalm 44

We have heard with our ears, O God,
  our fathers have told us
  what deeds Thou didst perform in their days,
  in the days of old.
Thou with Thy Own hand didst drive out the nations,
  but them Thou didst plant.
Thou didst afflict the peoples,
  but them thou didst set free.
For not by their own sword did they win the land,
  nor did their own arm give them victory.
But Thy right hand and Thy arm
  and the light of Thy countenance :
  for Thou didst delight in them.
Thou art my king and my God,
  Who ordainest victories for Jacob.
Through Thee we push down our foes.
Through Thy name we tread down our assailants.
For not in my bow do I trust,
  nor can my sword save me.
But Thou hast saved us from our foes,
  and hast put to confusion those who hate us.
In God we have boasted continually,
  and we will proclaim Thy name for ever.

Yet Thou hast cast us off and abased us,
  and hast not gone out with our armies.
Thou hast made us turn back from the foe;
  and our enemies have despoiled us.
Thou hast made us like sheep for slaughter,
  and hast scattered us among the nations.
Thou hast sold Thy people for a trifle,
  demanding no high price for them.
Thou hast made us the taunt of our neighbours,
  the derision and scorn of those about us.

Thou hast made us a byword among the nations,
   a laughingstock among the peoples.
All day long my disgrace is before me,
   and shame has covered my face,
   at the words of the taunters and revilers,
   at the sight of the enemy and the avenger.

All this has come upon us,
   though we have not forgotten Thee,
   or been false to Thy covenant.
Our heart has not turned back,
   nor have our steps departed from Thy way,
   that Thou shouldst have broken us in the place of
                                             jackals,
   and covered us with deep darkness.
If we had forgotten the name of our God,
   or spread forth our hands to a strange god,
   would not God discover this?
For He knows the secrets of the heart.
Nay, for Thy sake we are slain all the day long,
   and accounted as sheep for the slaughter.

Rouse Thyself! Why sleepest Thou, Yahweh?
Awake! Do not cast us off for ever!
Why dost Thou hide Thy face?
Why dost Thou forget our affliction and
                                   oppression?
For our soul is bowed down to the dust;
   our body cleaves to the ground.

Rise up! Come to our help!
Deliver us for the sake of Thy steadfast love!

Psalm 79

O God, the heathen have come into Thy inheritance.
They have defiled Thy holy temple.
They have laid Jerusalem in ruins.

They have given the bodies of Thy servants
  to the birds of the air for food;
    the flesh of Thy saints to the beasts of the earth.
They have poured out their blood like water
  round about Jerusalem,
    and there was none to bury them.
We have become a taunt to our neighbours,
  mocked and derided by those round about us.

How long, Yahweh? Wilt Thou be angry for
                                        ever?
Will Thy jealous wrath burn like fire?
Pour out Thy anger on the nations
  that do not know Thee,
    and on the kingdoms
      that do not call on Thy name.
For they have devoured Jacob,
  and laid waste his habitation.
Do not remember against us
  the iniquities of our forefathers.
Let Thy compassion come speedily to meet us,
  for we are brought very low.
Help us, O God of our salvation,
  for the glory of Thy name.
Deliver us, and forgive our sins,
  for Thy name's sake.
Why should the nations say :
  'Where is their God?'
Let the avenging of the outpoured blood of Thy
                                        servants
  be known among the nations before our eyes.
Let the groans of the prisoners come before Thee.
According to Thy great power preserve those doomed
                                          to die.
Return sevenfold into the bosom of our neighbours
  the taunts with which they have taunted Thee,
                                        Yahweh.
Then we Thy people, the flock of Thy pasture,
  will proclaim Thee for ever;
    from generation to generation
      we will recount Thy praise.

Psalm 83

O God, do not keep silence.
Do not hold Thy peace or be still, O God !
For lo, Thy enemies are in tumult.
Those who hate Thee have raised their heads.
They lay crafty plans against Thy people;
    they consult together against Thy protected ones.
They say : 'Come, let us wipe them out as a nation;
    let the name of Israel be remembered no more.'
Yea, they conspire with one accord;
    against Thee they make a covenant :
    the tents of Edom and the Ishmaelites,
    Moab and the Hagrites,
    Gebal and Ammon and Amalek,
    Philistia with the inhabitants of Tyre :
    Assyria also has joined them :
    they are the strong arm of the children of Lot.

Do to them as Thou didst to Midian,
    as to Sisera and Jabin at the river Kishon,
    who were destroyed at Endor,
    who became dung for the ground.
Make their nobles like Oreb and Zeeb,
    all their princes like Zebah and Salmunna,
    who said : 'Let us take possession for ourselves
    of the pastures of God.'
O my God, make them like whirling dust,
    like chaff before the wind.
As fire consumes the forest,
    as the flame sets the mountains ablaze,
    so do Thou pursue them with Thy tempest
    and terrify them with Thy hurricane.
Fill their faces with shame,
    that they may seek Thy name, Yahweh.
Let them be put to shame and dismayed for ever.
Let them perish in disgrace.
Let them know that Thou alone,
      Whose name is Yahweh,
      art the Most High over all the earth.

General Index

Aaron, 75, 85, 87,89, 95
Aaronic priesthood, 90
ABEL, F. M., 11n, 190n
Abraham 10; God's blessing on, 19-20; 53; chosen by God, 79, 80, 103 ; God's promise made first to him,   80, 81, 82, 93, 124, 127, 131, 171
Antiochus, 135
Assyro-Babylonian empire, 6; notion of 'corporate personality' in, 26-7
Audience, implied in the Psalms, 60, 64-6

Baalpeor, 77, 94, 162, 163, 167
Babylonian conquest of Juda, 135, 159
BAECK, LEO, 112n
BENTZEN, AAGE, 37n, 49
BEST, E., 9n
BEYER, 55n, 56n, 57n
Blessing, the, in Israelite custom, 54-8
BLINZLER, J., 110n
BURTON, ERNEST DE WITT, 122n

Cambridge Mediaeval History, 111n, 112n, 113n
Canaan, history of Israel in, 153-69; influence of Canaanite religion upon Israelite practice, 160-4, 166-9; theological significance to Israel, 169-90

CAZELLES, H., 16n, 80n, 171n
CERFAUX, L., 23n, 123n, 127n
CHENU, M. D., 197n
Christian-Jewish tension, 110-5; in early Church, 115-30; *see also* Old Testament: Christian attitude towards; Psalms: Christian attitude towards
Christian liturgical prayer, 67-72, 68n-70n
CLAMER, A., 12n, 16n, 80n, 97n, 99n, 173n, 193n
'Corporate personality', concept of: in Israel, 9-21, 28-9, 107, 108, 141, 150; in New Testament, 21-5, 27, 39; in other cultures, 26-7; in the Psalms, 29-40, 51
Crossing of the Red Sea: in the Psalms, 74, 75-6, 77; in the Pentateuch, 90-2, 95; *see also* Exodus
CULLMAN, O., 102n

Datham and Abiram, 20, 77, 93
David, defeats Edomites, 71; influence on Israel's destiny, 19, 21, 156, 157, 158; lament for Saul and Jonathan, 142
Deuteronomy, Book of 16, 24, 92, 135, 152n, 153, 170, 181, 184, 185n, 191
Dictionnaire de la Bible, Supplément, 98n, 107n

213

215

Index of References to the Psalms

218